THE STORY OF OUR SEASON

THE STORY OF OUR SEASON

The Official Manchester United
Players' Diary 2009–10

Edited by Steve Bartram

SIMON &
SCHUSTER

London · New York · Sydney · Toronto

A CBS COMPANY

First published in Great Britain by Simon & Schuster UK Ltd, 2010
A CBS COMPANY

1 3 5 7 9 10 8 6 4 2

Simon & Schuster UK Ltd
1st Floor
222 Gray's Inn Road
London
WC1X 8HB

www.simonandschuster.co.uk

Simon & Schuster Australia
Sydney

All photographs © Getty Images

A CIP catalogue for this book is available
from the British Library.

ISBN: 978-1-84737-909-2

Typeset by M Rules
Printed in the UK by CPI Mackays, Chatham ME5 8TD

This book is dedicated to the memory of Albert Scanlon,
now back with the Babes.

Contents

Introduction

Even before the dust had settled on United's epic 2008–09 season, you got the sense that 2009–10 would be a curious campaign. A world-record sale, a cross-city defection and a brush with terrorism all pre-dated August, and the plot twists kept on coming. United started the season bidding to win a historic fourth title in a row; by Christmas many had already written off the Reds' chances.

Then, in time-honoured, indefatigable style, Sir Alex's men seized control of the title race. But even a spate of own goals in United's favour hardly helped shake the nagging doubt that fate was not onside. As it transpired, it lay with Chelsea (having been dubiously flagged onside), as United fell foul of crippling injuries and questionable decisions at key times. Plus, of course, there was that frustratingly slow start to the season.

Yet despite missing out in excruciating fashion on the Premier League and Champions League trophies, 2009–10 yielded myriad talking points and memories. Few teams could cope with selling the reigning Ballon d'Or holder, but the evolution of Wayne Rooney as a penalty-area predator ensured the Reds' highest goals-per-game ratio since the mid-1960s. A rough-diamond-turned-crown-jewel, United's talisman is now a genuine shout as the best all-round player in existence.

And lest we forget the rest of a glittering ensemble cast. Antonio Valencia made a seamless transition from Wigan; Patrice Evra and

Darren Fletcher were models of consistency and some of the club's bright young talents took turns to shine. At the other end of the age scale are United's living legends: Ryan Giggs, Gary Neville and Paul Scholes. With more than 2,000 appearances between them and a combined age of 106, the trio continue to cut it at the highest level and remain vital components of the team.

Then there was the consuming sub-plot of the Manchester derby's resurgence. The Blues' emergence as arguably the richest club in the world ramped up an already intriguing fixture, and suddenly the whole country wanted a ringside seat for our local domestic. History will never forget three injury-time winners in four derby meetings, one of which primed the Reds to take yet more silverware and become the most successful team in domestic football history. And as for April's last-gasp win at Eastlands, all the trophies in the world couldn't replicate a feeling so sweet.

This is an account of the season told through the words of those who were closest to the action: Sir Alex Ferguson and his players. From Ronaldo's dressing-room farewell in Rome to new-dad Wayne Rooney facing CSKA Moscow despite severe sleep deprivation; from narrowly averted fisticuffs at Eastlands to the aftermath of 'that' kiss between Gary Neville and Paul Scholes. Patrice Evra even talks about mid-match vomiting.

It was a season that scaled peaks and plumbed depths, deceived and discombobulated. If you thought it was a rollercoaster on the terraces, try being inside the dressing room.

Enjoy.

Steve Bartram
Manchester, June 2010

The Pre-Season

It is the stench of failure, rather than success, which lingers longest at Manchester United.

The 2008–09 season had been another silver-laden marathon in which Sir Alex Ferguson and his players contested seven trophies. Come mid-May, the Reds were world champions, Premier League champions and winners of the Carling Cup and Community Shield. And yet the memory of Pep Guardiola and his Barcelona side joyously manhandling the Champions League trophy still gnawed away at fans and players alike.

'We had a great season, but because we lost our last game and it was the small matter of a Champions League final, it has a big impact on how you feel, especially during the first week of your holiday,' says Edwin van der Sar. 'After that, you reflect on everything you've achieved: winning the title again, reaching the Champions League final again, becoming world champions . . . But it's all in the past. You always think about the thing you lost, and it was a really major one to lose before we broke up.'

The wounds of Rome would take time to heal, but in the bowels of the Stadio Olimpico, mere minutes after the final whistle, the scene was already being set for United's 2009–10 campaign. Following his high-profile flirtations with Real Madrid in the summer of 2008, speculation had been rife for months that Cristiano Ronaldo would again attempt to secure his desired move to La Liga.

'To be fair, we really knew he would be leaving straight after the Champions League final,' admits Edwin. 'He thanked me for being a good guy and told me it had been an honour playing with me. When you hear that, you know it's inevitable he'll be leaving.'

Less than three weeks later, a fax from Real Madrid arrived at Old Trafford, confirming they were willing to pay a world-record £80 million transfer fee for the reigning Ballon d'Or holder. Like the Champions League trophy, another prized asset was bound for Spain.

'Shortly after the Champions League final, I was going over to FIFA for a meeting and I was approached by Real Madrid about Cristiano,' recalls chief executive David Gill. 'We discussed it and we indicated what we would want for the player. A lot of discussions had happened back in 2008 in terms of him wanting to leave. We resisted that at the time, but if it comes to a point where a player definitely wants to leave the club, then we need to be in a position to understand that. We were half-expecting it, and obviously we were in quite a strong position. He wanted to go, Real Madrid were desperate to buy him and we weren't willing sellers, so we ended up doing a deal which, from a club perspective, was a good deal.

'We spoke to them verbally and then that was followed up formally via fax. The deal was then announced the next day. There were phone calls with Alex and the owners and they all agreed it was okay, and that we should get on and do it. On the one hand it's a lot of money, on the other hand as the club we'd have much preferred Cristiano to stay. He was a great, great player for us and had six fantastic seasons. Alex, his coaches and the other players had helped make him into the player he was and is, so you prefer to have him in the team. We'd have been delighted if he'd wanted to extend his stay with us. He had three years left on his contract at that point and we'd have extended that. So on the one hand great, on the other not so good.'

Ronaldo's impending departure fanned the flames of conjecture. Franck Ribéry, David Villa, Sergio Agüero and even Liverpool's Fernando Torres were tipped as big-money arrivals as the world's football media worked itself into a frenzy of fantasy. The name of French international Karim Benzema cropped up more than most, however, and with Sir Alex Ferguson a confirmed admirer of Lyon's no-nonsense goal-getter, the story appeared to have credence.

Even at Carrington, the rumour mill was whirring. 'We normally hear rumours through a team-mate of someone or an agent of some-one, but you hear so many stories that you don't believe them until the medical's done and you see them stood in the jersey next to the manager,' says John O'Shea. 'There were so many big names being bandied about: Ribery, Robben, Benzema . . . you name it. You got the sense that the £80 million was burning a hole in the manager's pocket and he had to spend it at some point. But he had faith in the players that were here; he knew players would improve, so he was confident with what he had. You have to trust the manager, with all his experience.'

Nevertheless, the need for a new striker was exacerbated by the widely predicted departure of Carlos Tévez. The Argentinian's two-year loan at Old Trafford had lapsed – despite months of high-profile public soothing as all parties seemed intent on signing a permanent deal – and just eight days after Ronaldo's mooted departure he con-firmed he would not be joining United.

The announcement ended months of speculation over the Argentinian's future. 'The dressing room was probably split fifty–fifty over Carlos,' admits O'Shea. 'I wasn't sure, but there were plenty of people who thought he would end up staying.'

Among them was Patrice Evra, Tévez's closest ally inside the United dressing room. 'I never believed he was leaving,' says the Frenchman. 'It's a fact that Carlitos loves Manchester United and the fans loved him so much, and he felt that. But he made his choice. I don't know why he left the club. I wasn't there when he had his meet-ing with Sir Alex and David Gill. I respect his choice, though. The only thing I can say is that he was a great professional and he was loved in the United shirt. But I only believed he had left when I saw him posing in a Manchester City shirt.'

Upon completing a much-vaunted move across Manchester to Eastlands, Tévez was quick to announce: 'I didn't stay at United because Sir Alex Ferguson didn't do enough to keep me there.' Four days later, Manchester City unveiled a huge city-centre poster of the Argentinian – ironically celebrating a goal at Wigan that played a huge role in the Reds' 18th league title – complete with the slogan 'Welcome to Manchester'.

By then, and with far less fanfare, United's first summer signing had been secured. Like the Tévez deal, the arrival of Antonio Valencia from Wigan Athletic had been widely touted in the media. That didn't lessen its impact, however, and Sir Alex Ferguson was quick to talk up the virtues of United's new No. 25.

'Antonio is a player we have admired for some time now, having spent the last two years in the Premier League with Wigan,' he said, before confidently pronouncing: 'I am sure his pace and ability will make a significant contribution to the team.'

A reported £16 million of the Ronaldo fee had been spent within three weeks of the Portuguese's agreed departure, but replacing the reigning Ballon d'Or holder could not be achieved in a single manoeuvre. Valencia would bring pace and penetration to the flanks, but the Ecuadorian had netted just seven goals in almost three seasons at Wigan (and that tally, he admitted, 'probably included training sessions!'). United also needed a predator; sadly, an endangered species. And while Sir Alex stalked Lyon's Benzema with intent, the Frenchman was instead hoovered up into the talent vacuum of Real Madrid.

'We tried for Benzema because, at twenty-one, I felt there would be an improvement there,' said the United manager. 'He is tough, with a good physique and goalscoring record, so it was worth going a wee bit extra for him because of his age. But when it went to forty-two million Euros, it was beyond his value. We went to thirty-five million and I think that was fair.'

Never one to let the grass grow, the next day Sir Alex was on the phone to ex-Red Nicky Butt. The veteran midfielder remained a valued judge to his former manager, who asked him for his thoughts on Newcastle colleague Michael Owen. The England international striker was available on a free transfer, but was attracting few high-profile suitors thanks to the media-perpetuated reputation he'd earned as an injury-prone gamble.

On Butt's say-so, the United manager rang Owen, invited him to Chez Ferguson for a spot of breakfast and a chat, and the summer's unlikeliest transfer was secured over two hectic days. Just 48 hours earlier, racing enthusiast Owen had been rated a 20–1 long-shot to join the champions.

'The more experienced you get, the more you learn to deal with situations,' says Owen. 'But nothing really prepares you for playing for a club like this. Being asked to play for Real Madrid was fantastic, but this really was out of the blue. It was fantastic to be asked by the manager, and from there your thoughts turn from how fortunate I was to how I would make sure I performed. After that initial surprise of a couple of days, it was all about making sure I could contribute to the team.'

Among Owen's new team-mates, the prevalent air of shock mirrored that outside the club. Nevertheless, a goalscorer was on his way, and the squad quickly ushered the new, yet familiar, face into the fold. 'I think my reaction to the news was probably one of surprise at first, like everyone,' says Gary Neville. 'Obviously playing with him for England, you know his qualities. I don't think it took him long to settle in because he knew so many of us through playing for England. It's quite easy to settle in at this club. We make all new players welcome and it's an easy atmosphere for players to integrate into. There aren't any initiations for new signings. Younger players coming through the ranks into the first team have to sing a song or make a speech, but not the players who get bought in. That would be a tougher school!'

Owen's assimilation into life as a United player was not only hastened by existing friendships with international colleagues, he also found several new workmates with a shared extra-curricular interest in horse racing. 'It didn't take me long to get settled,' says the striker. 'There are a few lads who have their own shares in horses. Scholesy really loves it and obviously the Gaffer owns plenty of them as well. When I first started out in football, everybody's favourite thing was to go and play golf, but nowadays you get very few who do that, but there are plenty who are into horse racing. Everyone has to have a release and that's something a lot of players enjoy.'

An increasingly unpredictable summer's activity was far from finished. In came Gabriel Obertan from Bordeaux. Even former Red Laurent Blanc, the young winger's manager, admitted the move caught him off-guard. Making room in the Carrington dressing room were Manucho, Richard Eckersley and Lee Martin, while Senegalese striker Mame Biram Diouf signed for United and immediately rejoined Norwegian club Molde FK for the remainder of their domestic season.

Business concluded, it was now a case of how to deploy the new-look squad. A reversion to the Reds' traditional 4–4–2 formation was hardly akin to ripping up the rule book, but stripping back the tactical intricacies of an approach tailored to Ronaldo's strengths would still require a little adjustment.

'We knew we could never replace Cristiano,' says Sir Alex. 'No matter what anyone says about the lad, for my money he is the best footballer in the world. He was fantastic and you don't replace that. When you've had someone who is the best at what he does, it is no good trying to find someone to do the same job.'

Pre-season gave the coaching staff the perfect opportunity to tinker with and trial various tactical and personnel combinations, with the hefty fringe benefit of the fitness boost brought about by a four-game tour of Asia and a two-match stopover at the Audi Cup in Germany.

First up in a madcap fortnight was a 15-hour, 6,600-mile trip to Malaysia. Before the Reds could even touch down in Kuala Lumpur, however, the forensically planned tour was under threat. Two suicide bombings in Jakarta, the second stop on United's trip, had tragically killed nine people. The Reds had been booked into the Ritz-Carlton hotel, one of two buildings hit by the blasts.

'When we landed in Kuala Lumpur, the first text message I got was about the Jakarta bombings, so we had to make a quick decision to cancel the Indonesia leg of the tour,' says David Gill. 'It was disappointing, but it was the right decision and we settled in Malaysia with everyone pulling together to arrange a second game.'

United edged both games against a Malaysia XI, winning 3–2 through goals from Wayne Rooney, Nani and Michael Owen, before Owen and Kiko Macheda secured a 2–0 victory in the hastily arranged second fixture. Next came the seven-hour flight to South Korea. For Gary Neville, however, Incheon International Airport would become familiar surroundings. Two days after arriving, the United skipper was heading back to Manchester to receive treatment on a minor groin injury.

For those who remained in Seoul, the fanatical scenes were mind-boggling. On his first pre-season trip with the Reds, Dimitar Berbatov admitted: 'It's crazy, it's like being in the Beatles! Everybody's screaming and chanting Manchester United names. It makes you feel good that so many people want to come and see you. It doesn't matter where we go, we are always welcomed like we're the biggest club in the world.'

Even Sir Alex concurred: 'I'm still amazed sometimes when we arrive at hotels and there are thousands of fans hanging about. Then they're in the corridors and in the lifts! You have to admire that love of the club. In fact, it's typical of the whole Far East – we have a terrific fanbase and there's a great fanaticism here.'

Special affection was reserved for local hero Ji-sung Park, who joined the squad direct from his summer holidays. His presence ensured a sell-out 64,000 crowd at Seoul's World Cup Stadium, where United overcame the stern challenge of FC Seoul, winning 3–2 courtesy of goals from Rooney, Macheda and Berbatov.

The final inter-Asian flight took the travelling party just 650 miles to the Chinese city of Hangzhou, for the tour-capping finale against Hangzhou Greentown. While the previous three games had been relatively testing affairs, the Reds' 8–2 romp against the Chinese side was a cakewalk. Goals from Owen (2), Berbatov and Zoran Tošić had the Reds out of sight before half time, then Nani and a Ryan Giggs hat-trick – his first for the club in any senior capacity – ensured a goal-fest for the enraptured locals.

Soon afterwards, the United party bade farewell to Asia, making another sapping 5,500-mile trip to Munich for a two-day involvement in the inaugural Audi Cup alongside hosts Bayern Munich, AC Milan and Boca Juniors. More travelling for the players, but clocking up air miles doesn't detract from the experience of touring to far-flung hotbeds of United fanaticism, according to John O'Shea.

'It's always incredible to see the reaction we get,' says the Irishman, 'But it's also a key part of our preparations for the new season. With all the travelling you don't perhaps get as much quality time to train as you would at Carrington, but the intensity of playing games in such hot conditions really sets you up for the months ahead.'

After touching down in Germany, the Reds faced the Argentine giants in the opening match and maiden United goals for Anderson and debutant Antonio Valencia secured a hard-fought 2–1 victory. The reward was a berth against Bayern in the final, but a drab 90 minutes took the match to a penalty shoot-out. Not only did United eventually lose 7–6 in an epic contest, but Edwin van der Sar sustained a broken finger in saving Danijel Pranjić's effort. Not for the last time in 2009–10, United would leave Munich beaten, and carrying an injury to a key player.

Back in Manchester, scans confirmed the Dutchman would be out of action for two months, but in Ben Foster and Tomasz Kuszczak the club had two more-than-capable understudies. 'I did get the sense it was my chance,' says Foster. 'It was a good opportunity to come into the team and play some regular football, and that's how it worked out, really. It was a horrible injury for Edwin – he said it was one of the worst he's ever had – but nevertheless it did open it up for me and Tomasz a little bit.'

Polish international Kuszczak was preferred in the Reds' next pre-season outing, a 2–0 win over Valencia at Old Trafford, secured by goals from Wayne Rooney and Tom Cleverley, who joined Watford a fortnight later on a season-long loan. With the season just ten days away, Sir Alex conceded he had a goalkeeping conundrum. 'It is not an easy one for me,' he said. 'It's a little bit of a dilemma and I'll speak to both Ben and Tomasz about it.'

Foster got the nod for the summer's final preparatory game: the Community Shield against Chelsea at Wembley. It was a familiar foe, and the chance to secure a silver-lined start to the new season.

2

August

'When there's a trophy up for grabs it means everything to you to walk out of that stadium as winners,' said Rio Ferdinand, gearing up for the final match before United's third straight defence of the Premier League title began.

A trip to face Chelsea in the Community Shield would provide a barometer of the Reds' progress after exertions in the Far East and Germany but, although Ferdinand coveted the silverware, he was realistic enough about the lack of gravity attached to victory.

'Winning would be great, but it won't guarantee a successful season,' he said. 'You can't read too much into these things. Obviously, being in Asia for two weeks took a lot out of the team – it was a tiring trip – but we should be very close to peak performance by Sunday.'

Manchester United 2 Chelsea 2
(Chelsea won 4–1 on penalties)

Wembley Stadium, 9 August 2009

The first silverware of the 2009–10 season went to Stamford Bridge, but an injury-hit United side displayed all the pluck and guts of seasoned winners to dominate the first half and force a penalty shoot-out after Chelsea had gone ahead. Nani's opener and Wayne Rooney's injury-time equalizer flanked goals from Ricardo Carvalho and Frank Lampard for the Londoners, who strolled to victory on penalties after misses from Ryan Giggs and Patrice Evra.

After all the pre-match debate over the choice between Ben Foster and Tomasz Kuszczak in goal, United scarcely needed a goalkeeper during the first half. Foster got the nod, but he could only watch on as Petr Čech single-handedly kept Chelsea in the game. The giant Czech was powerless to prevent Nani's early thunderbolt, but produced a string of fine saves, most notably to keep out Darren Fletcher's curling effort, before Carvalho nodded home a scrappy equalizer early in the second half.

The Blues took the lead in controversial circumstances soon afterwards. Michael Ballack caught Patrice Evra with an elbow but, as the Frenchman lay prostrate, Chelsea played on and Lampard hammered home via the post. Evra and his colleagues were incandescent with rage, and that sense of injustice fuelled a late rally.

Just when the gig appeared to be up, however, Rooney latched onto Giggs's perfect through-ball and clipped a delightful left-footed finish over Čech, taking the game to penalties, where the Blues would have the final laugh. However, the manner in which the Reds had bossed matters for long periods – minus departed stars and a spate of injured players – augured well for the forthcoming season.

Team: Foster; O'Shea (Fabio 76), Ferdinand, Evans, Evra; Park
(Giggs 75), Fletcher (Scholes 75), Carrick, Nani (Valencia 62);
Rooney, Berbatov (Owen 75)
Scorers: Nani (10), Rooney (90)
Attendance: 85,896
Referee: Chris Foy

Only 90 minutes into the new term, and there was already a pivotal refereeing decision to discuss. Chris Foy's decision to allow Chelsea's second goal provoked a stormy response in the United camp, and Sir Alex was quick to offer his thoughts. 'That incident cost us the game,' said the boss. 'The referee saw it – Ballack elbowed Evra in the face – and the referee was clearly in line with the actual incident. I'm disappointed because he stopped the game twice before that for fouls, or for players lying down. Ballack was lying down and he got up within seconds but the referee thought it was serious, a serious foul.'

Sir Alex's irritation was hardly soothed by his side's profligacy in front of goal, which proved costly as the Blues eventually extracted a shred of consolation for their penalty hell in Moscow two seasons earlier.

'We played well for a lot of the game and we should have put it to bed in the first half,' said Sir Alex. 'Their equalizer was a poor goal from our point of view, I think we should have defended it better. Chelsea at that point had come into the game and were controlling it. Their second goal, as we saw, shouldn't have been allowed. Once they got that goal, Chelsea didn't look like losing the game. I thought they were in control, but we got the equalizer and then penalty kicks . . . Well, we've never been that great at penalty kicks. Only once, I think!'

With pre-season done and dusted, the United manager was pleased to see his side's fitness levels at a promising level, equipping them ideally for the rigours of the season ahead, and the task of sustaining success after the loss of Ronaldo. Not for the first time, youth would be given a chance to prove itself.

'It's a fresh start, a new challenge for us,' enthused Sir Alex. 'We have a lot of young players that want to do well. That's the area in which I am most encouraged. Our critics are misreading the situation with our young players developing and improving. There are good signs there. We have a very strong squad. We're where we want to be. The issue is how we progress as a team, in a different shape and a different way to when Cristiano was here. That is something I'm looking forward to and interested to see our progress and what this team can do. It will be different without Cristiano.

'You hope the nucleus of experience we have helps those young players develop, passing on everything they've picked up over the years. Whatever they have done in the past can be done by these players. They're at the right club and have the right motivation to win, with the right platform to succeed. That's the value of players like Paul Scholes, Ryan Giggs and Gary Neville. That transmits itself into these young players.

'There is no decline in our motivation. Our pre-season went well and our form is good. I think we should have won the Community Shield and we should have beaten Bayern Munich in the Audi Cup. But they're the games we needed. They brought good edge to our game and Sunday is the acid test of whether we're ready.'

Barclays Premier League

Manchester United 1 Birmingham City 0

Old Trafford, 16 August 2009

For the first time in three seasons, United's title defence began with a victory, albeit of the slimmest possible margin in a trying tussle with Alex McLeish's well-drilled Birmingham. Wayne Rooney's first-half tap-in, turned home from close range after his initial header had hit the post, won all three points for the Reds, who were also indebted to a wonderful late save from goalkeeper Ben Foster to keep out Christian Benítez's shot.

Pre-match expectations had been high going into a gloriously sunny afternoon clash against a team who had opened their previous season against Sheffield United in the Coca-Cola Championship. The Midlanders' steadfast resolve would soon become apparent during an impressive return to the top flight, but most supporters inside Old Trafford expected a one-way goal avalanche.

United made the majority of the first-half chances, as Joe Hart denied Dimitar Berbatov and Rooney – the latter after a sumptuous chip – before Nani crossed for Rooney to tap the hosts ahead at the second attempt, on 34 minutes. Try as they might, neither Rooney nor his colleagues could find another route past the visitors. On-loan Manchester City goalkeeper Hart did well to field Rooney's audacious 35-yard snapshot just after the break, while Berbatov was twice agonizingly close to opening his account for the season.

The solitary goal did little but fray nerves among the home support, however, and late anguish was only averted by the brilliance of Foster, who reacted superbly to turn away substitute Benítez's close-range effort with ten minutes remaining. Another sub, United's Michael Owen, was also thwarted by goalkeeping heroics in injury time, but it mattered little: the champions were off and running for the season. It was a victory achieved with equal measures of swagger and uncertainty. Few guessed then that it had set the tone for a capricious Premier League season.

Team: Foster; Fabio, O'Shea, Evans (Brown 75), Evra; Valencia, Fletcher, Scholes, Nani (Giggs 46); Berbatov (Owen 74), Rooney
Scorer: Rooney (34)
Attendance: 75,062
Referee: Lee Mason

Having played a major role in United's three-point haul, Ben Foster was predictably elated at full-time. 'I was happy with my contribution to the win, especially after last weekend at Wembley when I was disappointed with my performance,' he admitted. 'It was good to bounce back. The most important thing was to get the three points but I was pleased to keep a clean sheet and do fairly well.'

The England international also reserved praise for the stand-in members of United's injury-hit defence. 'Those who came in – John O'Shea and Jonny Evans – were fantastic, while Fabio on the right is playing beyond his years. He's a great talent,' added Foster. 'I think that shows we've got the players here. Whoever comes in can do a job just as well as the others can.'

The manner of United's victory was unexpectedly laboured, but the failure to fire a hatful of goals past Alex McLeish's Birmingham would become more understandable with time. 'It was a really tough game,' reflected Paul Scholes. 'Birmingham were a very well-organized team and they laid down a marker then that showed they were a tough team to beat. It was a sign of things to come for them for the rest of the season.'

With one promoted side vanquished, another awaited the Reds just three days later. Burnley's first taste of top-flight football in 33 years had yielded a routine 2–0 defeat at Stoke City, but Owen Coyle's side had been preparing for United's visit to Turf Moor from the moment the Premier League fixtures had been announced. 'Wednesday's match will be a tough one,' warned Foster. 'Burnley are going to be really up for it and their fans will give them an extra twenty per cent. We've got to go there, be professional, do what we did against Birmingham and hopefully keep another clean sheet.'

John O'Shea, speaking from experience, echoed those sentiments. 'I played at Turf Moor a few seasons ago in a League Cup game and the atmosphere that night was special,' said the Irishman. 'So I can only imagine what it'll be like for their first Premier League game. We know it will be a real battle, but it's up to us to make it as tough as we can for them.

'People looked at our first couple of fixtures and said they would be surprised if we didn't pick up maximum points. But we have to guard against that. Look at the last two seasons: we drew against

Reading and then Newcastle. We know teams that get promoted are on such a high in the first month, then they realize how tough the Premier League is. We have to make sure Burnley realize it a bit earlier than normal.'

Over at Turf Moor, Clarets skipper Graham Alexander voiced his side's determination to spring an almighty shock. 'I've never put [the Premier League] on a pedestal,' said the Scot. 'It's just a game of football against eleven men. We're used to being the underdog here and it's par for the course. We just have to work hard.'

With no small measure of that promised grit, the Clarets had established themselves as cup menaces for some of English football's leading lights over previous seasons, before returning to the top flight via the play-offs under Owen Coyle's leadership.

'Burnley is a fantastic story,' Sir Alex said at his pre-match press conference. 'They've been outside the top league for thirty-three years, which is a long time. No matter what happens this season, they won't forget this. It'll be a great experience. Over the years we've played promoted teams early on in the season, and this year's no different with Birmingham and then Burnley. It'd be nice to get off to a good start. We didn't do that well early on last season, so we need to change that this time around. It can be hard going to a promoted team's ground early on. You can imagine what the atmosphere is going to be like at Burnley – it's going to be red-hot. It'll be a flag day. It's going to be a big occasion for them. But hopefully that's where our experience helps.'

Barclays Premier League

Burnley 1 Manchester United 0
Turf Moor, 19 August 2009

Pre-match warnings and wariness went unheeded as Robbie Blake's first-half blockbuster sent the champions tumbling to a resounding first defeat of the season at Turf Moor. Those who had predicted a season of struggle for the Reds revelled as a string of missed chances – most notably a Michael Carrick penalty, saved by Clarets goalkeeper Brian Jensen – proved costly.

Long before kick-off, Turf Moor was a citadel of sound as a capacity 20,872 attendance whipped up a frenzied atmosphere. Despite the strident home support, United made the brighter start and should have moved ahead inside two minutes when Michael Owen, making his first competitive start for his new club, missed Patrice Evra's left-wing cross without a defender in sight.

The hosts grew in confidence, however, and took a shock lead on 19 minutes when Stephen Jordan's cross was headed out only as far as Blake, whose unstoppable volley hurtled past Ben Foster and into the net to put the Clarets ahead.

In the fashion of champions, United's response was merely to shake off the blow and hit back. While Burnley's defence largely provided an unyielding shield for Jensen, Owen was off-target with a free header and the back-tracking Blake conceded a penalty for a rash challenge on Evra. With no Ronaldo to rely on from the spot anymore, the usually unerring Carrick assumed the taker's duties, only to see his effort palmed to safety by Burnley's giant custodian. Cue further bedlam from a delirious home contingent, all eager to salute the efforts of a goalkeeper affectionately known as 'Beast'.

After the break, Jensen was at it again to deny Ji-sung Park and Ryan Giggs, while Dimitar Berbatov, Wayne Rooney and Evra all fired off-target in a draining, frustrating outing for the Reds. With every passing minute and each spurned opportunity, the sense grew that this was Burnley's evening. When referee Alan Wiley confirmed that unlikely outcome with the final whistle, the inquest immediately began.

Team: Foster; O'Shea, Brown (Neville 71), Evans, Evra; Park, Carrick, Giggs, Anderson (Valencia 59); Rooney, Owen (Berbatov 63)
Scorer: n/a
Attendance: 20,872
Referee: Alan Wiley

'We were too frivolous with the chances we had,' admitted Sir Alex afterwards, clearly irked. 'Sometimes we were taking touches on the ball instead of shooting quickly. And in the last twenty minutes, we rushed and made one or two bad decisions. It was a bad performance. If we'd scored the penalty, I think we'd have won the game. I think we'd have composed ourselves and taken our time in the second half.'

While irritated by his own side's shortcomings, the United manager was gracious enough to lavish praise on their conquerors, saying: 'You can't deny Burnley their victory. Every member of their team worked their socks off and the fans were fantastic – they got behind them all night, cheering every kick of the ball. To play Manchester United on their return to the top division after a long time, it was a great occasion for them.'

Assistant manager Mike Phelan (a former Burnley player) concurred that Carrick's penalty miss was a pivotal moment, but still saluted the midfielder's desire to step up and take the kick. 'He took the ball early – maybe there were a few others who wanted to take it – but he took the ball and had the courage to take it,' said Phelan. 'He was confident. Unfortunately he didn't put it in the net, which probably would have settled us down a bit just before half time. But it wasn't to be.'

For Carrick, the missed opportunity merely capped an evening to forget. 'We were pretty stunned in the dressing room afterwards,' he says. 'You could say that it was the wrong time to play Burnley, so early in the season, but at the same time we shouldn't have lost that game. That was their first home game in the Premier League, and obviously us coming to town was massive for them. But we just weren't firing on the night, I missed a penalty and everything added up to a really disappointing night for us. We couldn't move on quick enough.'

Inevitably, United's misfortune yielded countless column inches over the following days. Media outlets were awash with theories on how the champions had come unstuck against such unfancied opposition, and why the usually free-scoring Reds had mustered only a single goal in the opening two games. The general consensus predictably fingered the club's transfer activity: no Ronaldo, no Tévez, no chance. Within the confines of Carrington, however, there was no panic. After some fierce training sessions, Burnley was out of the players' systems, and attentions switched to the short trip to Wigan Athletic's newly named DW Stadium.

'Bad starts are possibly part of our history,' Sir Alex told his pre-match press conference. 'But we don't like losing, and we don't like losing in a situation where we feel we should have won. We've dom-inated two games of football, but of course we'd like to score more goals. Our ratio of goals dropped last season: it was our poorest for fifteen years in terms of goal difference. That was an issue last year and will be again unless we step up to the mark, which I'm confi-dent we will do. We'll win games because this is a good squad of players.

'You can't lose too many games in this league and we've already lost one. It's another day in the history of Manchester United. It's not a part of us that we like, but none the less it's a part of us. It's hap-pened before and it'll happen again. At this club, whenever we have a defeat it's about what you then go and do. On Saturday, as is always the case in football, we have an opportunity. Four days after a bad defeat we can do something about it.'

Sir Alex's cautious optimism was fuelled by the return from injury of Nemanja Vidić and skipper Gary Neville. Although Rio Ferdinand was expected to miss another month of action, having the squad's defensive options bolstered by such seasoned, reliable performers proved a huge boon.

'Experience is important,' said the manager. 'And the kind of experience that Gary brings is great for us, while Vidić's performance levels since he's been with us have been outstanding. So you'd always want Nemanja in your team. We'll get that back on Saturday and that'll help us.'

Barclays Premier League

Wigan Athletic 0 Manchester United 5

DW Stadium, 22 August 2009

United not only returned to winning ways, but were back in the goalscoring groove with a second-half annihilation of Roberto Martínez's Wigan Athletic.

Wayne Rooney reached and passed a ton of Premier League goals with a quickfire brace, while Dimitar Berbatov, Michael Owen and Nani all found the net as the Reds ran riot at the DW Stadium.

Sir Alex Ferguson made seven personnel changes after his side's shock reverse at Burnley. One of those, Darren Fletcher, was only prevented from giving United the lead inside four minutes when Titus Bramble cleared his effort off the line.

Paul Scholes lashed over the bar from just inside the area and Rooney chanced his arm twice in a minute, while the Latics served belated notice of their presence as Jason Koumas brought a wonderful save from Ben Foster with a curling 25-yarder.

Missed chances had almost cost United for the second time in two games. After the interval, however, the Reds were remorseless in front of goal. Former Wigan winger Antonio Valencia, enjoying a mixed reception from the home support, crossed superbly for Rooney to nod in his 100th Premier League goal, before Berbatov capped a delightful move by lobbing the ball over Chris Kirkland and volleying in.

Rooney doubled his haul with a deflected effort before Owen, on for the England striker, bagged his maiden United goal with a trademark clinical finish. Having timed his run to perfection, the former Liverpool and Real Madrid star latched onto Nani's through-ball and dispatched a cool strike into Kirkland's far corner.

Portuguese winger Nani put the gloss on a five-star performance with a dipping 25-yard free-kick in the final minute of stoppage time,

20

ensuring the perfect riposte for any detractors looking for further flaws in the champions after that unlikely Turf Moor setback.

Team: Foster; Neville, Vidić, Evans (O'Shea 72), Evra; Valencia, Fletcher, Scholes (Gibson 72), Nani; Rooney (Owen 72), Berbatov
Scorers: Rooney 56, 65, Berbatov 58, Owen 85, Nani 90
Attendance: 18,164
Referee: Howard Webb

Wayne Rooney was understandably delighted to have notched a personal milestone with his DW Stadium brace, but conceded that posting a handsome victory was of greater importance. 'Of course it's nice to score a hundred goals, especially for a team like United,' he said. 'But the most important thing is the three points. It's nice but it's something I'll look back on when I've finished playing. I've got a lot of games and a lot of goals left in me, so it's not something I'm too concerned with at the minute.

'We played some great football. The first half was frustrating because we had chances to score and never took them. In the second half we took the game to Wigan and they couldn't live with us. Everyone's delighted that Berba and especially Michael scored. It's a great feeling for the three of us to score, and Nani at the end. Scoring five away from home isn't easy.'

While one United goalscorer celebrated his 100th goal for the club, another was equally elated to have notched his first. 'It was certainly a great feeling to score,' beamed Michael Owen. 'I'd got a few in pre-season, but there's nothing quite like doing it in a competitive game. And I probably scored the hardest chance I've had! I had two chances at Burnley and one against Birmingham, but this was the fourth real opportunity I've had.

'I don't think I missed a chance in pre-season, but I've missed a couple since the season started and, as ever, everyone is quick to write you off. It was as if I hadn't scored for a couple of years! That's something I've had to deal with for years now and I don't think that will change until I hang up my boots. But I'd be disappointed if people didn't think I could go on from here. I obviously believe I can, as I have done throughout my career and I certainly expect to score more goals in the Red shirt.'

For Sir Alex, a five-star return to form was rendered even sweeter by the identity of his goalscorers. With all three senior strikers off and running for the season, the United manager could call upon predators driven by the taste for blood. 'Our strikers have scored the goals today, and that's the important thing,' he said.

'That can only do us the power of good, because you know what strikers are like – when they're not scoring they're not the same people. If Dimitar and Michael can weigh in with the goals that we expect of Wayne Rooney, then it will make a difference to our game. It's terrific for a young lad like Wayne to reach a hundred goals at his age. We've had players over the years who've taken many years to get to one hundred. For a young lad to do it, it's great.

'Michael's was a fantastic goal: great run and excellent movement, and a good pass from Nani. Michael Owen has proved himself over the last ten years to be the best goalscorer in England and today he showed that again. I think it will do him the world of good. Obviously coming to the club and after all the discussion around him joining United after being at Liverpool, it was important to get a goal like that, and the crowd were great with him. That was fantastic.'

Upon opening his United account, Owen rejoiced in front of the thousands of travelling supporters, who signalled their acceptance of the former Liverpool prodigy with ironic renditions of an anti-Liverpool anthem, much to the amusement of all those of a Red persuasion.

'I enjoyed it,' smiles Owen, looking back. 'To be honest, whatever they sang about me, it's great. You always want to enjoy an affinity with the crowd. You always play better when you feel as if you're wanted and liked – that doesn't just go for football, that's in any walk of life. If you feel good and confident in your job, you're going to perform better. The minute the fans chant your name, you get a lift and feel better about yourself, and obviously there's a lot of irony in that chant for me.'

With the goals flowing again, both individually and collectively, United's outlook was altogether rosier. Rooney revealed in his post-match interview that he and his fellow players are thick-skinned enough to combat the flak that flew after defeat at Turf Moor. 'To be honest, we're not that concerned what anyone outside the club has to say,' he responded. 'The people who matter speak to us and that's who we listen to – we don't listen to anyone else.'

The most prominent voice, that of Sir Alex, added a closing dose of perspective just before the Reds left the DW Stadium. 'We can't worry about these things,' he said of the public furore that followed the humiliating defeat to Burnley. 'We've got to look at the reality of what we're talking about, and the reality of Wednesday was disappointing. We're not going to kill ourselves because of it, but we're going to take reminders of it, lessons and experience from it. We all know we've got players with great experience at our club. We still aren't prepared for the kind of setback we got on Wednesday. It shouldn't have happened, but it did happen and we had to do something about it. You're always looking for a response, and we got a good one.'

With seven days before the next outing, a mouth-watering visit from Arsenal, Carrington became a hive of preparation. But, for a small party of club staff, including chief executive David Gill, the latter part of the week was spent in Nyon, Switzerland, for the annual glitzy draw for the group stage of the UEFA Champions League.

For the fifth season in a row, United's representatives were joined by their counterparts from Arsenal, Chelsea and Liverpool. But for all the familiar faces on show, the selection process would incredibly pit the Reds against three completely alien opponents: Russia's CSKA Moscow, Turkey's Beşiktaş and Germany's VfL Wolfsburg. A trio of trips into the unknown lay ahead, two of which would involve jaunts to the very edge of the continent.

Gill, however, was bullish about the Reds' hopes, especially after reaching two successive finals. 'I think you can get psyched out by travel and that sort of thing,' he said. 'I'm sure it won't affect those European games or the Premier League games either side of them. We're looking forward to going back to Moscow – there were great scenes there back in 2008 so we're excited by that. It's a new season and we're looking forward to it. It's important to win the group so you have the advantage of playing at home in the second leg of the first knock-out game. I'm sure the guys are now beginning to do their homework and assess the teams, so Sir Alex has the information he needs.'

Sure enough, back at Carrington, the United manager had arrived at his assessment of the challengers. 'These are difficult ties,' Sir Alex said. 'CSKA have developed strongly in the last few years and games in Turkey are always difficult. We also know the quality we're up against with Wolfsburg, with what they achieved in the Bundesliga last season. I think it's a difficult group and certainly the toughest of all the English teams. It's difficult, especially as after two away games we come back to important games in the Premier League against Manchester City and Liverpool.

'I think Russian teams have improved a tremendous amount in the last few years, with a big financial investment in their football. There are a lot of Brazilian players playing in the league, so we can expect a difficult game there. We've had experiences of playing in Turkey in the past and it is never easy. The atmosphere is quite volatile. Then our last game is against Wolfsburg, who won the Bundesliga last season. Their home record is very good.'

Ominous indeed, but the Reds' travelling party weren't just returning to Manchester with a tricky schedule to fathom: on board was UEFA's prestigious award for Edwin van der Sar, voted the best goalkeeper in Europe.

'The award couldn't have gone to a better professional,' said Sir Alex. 'Edwin's dedication to football in the last few years has been absolutely unbelievable. It's an award that is thoroughly deserved and I think everyone in football will applaud that.'

For neutrals and those of a partisan persuasion, United's clash with Arsenal, which loomed the day after the Champions League draw, was a tantalizing spectre. For much of the Premier League era, the two clubs had jostled one another for silverware. Although Arsene Wenger's side have failed to snare a single trophy since mugging United in the 2005 FA Cup final, Sir Alex conceded the fixture still retained special significance.

'Games against Arsenal are never easy, but they're always interesting,' he said. 'Over the years United–Arsenal matches have been the feature of the Premier League. For a long time we were both competing for the same number-one spot. Some of the games were very feisty, but I think the character and the personalities within the teams have changed. We don't have a Keane or a Vieira. There's been a material change in that sense. They were both volatile characters and dominant figures in the team and the captains in the sides. That said, even the last game of the [2008–09] season, which finished 0–0, got a bit heated at times. So it won't be any less competitive.'

Arsenal travelled north after an eye-catching start to the season, having roundly thrashed Everton 6–1 at Goodison Park, strolled to home and away Champions League qualifying victories over Celtic and pummelled Portsmouth 4–1 at the Emirates Stadium.

Regardless of the visitors' menacing form, Sir Alex and his players conceded that United's record in seismic clashes against Arsenal, Chelsea and Liverpool needed to improve on the previous season's return. 'Some seasons we've won those games and lost the league and other times we've lost those matches and won it,' said Gary Neville. 'Last season we lost twice to Liverpool, drew against Arsenal at home, lost away at the Emirates and drew away at Chelsea. So they didn't play too much importance last season.

'It's about being consistent over the whole campaign, but obviously if you can take points off your major rivals it can only be good, especially when the games are later on in the season. If the matches are early you at least have time to recover. But as we've seen, winning them doesn't necessarily mean you're going to win the league. Saying that, of course, we want a good result on Saturday.'

Barclays Premier League

Manchester United 2 Arsenal 1

Old Trafford, 29 August 2009

One of the most memorable own goals in recent memory gave United a vital early-season victory over perennial title rivals Arsenal at Old Trafford.

Abou Diaby's inexplicable header past Gunners goalkeeper Manuel Almunia completed a quickfire turnaround for United, who had drawn level through a Wayne Rooney penalty after Andrei Arshavin opened the scoring.

Encounters between England's most expansive, entertaining teams are invariably engaging affairs, and this game predictably ebbed and flowed from end to end. However, attacks were often launched by opposition mistakes, with both sides uncharacteristically sloppy in possession throughout the first half. Darren Fletcher, whose tough-tackling, sweat-soaked shift in midfield laid the foundations for victory and later prompted an indignant outburst from Gunners boss Arsene Wenger, lashed a volley over the bar early on, while Rooney's free-kick inched just past the post with Almunia beaten.

Arshavin and Robin van Persie had already come close for the visitors, however, and it was the little Russian who opened the scoring five minutes before the break. Taking advantage of space to turn and advance on goal, Arshavin smashed a 25-yard shot that flew through the stretched fingertips of Ben Foster. Were there any hint of blame attached to the United goalkeeper, it evaporated shortly after half time when he pulled off an incredible reaction save with his left foot to deny van Persie a potentially decisive second goal.

That moment proved pivotal. Just three minutes later, Rooney reached Ryan Giggs's threaded through-ball just ahead of Almunia, tumbled under the Spaniard's challenge and emphatically converted the resulting penalty into the Stretford End goal.

Within five minutes the scoreline had completely flipped. Giggs's inswinging free-kick dropped between Almunia and his defence and, under no pressure from anybody in a Red shirt, Diaby's decisive act was to thump a header past his own goalkeeper and tee up a vital win for the hosts.

The nature of the rapid turnaround devoured Arsenal's confidence, and both Dimitar Berbatov and Nani spurned presentable chances to further extend the lead. In true United fashion, however, there was still time for a late flirtation with danger, as van Persie lashed home a finish in the 96th minute, only for an assistant's flag to correctly rule that William Gallas had been offside in the build-up. Incensed, Arsene Wenger booted a stray water bottle on the touchline and was promptly banished to the stands for his outburst. Bizarre scenes unfolded as the Frenchman clambered atop the ledge between the two dugouts, apparently uncertain of just how he was meant to reach his new vantage point. Seconds later, the sideshow and main event were both ended by referee Mike Dean, putting a suitably odd gloss on a peculiar, yet crucially successful, afternoon's work for the Reds.

Team: Foster; O'Shea, Vidić, Brown, Evra; Valencia (Park 63),
Fletcher, Carrick, Giggs (Berbatov 86), Nani; Rooney
Scorers: Rooney (59 (pen)), Diaby (64 (og))
Attendance: 75,095
Referee: Mike Dean

Much of the post-match debate centred around the contribution of Darren Fletcher. The Scottish midfielder's relentless display broke up the Gunners' rhythm and inspired his team-mates to a gutsy victory. Upon learning that Wayne Rooney had landed Sky Sports' man-of-the-match award, Sir Alex laughed: 'I think Wayne will give it to

Darren! He was the outstanding performer on the field. He really was outstanding. He always does well on these big occasions because he's a big-game player.'

Rooney concurred: 'I've said many times, forwards score goals and tend to get the man-of-the-match award. But Fletch was head and shoulders above anyone else on the pitch.'

Looking back, Fletcher is faced with mixed memories of an afternoon when he drew plaudits and criticism in equal measure, from both sides of the divide. 'Arsenal played very well that day and we were probably a little bit fortunate to get the win,' he says. 'In the first half, they played really well and took the lead with an unbelievable goal from Arshavin.

'In the second half, we really battled more than anything and clawed our way back into the game. Looking back we could've played better, but the most important thing was the victory. It was about us showing great attitude. It mightn't have been pretty, but we were dogged and resilient and battled our way back into the game. To be honest, I remember the game more for Arsene Wenger's comments about me and what that meant over the coming weeks.'

The Scottish midfielder was referencing the Arsenal manager's thinly veiled dig about what he perceived as a string of unpunished fouls against his players. 'I have seen today a player who plays on the pitch only to make fouls,' said the Frenchman. 'For me, this is a point that is more urgent than diving, the players who are never punished and get out of the game without a yellow card. I think it is anti-football. I don't know why it is. You should ask the referees. Look at how many deliberate fouls some players get away with. That's a bigger problem because it cuts the flow of the game. And people pay to see football, not free-kicks.'

While Fletcher concedes some understanding of Wenger's indignant outburst, he remains adamant that the accusations sit on unstable foundations. 'I know I'm not a dirty player,' he says. 'I try and win the ball back and tackle, but it's all fair. It's never done to hurt anyone – it's just part of the British game. We love to see it in

28

England. We love to see players tackling and committed and closing down; it's an important part of the game. But I know also that when the ball comes to me, I'm able to play a little bit as well. That's the idea of being an all-round midfielder, you try and work hard and achieve that every day to try and be an all-round player.

'I can understand Arsenal's stance. They're all about total football and they play some great football, but when teams play against great football they have to beat them other ways. I'm not saying people go to kick them or anything like that, but if you stand off these players they're going to do you a lot of damage. You have to get up against them. It's more about that than kicking them. You get up against players all the time and there are going to be fouls given away.

'If you just stand off Arsenal, they'll pass you to death and beat you comfortably. If you get up against them and make it difficult for them, then you've got a chance of winning the game. If you look back, they've been on the wrong end of a lot of bad injuries, which maybe is a reason they get a little bit defensive, and understandably so. But no United player has the mentality of going out to hurt someone.'

Wenger's irritation wasn't helped by the farcical scenes in which he was needlessly banished to the stands. The faintly ludicrous memory of Arsenal's manager atop the South Stand tunnel was a lingering one.

'As a player, you don't really see too much because you're just focusing on the game. But I saw a bit going on, saw the fans going mad for it and it was quite surreal to see Arsene Wenger standing up there on the dugout, with his arms out, shrugging,' grins Ben Foster. 'I think he was a little bit bewildered by it all as well!'

Although not every game boasts such bizarre scenes, the England goalkeeper had enjoyed another eventful taster of life in between the sticks for United. Despite question marks over his failure to repel Arshavin's opener, his breathtaking stop from van Persie laid the platform for the Reds to save the match.

'I was disappointed with the goal I let in,' he admits. 'I thought

I should've saved it. You don't get too many chances in the United goalkeeper's jersey. You might make a mistake and sometimes you don't get anything else to do in the game so it doesn't reflect well on you. Thankfully I had a good save to make and I felt in some ways that helped me redeem myself. I was quite happy with it as a reaction save. Van Persie was quite close and he hit it with pace but I just managed to stick out a foot and turn it away. Plus it was one–nil at the time, and if that goes in it could've been over. Luckily I kept it out, we did well to get back into the game and it was a massive win for us.'

For the first time – but not the last – during the course of the 2009–10 campaign, United would be given a helping hand by an opposing player. In a record-breaking campaign in which the Reds benefited from 12 own goals, the first, from Abou Diaby, was perhaps the most spectacular.

Ryan Giggs has seen most things in football during his epic, unparalleled career, but seldom has he delivered a free-kick and watched an opponent emphatically convert it at the wrong end.

'Basically, I don't try and pick anyone out when I take a free-kick. I just aim to put it into an area where players are going to be,' says the Welshman. 'I put it into a decent area and I was thinking: "Why is there no one in there?" Next thing I know, it's in the back of the net. It's just one of those fluke things that happen sometimes. If you put it in the right area anything can happen, I suppose. It was an unbelievable finish. I was in shock because there wasn't anyone near him. You could understand it if he gets a nudge or just puts the ball where he didn't want to, but there was nobody near him. Nevertheless, we were happy to take it!'

Three priceless points and a dent in a fellow title contender's ambitions constituted a highly satisfactory end to August. 'The dressing room is always a special place after a victory,' admits John O'Shea. 'But it's always that little bit more enjoyable when it's a really important win or you've beaten your local rivals or a big team like Chelsea or Arsenal.' Not that United's players would be celebrating for too long: another round of World Cup qualifiers required 17 members of the first-team squad to meet up with their respective countries, hitting the pause button on United's season just as it was starting to click into gear. Perched third in the table, only Chelsea and Tottenham, with their unblemished records, could claim to have made a better start to the season. Ominously, the latter would be United's first opposition in September.

3

September

Usually a hive of activity, with players and staff filing down corridors and popping out of side doors, Carrington turns into an altogether more serene setting during international breaks. Usually. During the two-week hiatus from club football that opened September, however, it remained a milling nerve centre of bustle. There were the usual suspects: Ryan Giggs and Paul Scholes, both long since retired from international football, and Gary Neville, without an England appearance since February 2007, owing to injury and the emergence of reliable replacements. In addition, Rio Ferdinand continued his rehabilitation from injury, while Michael Owen, Anderson and Fabio also lent further first-team presence to proceedings.

'We've got a good group of players training here while the internationals are on,' said Sir Alex. 'In fact, it's unusual to have that many players here.' Although the United manager has had his share of scrapes with national football bodies – not least England's Football Association – he still roots for his players when they pull on their countries' shirts.

'It's important the players represent their countries and we want them to do well,' he said. 'When they are competitive matches we

32

don't have any complaints, because every player at our club is conscious of the fact that they have important games coming up.' Of the glut of Reds on duty, only Antonio Valencia tasted defeat in the first half of the two-match break, as Ecuador lost against Colombia.

For United, less positive overseas action was brewing in France, where Le Havre AC president Jean-Pierre Louvel publicly accused the Reds of offering financial incentives to coax highly rated teenage midfielder Paul Pogba to England. It didn't take long for the club to release the following statement:

'In response to the wholly unfounded comments widely reported in the media of Le Havre AC president, Jean-Pierre Louvel, Manchester United wishes to categorically confirm that, as a matter of club policy, and in accordance with the applicable football regulations, it does not offer inducements to the parents of players that sign for the club, such as monetary payments or the purchase of houses.

'Manchester United has today written to Le Havre AC to put it on notice that action will be taken if such allegations are repeated in relation to the transfer of Paul Pogba. Manchester United is entirely satisfied that the transfer of Paul Pogba has been conducted in accordance with the regulations set down by the world governing body, FIFA. Manchester United is ready to defend any claim brought against it by Le Havre at FIFA.

'It is to be noted that all contractual documentation relating to the player's registration with the club has already been fully ratified by The Football Association and the Premier League.'

Just a week earlier, Chelsea had been banned from signing players for two transfer windows after FIFA found them guilty of 'tapping up' former Lens midfielder Gaël Kakuta. Sir Alex quickly threw his own weight behind United's defence. 'There has been a lot of jumping on the bandwagon, but I can assure you Manchester United have behaved absolutely correctly in all our dealings with young players and their parents,' he said.

'There has never been a case, ever, that we have paid parents. It would be crazy to even contemplate that because paying a parent would be the biggest headache you could ever have. This was levelled by some frustrated director at the French club and he's now going to have to retract [his comments]. People were always going to bring us into it because we are the biggest club, but [Le Havre have done so] without any foundation, without any knowledge of the situation. What other clubs do is subject to a lot of controversy at the moment but I'm confident in our own club.'

While a storm raged around the prospective arrival of one French youngster, another was already hard at work in an attempt to reach full fitness and make a name for himself at United. Gabriel Obertan was a relative unknown when he signed from Bordeaux, but it soon became clear his development throughout his late teens had been hindered by an undetected back injury.

'At sixteen he was one of the outstanding young talents in Europe, and he's told us that over this last year and a half he's been playing with this back injury and no one thought about getting a scan,' revealed Sir Alex. 'We're taking our time with him because we want him back and at a hundred per cent. He's very quick, he can play on both sides or through the middle and he brings a real versatility to us. We expect big things from him.'

While Obertan's recuperation was a case of more haste, less speed, the recovery work of Rio Ferdinand and Gary Neville was reaping rewards. Neville's 90-minute outing for Ole Gunnar Solskjaer's Reserves just before the international break had gone flawlessly, and he was fully recovered from a calf injury. Ferdinand, meanwhile, was in line for a return at Tottenham after a week of training unhindered by his thigh injury.

The pair's involvement hinged on the flow of international stars returning to Carrington. After the second round of fixtures with their respective nations, some entered the premises assured of a berth at the 2010 World Cup, while others' fates were terminal or undecided. As ever after international breaks, the coaching staff's preparations would hinge on the dribs and drabs of players filtering home, nursing bumps and bruises sustained around the globe.

Even with a full squad available, United had the daunting prospect of travelling to White Hart Lane to face a Spurs side with a 100 per cent record and a spot atop the Premier League table. Having done his research, Sir Alex was not surprised by the Londoners' lightning start to the new term.

'I watched a couple of videos yesterday and they'll be a handful for us,' the manager told his pre-match press conference. 'But that's the nature of the Premier League. Hopefully I can pick the right team and get a good result. I think Tottenham can break into the top four. Harry Redknapp has brought in a few of his own types of players, players he's familiar with, like Peter Crouch and Jermain Defoe. He's now got Niko Kranjčar as well from Portsmouth and Wilson Palacios from Wigan, who was a good signing and brought some steel into the midfield.

'They've really started well this season; there's a good degree of experience there. I think Tottenham definitely have a realistic chance of breaking into the top four. They and City are ahead of the rest, I think . . . Then it's Everton and Aston Villa.'

Ryan Giggs, a veteran of United–Tottenham clashes down the years, was prepared for another absorbing encounter between two clubs that have traditionally clung to the need to entertain. 'They've got a lot of players who are on song, like Aaron Lennon and Jermain Defoe, who's scoring the goals for them,' said the winger. 'Spurs are also good defensively and this season they've started really well. Over the years there have been some great games between us. It's a fixture famous for two teams who like to play football the right way. White Hart Lane is a great place to go, but it's always a tough game. We know we'll have to be at our best because we're playing against a very good side.'

Barclays Premier League

Tottenham Hotspur 1 Manchester United 3
White Hart Lane, 12 September 2009

Despite a rip-roaring start from the in-form hosts and the dismissal of Paul Scholes, United posted one of the season's finest away performances with a swaggering comeback victory at White Hart Lane. Jermain Defoe's superb strike gave the hosts a dream start, but the Reds' slick, incisive passing had Harry Redknapp's side chasing shadows throughout the game, and goals from Ryan Giggs, Anderson and Wayne Rooney earned United three impressive points.

Four wins from four previous games had Spurs – unbeaten at home throughout 2009 – atop the Premier League table as the champions arrived in North London, and Defoe's record of four goals in as many games pinned him as the hosts' main threat. His breathtaking opener, a marvellous close-range overhead kick inside the first minute, merely confirmed his billing.

Despite the early setback, United could have levelled just a minute later as Carlo Cudicini did well to parry away Darren Fletcher's effort. Peter Crouch twice fired off-target as the game flowed from end to end, but the visitors' crisp passing carried greater menace, with Scholes and Giggs in devastating form. Making his 700th United start, the latter restored parity after 25 minutes, curling a 20-yard free-kick superbly into Cudicini's top left-hand corner.

The deserved leveller threatened to burst the dam, as Cudicini superbly denied Dimitar Berbatov and Rooney, before Berbatov fired over after a goalmouth scramble in which his initial shot had been cleared off the line. Spurs' resistance was broken again five minutes before the interval, when Scholes's blocked shot ricocheted back to the edge of the area and Anderson hammered home his first goal for the club after more than two seasons of close calls.

Redknapp introduced Jermaine Jenas at half time and the England midfielder drew a stunning fingertip stop from Foster with a curling effort from 25 yards. It was a save goalkeeper coach Eric Steele would later label the best of the season. From the subsequent corner, Crouch nodded over via the crossbar.

Tottenham's hopes were boosted by the dismissal of Scholes for picking up a second booking, and former Spur Michael Carrick replaced Berbatov as United adopted a 4–4–1 line-up. Lone striker Rooney had an effort acrobatically tipped onto the woodwork by Cudicini as United continued to forge the clearer openings, before the No. 10 added the killer goal 12 minutes from time when he latched on to Darren Fletcher's through-ball, turned inside Alan Hutton and slipped a shot between Cudicini's legs.

Comfortable victors at one of the Premier League's most unforgiving venues, United's season was gathering momentum.

Team: Foster; O'Shea, Ferdinand, Vidić, Evra; Fletcher, Anderson (Nani 82), Scholes, Giggs; Berbatov (Carrick 62), Rooney
Scorers: Giggs (25), Anderson (41), Rooney (78)
Attendance: 35,785
Referee: Andre Marriner

'I think it was always going to be a hard game,' admitted Sir Alex. 'Spurs are in great form at the moment and they got off to a fantastic start by scoring in the first minute. It was a marvellous finish from Defoe, but it was early in the game and there were still ninety minutes to play. We had to gather our game and show our composure and I thought our football was fantastic.'

At the heart of United's display was another superlative-stretching effort from Ryan Giggs and Paul Scholes, even if the latter was harshly removed from the fray by referee Andre Marriner.

Looking back, Scholes states: 'It was probably one of our best performances of the season. We did really well to go in ahead at half time, especially after falling behind inside a couple of minutes to a very good goal from Defoe. We fought back and played really well.

White Hart Lane is always a tough place to go and this season it has been a better Spurs team than I can remember. It was a great result for us. I got sent off when I never should have done. It was never a foul for the second booking, but thankfully Wayne popped up with a third goal to make the game safe.'

The match achieved landmark status in the career of another midfielder, who finally ended his goalscoring duck. Inevitably, Anderson's colleagues were swift to acknowledge the achievement, and pour a small measure of scorn over his impromptu celebration of firing double-barrelled fingers at the home support.

'He's had a bit of stick about his celebration,' said Giggs. 'But we're all pleased. His performances have been really good since he's come to the club. He's a top player. He knows he needs to add goals to his game and hopefully he'll score a lot more.'

'I think the lads have seen it coming,' added Rio Ferdinand. 'The international break gave him plenty of time to train and we've seen glimpses of what he can do. He scored a good goal for the Reserves and I think he's got the knack now of scoring. Hopefully he can go on a good run now and score more because if he does he'll be a top-class player.'

The Reds' equalizing goal provided another talking point, with further proof that Cristiano Ronaldo's set-piece prowess could be replicated. 'I've been a bit rusty at free-kicks,' said Giggs. 'Nani's already scored one this season, Wayne and myself can both take them. We've got plenty of options, but we didn't have a look-in for four or five years, with Cristiano being about!'

With a flight to Turkey less than 48 hours away, the Reds remained in London and flew to Istanbul from Stansted. The euphoria of reaching such fine domestic form was quickly quelled by a return to European duty for the first time since losing out to Barcelona four months earlier.

Defeat in Rome had not only cost Sir Alex's men their most prized possession, it had reintroduced the Reds to defeat in Europe. In reaching two successive finals, United had set a new competition record of 25 games unbeaten, five games longer than Ajax's previous stint. To be brushed aside by Xavi, Iniesta et al. in Italy stung, and still rankled.

'I'm a winner – I like to win – so I still think about what happened in Rome,' said Patrice Evra. 'Everybody says we did well last season and we won three trophies, but when you lose the final in the manner we did, without giving a true account of ourselves, it's very frustrating. We didn't show people the real Manchester United and we were very upset with ourselves. We missed a big opportunity in Rome and that's a real shame. It killed all my dreams last year. When I think about last season now I don't think about winning the league or the Club World Cup or the Carling Cup; all I think about is losing in Rome and that's made me determined to do well this year and make up for that.'

Quite how thoroughly those ambitions would be examined in the Inönü Stadium by an out-of-sorts Beşiktaş side remained to be seen. As previous trips to Turkey had demonstrated, however, local sides can always call upon a boisterous 12th man to chip in from the stands.

'We've been here a few times and it's always an experience,' Sir Alex said at his pre-match press conference. 'We expect much of the same tomorrow in terms of the atmosphere. I think the type of atmosphere you experience in Turkey is unique and incredible. It really shows the fanaticism of the supporters. I remember a previous trip to Istanbul when the home fans were in the stadium from midday, many hours before kick-off. That was amazing. It shows you the devotion they have for their football club. Hopefully we can play our game and try to quell the atmosphere – we'll use our experience to do that.'

Champions League Group B

Beşiktaş JK 0 Manchester United 1
Inönü Stadium, 15 September 2009

United rode out a tricky opener to the new Champions League season with a commanding 1–0 victory over Beşiktaş in a baying

Inönü Stadium. The Reds regularly play in front of crowds almost thrice the 26,448 who packed the Turkish champions' home stadium, but have rarely sampled atmospheres to rival that which soundtracked a cagey, cat-and-mouse encounter.

Paul Scholes settled matters with a late header, nodding in via an upright after Nani's powerful shot had been saved by Hakan Arikan, but the Reds could easily have made a more emphatic return to winning ways in a first European outing since being humbled by Barcelona in Rome.

United's European experience showed throughout a calm, collected performance. Neither side forged openings of note during the first period, although Nani and Antonio Valencia were constant pains for their opposing full-backs. The Ecuadorian twice came close to reaching crosses and Michael Carrick's shot forced a save from Arikan, but half time came and went with neither goalkeeper severely troubled.

Just after the hour mark, with his side in total control but enjoying possession without penetration, Sir Alex Ferguson reverted to 4–4–2, introducing Michael Owen and Dimitar Berbatov for Wayne Rooney and Carrick. United's threat grew as a result of the reshuffle and the deadlock was finally broken on 77 minutes when Valencia fed Nani, Arikan palmed out the Portuguese's blockbuster and Scholes obliged by nodding into the untended goal. Time remained for Owen to fire narrowly off-target as United continued to press, but a victory, procured with a clean sheet and a seamless switch of formation, augured well in the Reds' first Continental outing since Rome.

Team: Foster; Neville, Evans, Vidić, Evra; Valencia (Park 84),
    Anderson, Carrick (Berbatov 63), Scholes, Nani; Rooney (Owen
    64)
Scorer: Scholes (77)
Attendance: 26,448
Referee: Nicola Rizzoli

Draw the sting, kill the crowd, win the game. United's usual three-point plan for European away trips was only two-thirds completed, but Scholes's late winner ensured the spoils for the visitors, even if almost all post-match talk centred around the contribution of the incessant home support.

'It was a great atmosphere to play in and a few of the lads applauded their fans when we came off because you have to appreciate support like that,' said Jonny Evans, making his first concession to an unyielding evening's work. 'Each European game differs – the stadiums, the pitches, the atmospheres . . . We knew it was going to be hostile, but it was a great atmosphere and you learn from experiences like that.'

Even Wes Brown, veteran of 11 European campaigns, was floored by the Turkish support. 'It was one of the best atmospheres I've ever experienced. For half an hour one section of the ground wasn't even watching what was happening on the pitch – they were just singing and chanting at each other!'

The only brief lull was prompted by Scholes's solitary strike, and Sir Alex was keen to emphasize his side's professional second-half display. 'I think we had a bit more urgency in the second half. We started it very well, almost scoring from the first attack and I think that gave us a bit of impetus,' said the boss. 'We said that if we get into a scoring position, we should have people up in support. Paul has been fantastic at that over the years. It was a very important goal.

'I thought the players did well most of the time. We had good possession and were the better team, and we played with good concentration because the atmosphere's something you have to deal with. I thought it was a fantastic atmosphere and it's a test of the players' concentration, test of their nerve and I think they've done OK.'

The Reds returned to Manchester after five nights away from home, eager to lay a marker on local territory over the following days. Never before had a Manchester derby attracted such hype and worldwide attention. Sub-plots were plentiful and the scene-setting was further aided by the top form that had galvanized both United and City. While the Reds had caught the eye at White Hart Lane, the Blues' 4–2 thumping of Arsenal at Eastlands had also set tongues wagging.

The actions of ex-Gunner Emmanuel Adebayor against his former employers – the Togolese striker raked his studs down the face of Robin van Persie – ensured he had no involvement at Old Trafford, but doubts over fellow striker Carlos Tévez never rang true. The little Argentinian was struggling with an ankle injury, but always seemed likely to feature against his former employers. Rio Ferdinand's involvement would be determined by a late fitness test, while Ji-sung Park prepared for the game by penning a two-year contract extension, a deal that tied him to Old Trafford until at least June 2012. In the run-up to the game, however, United's issues only warranted minor mention. All talk was of Tévez.

At his pre-match press conference, a defiant Sir Alex declared: 'Whether Tévez plays doesn't bother me one bit. Their best player is not playing. Emmanuel Adebayor has been their star player, no question about that. He has scored in every game and his absence is a loss.'

Giddy at the chance to pick the manager's brains on the perception of a changing landscape in local and national football, the journalists hurried the topic along to City's confrontational 'Welcome to Manchester' poster.

'It's City, isn't it?' snapped Sir Alex. 'They are a small club, with a small mentality. All they can talk about is Manchester United, that's all they've done and they can't get away from it. It is a go at us, that's the one thing it is. They think taking Tévez away from Manchester United is a triumph. It is poor stuff. I thought he would go to City a long time ago. I don't look upon City as my biggest challengers. For all the buying they have done, they still have to pick a team with balance.'

Asked whether City's new-found wealth would wrest local rule from his side, a laughing Sir Alex signalled an end to the press conference by leaving his chair and adding: 'Not in my lifetime.'

Barclays Premier League

Manchester United 4 Manchester City 3
Old Trafford, 20 September 2009

It needed something special to justify the weeks of posturing and hype over the first instalment of a new, improved era of Manchester derbies. After a captivating clash instantly established as an all-time classic, it seems this fixture will never be the same again. Goals, controversy and incident alternated with dizzying regularity throughout an absorbing affair, but Sir Alex Ferguson's assertion that he had just witnessed the greatest Manchester derby in history was perhaps swayed by events well after normal time had ended.

Michael Owen, in the 96th minute, at the Stretford End, after United had been pegged back three times by Mark Hughes's stubborn Blues, catapulted himself into Old Trafford folklore with the most dramatic of winners. When Owen stabbed home his unerring late winner, he finally settled almost 100 minutes of enrapturing football. Rooney had needed less than two to open the scoring.

As United started with glaring intent, Patrice Evra latched on to a quick Ryan Giggs throw-in and squared for Rooney, who outfoxed two defenders before slipping the finish underneath Shay Given. Old Trafford had previously resounded with jeers and catcalls for the returning Carlos Tévez. Suddenly it shook with joy. The local pecking order appeared very much intact and the home support was revelling in the chance to bait its near neighbours. Alas, the 3,500 Blues in attendance were soon creating their own din, with Tévez a major contributor as he dispossessed Ben Foster at the second attempt and picked out Barry, who calmly slotted a finish between the post and Nemanja Vidić.

Stunned more by the manner of the equalizer than by being pegged back, United's dominance diminished as the first half wore on, and City would have gone into half time ahead if Tévez hadn't curled against the outside of Foster's post under pressure from Evra. Instead, the hosts used the interval to regroup and shortly after the restart Sir Alex's men rediscovered their dominance and quickly retook the lead. Giggs stuck to the left flank, terrorizing Micah Richards, and the Welshman crossed superbly for the onrushing Fletcher to nod United back ahead on 49 minutes.

The game's tit-for-tat nature continued when Bellamy struck a stunning leveller three minutes later, taking advantage of space before unleashing an unstoppable drive into the top corner. Undeterred, United piled on the pressure. Clearly identifying City's weakness from wide areas, Giggs and substitute Antonio Valencia, on for Park, sent in a barrage of crosses to cause havoc in the visitors' defence. Given repeatedly had to bail out his back four, saving superbly from two Dimitar Berbatov headers and a Giggs piledriver.

Inevitably, a Giggs cross helped put United ahead for the third time, as Fletcher rose to glance in a left-wing free-kick on 80 minutes. But still there was time for another twist. Or two.

After Shaun Wright-Phillips and Martin Petrov had both fired narrowly off-target, it appeared United would see out the few remaining seconds of normal time, plus any injury time added by referee Martin Atkinson. Instead, Rio Ferdinand's casual pass was intercepted by Petrov, who released Bellamy to race into the area and slot past Foster from a tight angle.

Amid scenes of great contrast – City delirious on the field and in the stands, United players on their haunches, home supporters clasping hands behind heads – fourth official Alan Wiley broke the news that there would be a minimum of four added minutes. Tack on time for City's celebrations and a subsequent substitution – Michael Carrick on for Anderson – and there was plenty of time for a definitive solution to the game.

Midway through the 96th minute, a long punt from Rooney was cleared only as far as the untouchable Giggs. Substitute Owen, introduced earlier for Berbatov, had peeled away into a yawning gap and was bellowing for the pass. Giggs duly delivered an inch-perfect half-volley matched in its flawlessness only by Owen's stunning first touch and subsequent stabbed finish.

Cue pandemonium. United's bench poured into the technical area, with substitute Gary Neville star-jumping up the touchline in front of the stunned away support; all around them Old Trafford heaved and writhed in jubilation. Seconds later, the full-time whistle prompted another wave of celebrations, as all those of a Red persuasion spent their last energy milking a truly classic encounter. The status quo has rarely felt so satisfying.

Team: Foster; O'Shea, Ferdinand, Vidić, Evra; Park (Valencia 62), Anderson (Carrick 90), Fletcher, Giggs; Berbatov (Owen 78), Rooney

Scorers: Rooney (2), Fletcher (49, 80), Owen (90)

Attendance: 75,066

Referee: Martin Atkinson

'I don't know where you start,' a drained but elated Sir Alex said afterwards. 'We've had a fantastic performance. We made three horrendous mistakes – mistakes you don't even half-associate with our team – and it kept City in the game. Every time we scored, we made a mistake and let them back in it. If you do that you can end up losing the match. Fortunately we got the break. Michael Owen scored a fantastic winning goal and we deservedly won the game.

'I am unhappy because the errors spoiled an emphatic victory. We could have won six–nil or seven–nil today and the fact we made those mistakes made it probably the best derby game of all time. You're left pondering what you'd rather have: win six–nil or win the greatest derby game of all time. I'd rather win six–nil!'

After winning the first Manchester derby of the season, Sir Alex admitted he was delighted with his side's determination to mark their territory. 'For us it's unusual to accept that they're top dogs in terms of media attention,' he said. 'But sometimes you have a noisy neighbour and you have to live with it. You can't do anything about them, they keep making noise, but what you can do – as we showed – is get on with your life. Put your television on and turn it up a bit louder!

'As far as the players are concerned, they showed their playing power. In the second half we were outstanding, absolutely magnificent. I've got to cling on to that performance as the real playing power of Manchester United, and that's the best answer of all.'

While the manager would rather have provided a more emphatic answer in terms of scoreline, Patrice Evra preferred to savour the flaws and imperfections that contributed towards an unforgettable occasion. 'Sometimes we need mistakes to have a great game like this,' said the Frenchman.

'We could have killed the game early on, but when we scored we started to make mistakes. I think for everybody it was an amazing day. To score like this in the last second of the game was just amazing. The players on the bench were coming on the pitch, the fans, the atmosphere . . . This is why I say thanks to God I play in the Premier League and for United. A day like this is just amazing.'

For Evra, the occasion carried a surreal undertone through his clash with close friend Tévez. 'It's difficult to play against Carlitos,' admits the Frenchman. 'Even though he moved to City, I still see him, go round to his house and go out to restaurants with him as well. He's still a close friend and he will be for ever. Just because he went to City doesn't mean he won't be my friend anymore. When Carlitos was here he was just like a brother.

'Still,' he adds, with typical mischief, 'it was very good to wind him up. I was texting him before the game, telling him he would never win against us. He threatened to get me with a bad challenge, but I know he'd never do that. Then during the game I kicked his face – by accident – and he asked me what was going on. Afterwards we were just laughing about it on the pitch, but at the end I couldn't resist squirting him with water, celebrating the win.'

The game sealed a spot in club folklore and Michael Owen had played an indelible part in proceedings. In killing Ryan Giggs's pass and stabbing home at the Stretford End, he had punctured

City's inflated ambition and made himself an instant Old Trafford hero.

'It was one of those games that had virtually everything,' grins the striker, looking back. 'I would think it'll go down as one of the most exciting Premier League games of all time, and certainly one of the most exciting derbies of all time. I was on the bench, watching the game swing to and fro. Tensions were building and it was one of those games you are dying to be a part of. You always envisage yourself coming on and scoring the winner in a game like that, but rarely does it happen.

'This time Giggsy spotted with me a great pass. Sometimes you have a bad touch and you don't score, sometimes you do. I was just fortunate that on an occasion like that it was a good touch and a good finish. I don't remember much of the aftermath, but it was definitely one of the most exciting moments of my career.'

The euphoria continued long after the final whistle. 'We were absolutely buzzing in the dressing room afterwards,' recalls John O'Shea. 'We were so happy and relieved to have won, but we were all up on adrenalin, I think. It was a classic rollercoaster game and the emotions were so up and down – it was incredible. We couldn't believe we'd let it get that far, to go to the very last minute of injury time. We were wondering how we hadn't won it easier, but I suppose it made it special to have done it in such a dramatic fashion.'

For all the euphoria inside the home dressing room, there were a couple of forlorn figures. A relieved Rio Ferdinand was indebted to Michael Owen's winner after gifting possession to City in the build-up for Craig Bellamy's equalizer ('I said a big thank-you to Michael at the time and texted him again later that night,' he later revealed), while goalkeeper Ben Foster was left to reflect on a display that raised questions over his credentials as the long-term heir to Edwin van der Sar's throne.

'I was absolutely distraught afterwards,' recalls Foster. 'I've never felt so bad after a game, and we'd won! It was a personal horror show. Nothing I did seemed to go right for me and I know I should have done better with two of City's goals. The first one was shocking and on the last one I've slipped and Bellamy just put it past me. It was one to forget.'

Foster wouldn't have the opportunity to get the shocker out of his system in United's next game, as the ever-patient Tomasz Kuszczak was readied for his first outing of the season.

With local authority established once more, United could quickly pan out to the bigger picture: silverware. The Reds' Carling Cup defence began against newly promoted Wolverhampton Wanderers at Old Trafford. And having played a major role in winning the 2008–09 trophy, budding midfielder Darron Gibson was itching to get involved against Mick McCarthy's men, with the added motivation of going up against a side he had joined on loan two seasons earlier.

'The Carling Cup's an important tournament for the young lads, because it's where we get most of our first-team opportunities,' said the Irishman. 'We know we'll need to perform to our best because Wolves will bring a strong side. There's always pressure at United, but there will be a bit more on us because we're defending the trophy and we're up against Premier League opposition. To win the Carling Cup again would be a huge achievement and it's what we want. Last season gave us a lot of confidence because we now know what it takes to win a major competition.'

As is customary, the early stages of the Carling Cup continue to provide a proving ground for the club's twinkling talents. Sir Alex hinted at a continuation of that policy the day before Wolves' visit, when he handed senior squad numbers to Norwegian prodigies Joshua King and Magnus Eikrem. Youth would again be given its chance.

Carling Cup Third Round

Manchester United 1 Wolverhampton Wanderers 0
Old Trafford, 23 September 2009

Despite having to cope for more than an hour with only ten men, the Carling Cup holders marched into the fourth round after a superbly taken goal from Danny Welbeck. The England youth international slotted home clinically after a sharp exchange with Michael Owen, as the Reds coped admirably after Fabio was dismissed for hauling down Michael Kightly as he bore down on goal. In keeping with tradition, Sir Alex Ferguson made wholesale changes from the team that edged the Manchester derby, with entirely different starting sides selected. Senior squad debutants Joshua King and Magnus Eikrem were both named on the bench.

Despite United hogging possession early on, it was a former Red who almost opened the scoring. Sylvan Ebanks-Blake, a scorer in his only United start four years earlier against Barnet, curled just over Tomasz Kuszczak's goal from 20 yards. Wolves' sporadic menace on the break dealt the Reds a significant blow just before the half-hour mark as Kightly burst onto a loose ball and raced towards Kuszczak, only for the stumbling Fabio to trip and fall, taking the attacker down with him. The inevitable red card prompted the introduction of Ritchie De Laet for Kiko Macheda, and only a fine save from Kuszczak prevented David Jones – another ex-Red – from curling Wolves into the lead from the resulting free-kick.

Despite the numerical shortfall, United forged the clearer openings. Owen, Welbeck and Michael Carrick all chanced their arm before the break, and Welbeck broke the deadlock with his first goal of the season just after the hour. Darron Gibson found the striker in space, before Welbeck swapped passes with Owen and steered home his fourth goal in a United shirt.

Although Kevin Doyle twice came close to forcing extra time, substitute debutant King, 17, almost had the final say when he tested Marcus Hahnemann's reflexes with a ferocious late drive. One goal was enough, though, to see the holders off and running on another cup defence.

Team: Kuszczak; Neville, Brown, Evans, Fabio; Nani, Carrick, Gibson, Welbeck (King 81); Owen (Valencia 69), Macheda (De Laet 31)
Scorer: Welbeck (66)
Attendance: 51,160
Referee: Peter Walton

'We're very pleased,' Sir Alex said at the final whistle. 'We kept our discipline and the players worked their socks off. I thought prior to the sending-off Wolves were a handful. They played a lot of good one-twos in and around our box and were a real threat. But after the sending-off we were better organized, kept our shape well and managed to get a result.

'It was a fantastic goal. There was real quality in the passing from Darron up to Danny, then in to Michael and back again for Danny to put it into the net. It was a tremendous goal. It was a great pass from Michael, too. The angle he made for Danny made it easier for him to score. I think one goal was always going to win it and after we went ahead we showed good resilience with enough experienced defenders to see it out.'

Fresh from bagging his first goal of the season – and celebrating by lampooning sprinter Usain Bolt's famed stance – Longsight teenager Danny Welbeck was understandably elated. 'I'm just like any other normal Manc boy, really,' he said. 'To be given the chance to play for United is a dream. Tonight, it was great playing with Michael Owen, because Michael Owen's Michael Owen. You can always learn from his movement, it's unbelievable. I just knew he was around the corner and he knew where I was going next. He played it there and I finished it off well.'

Even at just 18, Welbeck could boast more experience than fellow striker Joshua King. The Norwegian forward, with a powerhouse physique, also showed a maturity to belie his 17 years when he summed up his contribution. 'It's a big step up, obviously, but now I've just got to keep training hard and working hard and I might get a chance in the next Carling Cup game,' he said. 'It was a big day for me. I maybe should have scored, but I thought I did well.

'It was quite nervy at the start, like when I found out yesterday I got a squad number and that I might be in the squad. But as soon as I went on the pitch the nerves flew away and I got on with it.'

For King and the vast majority of the team who had secured a fourth-round trip to Barnsley, the stage exit would again beckon as

United prepared for a trip to Stoke City. In just one full season of Premier League football, Tony Pulis had established his side as one of the division's least accommodating hosts. Long throw-ins and physical football had been quickly tagged as the Potters' main attributes, but strict discipline, hard work and sporadic brilliance in attack meant a trip to the Britannia Stadium could not be taken lightly.

'The derby win was amazing, but that will soon be forgotten come Saturday when Stoke are getting in and about you,' warned John O'Shea. 'Stoke have really improved over the last year and made some good signings. They don't just have good battling qualities, they've got good footballing qualities, too.

'We know we'll have plenty of work to do. We know from last season how tough a place it is to go. We're under no illusions, but we're playing well at the moment and hopefully we can pick up another three points.'

Although the mood in the camp was already sky-high after a string of impressive results, spirits were further lifted when Owen Hargreaves returned to Carrington to continue his recovery after several months spent in Colorado.

'All the lads have been delighted to have Owen back around the place,' said Darren Fletcher. 'As players, we all know how frustrating it is to be out for a couple of weeks, but he had almost two years out. We're all really supportive of Owen and we want him back because we know he's a fantastic player and no one deserves injuries like that. He didn't get a special welcome back or anything, he just got the usual round of applause from everybody, plus Albert [Morgan, kitman] did his old trick of trying to blow the dust off his strip and his boots!'

Hargreaves's return provided a significant boost for Sir Alex and he outlined the road ahead for the midfielder during his pre-Stoke press conference. 'Hopefully the boy gets a break and continues his progress without any mishaps,' he said. 'He's been out for a long time, but he has the resilience to see it through. The good thing is that he is young enough to come back from an injury like this.'

While Hargreaves was focused on the coming weeks and months, his manager could only concentrate on the immediate stern test of his side's title credentials.

Barclays Premier League

Stoke City 0 Manchester United 2

Britannia Stadium, 26 September 2009

United stormed Stoke's Britannia Stadium stronghold with consummate ease, as Ryan Giggs rolled back the years once again with a pair of assists for Dimitar Berbatov and John O'Shea. The Reds were always in control of an evenly poised game, but required the introduction of veteran winger Giggs to tip the balance. He needed only five minutes to tee up Berbatov to open the scoring, and soon afterwards curled in a perfect free-kick for O'Shea to glance in the clincher.

In a tight opening to the game, chances were few and far between. It took a rare defensive lapse for the first notable opening, as ex-Red Ryan Shawcross lost possession to Antonio Valencia, only for the Ecuadorian to clip his finish just past Thomas Sorensen's far post. The Danish goalkeeper then thwarted Nani with a spectacular save from the Portuguese's curling effort, as United continued to dominate possession either side of the interval.

Stoke's chief threat was an aerial bombardment from long balls and set pieces, but United's defence repelled all that fell from the sky, with goalkeeper Ben Foster rarely tested. Giggs was introduced for Nani just before the hour mark and he soon latched on to a superb through-ball from Darren Fletcher and squared for Berbatov to slot home from inside the six-yard box. It was beautifully simple and a by-product of Giggs's unwavering functionality and incision.

The Welshman's high standards did briefly slip when he fired off-target under pressure from Sorensen soon afterwards, but his magnificent right-wing free-kick gave O'Shea the chance to glance home a clinical header and seal the points. By virtue of Chelsea's shock defeat at Wigan, the Reds' seventh successive victory in all competitions ensured top spot for the first time in the 2009–10 Premier League campaign.

Team: Foster; O'Shea, Ferdinand, Vidić, Evra; Valencia, Fletcher, Scholes (Carrick 81), Nani (Giggs 57); Berbatov, Rooney (Owen 81)
Scorers: Berbatov (62), O'Shea (77)
Attendance: 27,500
Referee: Howard Webb

It was another ageless, match-winning display from Ryan Giggs that had the world's football media thumbing through thesauruses after the match. Even Sir Alex Ferguson struggled to articulate the 35-year-old's enduring class and ability. 'I felt his intelligence would give them a bit of bother on that side of the pitch,' said the manager.

'I think Nani did his job quite well. He kept penetrating and keeping them pinned back, but Ryan brings you something else. The horrible part of being a footballer is that at some stage you are finished with the game – age catches us all. When someone like Ryan is playing at the level he is at, he realizes that to stay there he has to prepare himself in the right way. He has to look after himself and do the right things.

'It's a lot to do with how he lives his life and prepares for games, and he's helped by the fact he's got a good physique. He has never carried any weight and has always been a slim athlete. It's not a matter of him defying his age. It's more a case that there is no discernible deterioration in his game. It is remarkable. I don't know what else there is to say about him.'

Dimitar Berbatov, the beneficiary of Giggs's movement and ability in teeing up the opening goal at the Britannia Stadium, celebrated by encouraging the United supporters to recognize the assist, and he was similarly gushing over the winger's contribution afterwards.

'The game changed when Ryan came on,' said the Bulgarian.

'You can see the years he has been playing for Manchester United. They really help when you come on to the pitch and make decisions. That's what gave us the three points: his decisions. He played the pass to me to score and then the free-kick for Sheasy's header was another assist for him. We needed the three points and we deserved them. Stoke threw everything they had at us, and it was a difficult game, but in the end we deserved to win because we attacked them. We wanted to score and we eventually did.'

'Thankfully Giggsy listened to me for once,' adds John O'Shea, referring to his first, and only, goal of the season. 'I went over to him before he took the kick and told him to just get it over the first defender and I'd be there, waiting for it. Thankfully he listened and I was able to put a nice little flick in the corner and seal the win.'

Top of the league and boasting all the hallmarks of champions, the Reds were well set domestically. Attentions could switch to another venture into the Champions League, with German champions Wolfsburg travelling to Old Trafford for their maiden away trip in the competition.

The Reds' research revealed a team full of goals and one keen to attack at any opportunity. Strikers Grafite and Edin Džeko had terrorized the Bundesliga *en route* to securing their first league title in 2008–09, and the Brazilian had plundered a hat-trick against CSKA Moscow on Matchday One. With no first-hand experience to draw on, United's players were relying on the reconnaissance work of the club's coaching staff.

'When you don't know teams or players that well you don't always know what to expect in games,' said Nemanja Vidić. 'But that's why we have people at the club who show us the videos before the game so we can work out exactly how they play. It's a very important part of our preparation – we need to know what to expect from the players we'll be up against because it's the small details that can make the difference.

'It'll be a hard game and I think we'll be the two teams fighting for top spot in the group. Everyone wants to play well against Manchester United and try to beat us. It's the biggest stage to play on and other teams want to show what they can do. It's nothing new

Cristiano Ronaldo and Carlos Tevez say goodbye to each other, and United, after the Reds' Champions League final defeat to Barcelona.

Sir Alex Ferguson parades his three summer signings – Gabriel Obertan, Michael Owen and Antonio Valencia – before the world's media at Carrington.

Wayne Rooney celebrates opening the scoring against Birmingham in the 34th minute, ensuring a winning start to the Reds' Premier League title defence.

Patrice Evra is felled by Burnley's Robbie Blake. Michael Carrick misses the subsequent penalty, rendering Blake the match-winner in an almighty upset.

Bizarre scenes punctuate United's 2-1 win over Arsenal, as Arsene Wenger is banished to the stands – to the bemusement and delight of the home support.

Ryan Giggs curls home a superb free-kick to bring United level at White Hart Lane midway through the first half, en route to a swaggering 3-1 win over Tottenham.

Nani joins Paul Scholes to celebrate the veteran midfielder's late winner at Besiktas, getting the Reds' Champions League campaign off to a flier.

Old Trafford erupts in joy as Michael Owen settles a captivating Manchester derby with the latest of late winners, and takes his place in United folklore.

Patrice Evra is mobbed by Nemanja Vidic and Nani after his shot is deflected in by Sunderland's Anton Ferdinand, securing the Reds a hard-earned point in the last minute.

Antonio Valencia caps a fine passing move by hammering home his first United goal – the decisive strike in October's 2-1 win over Bolton.

Jamie Carragher bemoans his booking from Andre Marriner for hauling down Michael Owen, but the Liverpool skipper is fortunate to avoid dismissal in his side's 2-0 win over United.

Edwin van der Sar leads United's protests after John Terry's controversial header gives Chelsea a vital win at Stamford Bridge.

Match ball in tow, Wayne Rooney jokes with referee Mike Dean after the Reds' comprehensive 4-1 victory at Portsmouth.

Darron Gibson takes the plaudits for his superb brace against Tottenham in December, booking United a place in the Carling Cup semi-finals.

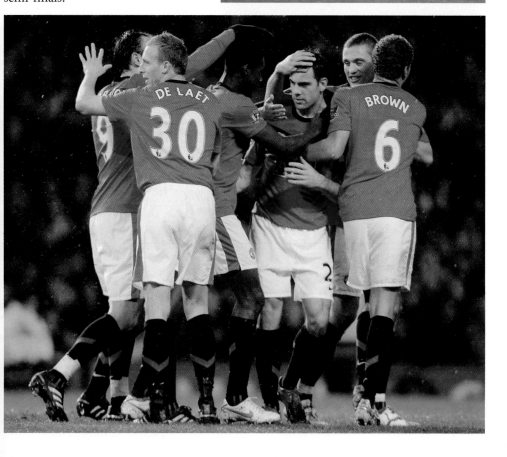

Michael Owen celebrates hitting his first Reds hat-trick as a patched-up United side storms to victory at Wolfsburg.

Wayne Rooney turns away in frustration after thudding a shot against the bar, during a shock home defeat to Aston Villa.

for us – we just have to concentrate on ourselves, work hard in training and keep improving.'

Injured pair Ji-sung Park and Michael Owen missed the Reds' final training session before the game, but Sir Alex was nevertheless relishing the chance to pit his side against a visiting team that he expected would play with refreshing abandon.

'I think they are the key threat in the group,' he said. 'The number of goals they score is quite amazing. Their two strikers scored seventy-one goals between them last season, which is incredible. It says a lot for Wolfsburg's ambition and progress that they won the league last year, and they did it in a very positive way, in terms of goalscoring. It wasn't a matter of winning the league by the odd goal. They went out to prove that their way of playing was the right way. I think it's positive the way they play and we admire that. It reflects our beliefs in the game, too, so it may be a very open game.'

The open, light-hearted mood of the press conference was enhanced when Jonny Evans was put on the spot by his manager, who stated that Wayne Rooney was benefiting from married life, with a child on the way.

When asked about his own plans for matrimony, Evans grinned: 'I don't really want to talk about that, especially because my girlfriend's sat in the middle of you all – she's on a placement at ITV this week!' Rather than shield the young defender, Sir Alex bellowed to the floor: 'Get him tied down, dear. Rings are cheap now!'

The laughter didn't last long, however. Not with a glaringly tricky encounter with Germany's finest to negotiate.

Champions League Group B

Manchester United 2 VFL Wolfsburg 1
Old Trafford, 30 September 2009

Old Trafford's first Champions League action of the season provided a stern examination of United's European credentials, as the Reds had to come from behind to dispose of Wolfsburg. Edin Džeko headed the Bundesliga champions ahead early in the second half, only for a deflected Ryan Giggs free-kick and a late belter from Michael Carrick to give United a three-point lead at the head of Group B.

Wolfsburg had insisted pre-match that they would throw caution to the wind in their first Champions League campaign and a bright start bore out that promise. Determined in defence and ambitious in attack, the Germans gave as good as they got for long periods. United's gameplan was hardly helped when Michael Owen limped off with a recurrence of the groin injury that had hampered him in training. However, his replacement, Dimitar Berbatov, quickly began pulling the strings in attack for the hosts and soon crossed for Wayne Rooney to convert, only for a harsh offside call to rule out the goal.

The Bulgarian continually provided openings for his colleagues, only for Wolfsburg goalkeeper Diego Benaglio to provide an impenetrable last line of defence by turning away efforts from Carrick, Antonio Valencia and Anderson. The Brazilian was denied again just after half time, before the visitors took a shock lead when Makoto Hasebe's neat back-post cross gave Džeko the opportunity to nod past Tomasz Kuszczak.

Galvanized by the upped stakes, United were level within four minutes as Giggs's free-kick deflected off the visitors' wall and spun into the far corner for the winger's 150th Reds goal. Giggs had goal 151 chalked off for offside as United continued to press, but the winner duly arrived when Berbatov and Giggs combined to tee up Carrick, who curled a sumptuous finish high into the Stretford End goal. Two wins from two, then, and an ominous message that United were determined to seize back the mantle of Europe's finest team.

Team: Kuszczak; O'Shea, Ferdinand, Vidić, Evra; Valencia (Fletcher 82), Anderson, Carrick, Giggs; Owen (Berbatov 20), Rooney
Scorers: Giggs (59), Carrick (78)
Attendance: 74,037
Referee: Viktor Kassai

Another game, another spell in the spotlight for Ryan Giggs. Having laid on a spate of assists in previous games, the winger curled home – albeit fortunately – a vital equalizer to tee up a come-from-behind victory and reach his 150th United goal.

'I'm proud to have scored that amount of goals, but it was more important we got back in the game so soon after they went ahead,' he said. 'It was a poor free-kick, to be fair, but we got that little bit of luck with the deflection. We played well in the first half, but we were lacking that quality pass in the final third. They're a good side and their two strikers are a real handful. But thankfully we got that bit of luck with our first goal and showed great character to come back and win it.'

Fellow goalscorer Michael Carrick also identified the team's resolve as a key component of the victory, insisting that inherent self-belief won the day. 'When we went a goal down we stepped up and still believed we could win the game,' said the midfielder. 'There's a lot of belief, confidence and trust in each other in our squad, and I think that's shown this season through the amount of goals we've scored in the latter stages of matches. Fitness helps, too, but the character and mental strength we have certainly helps. It's never ideal going a goal down, but when it does happen we always believe we can bounce back.'

Having seen his side fight back and overcome a stern examination to take a stranglehold of Group B, Sir Alex Ferguson was in high spirits afterwards, even if he would be shorn of the services of Michael Owen for United's next run-out.

'We knew Wolfsburg were a good side and it was a test in the sense that their front players are very difficult to play against, especially Džeko,' he said. 'He's a big lad and a real handful, and despite being up against two very good centre-backs he continually gave us problems. I was pleased with our performance and some of our football was fantastic. We played very well, the penetration was terrific and we could have scored a lot of goals. We're delighted with the two wins. Getting points on the board early on is always a bonus and it helps take the pressure off a bit for the trip to Moscow next month.'

Having built a three-point lead after just two games, United had made a powerful start to a tricky Group B campaign. Only goal difference separated the Reds from second-placed Chelsea in the Premier League, but the Blues' shock slip at Wigan had unexpectedly demonstrated fallibility in Carlo Ancelotti's side. Atop two tables, and off and running in the defence of the Carling Cup, all was well for the Reds going into the autumn.

4

October

With United at home to Sunderland and perennial title rivals Chelsea and Liverpool due to meet at Stamford Bridge, the Reds had an opportunity to take early charge of the title race. Black Cats boss Steve Bruce had enjoyed a successful start to life at the Stadium of Light, with summer signing Darren Bent rewarding his new club with a spate of early season goals. As Bruce prepared to bring his side to Old Trafford, Sir Alex was keen to champion the former United skipper's attributes.

'He was a great player for us,' the manager said. 'The fantastic thing about Brucey was that he had this great ability to play on with injuries. He was always hobbling about the training ground with knocks or hamstring strains. He'd just rub it better and play. It was unbelievable.

'Steve has galvanized Sunderland really well, and you can see something happening there – just hopefully not on Saturday! Everyone's a threat if you don't approach games the right way. We have to approach this game the right way and make sure the attitude and the character of the team is there. It will be. We have no problems there. The team is playing well and hopefully we'll get the result we want.'

Michael Owen's hamstring injury ruled the striker out, although there was promising news on that front, with the 29-year-old tipped to make a quicker-than-expected recovery. And as Edwin van der Sar and Rafael inched towards full fitness Sir Alex conceded he had an embarrassment of riches. 'We've got a strong squad,' he said. 'The problem with having everyone fit is picking the right team.'

Whatever Sir Alex's selection, there was plenty of confidence around Carrington in the Reds' ability to notch another important victory over Sunderland. 'We've got a good level of belief and strength,' said skipper Gary Neville. 'The main thing is that we all stay fit and keep the squad together. Since the last international break, we're looking healthier in terms of players having more training and games. You could see our attacking flair against City and Tottenham, our resilience against Arsenal and Beşiktaş . . . The performances since we came back from the break have been really good.'

Good, but not perfect, according to Nemanja Vidić. Like his skipper, the giant Serbian had been impressed with the upturn in United's fortunes. But he insisted there was more to come. 'At the moment we're doing well and we've had the best start to a season in my time here. We've played some big games and done well, so we're pleased. But we know we can always improve and we haven't hit our best form. I think that's a good thing, though – the season is not a sprint, it's more like a marathon.

'We have quality players, but it's the small details that determine who wins the titles and cups. You therefore need to make sure you are also ready for the final part of the season when you have very important games.'

In order to enter the final straight with a shout of winning honours, however, the Reds could scarcely afford to drop any points *en route*. Any slip-ups against Sunderland, regardless of the Black Cats' impressive recent form, would raise eyebrows and allow Chelsea the chance to re-take top spot in the Premier League.

Barclays Premier League

Manchester United 2 Sunderland 2

Old Trafford, 3 October 2009

United were shocked by Steve Bruce's voracious Sunderland side as a seven-game winning streak was curtailed, but the Reds' never-say-die spirit still procured a dramatic point. Having fallen behind to goals from Darren Bent and Kenwyne Jones, the hosts hit back through Dimitar Berbatov's sublime scissor-kick and a last-gasp own goal from Mackems defender Anton Ferdinand. The point, hard-earned against a visiting side who snapped into challenges and fiercely contested every loose ball, was just about deserved for the Reds' second-half rally.

Sir Alex made seven changes to the team that overcame Wolfsburg – most notable was a second league start for Danny Welbeck – and it was the visitors who settled quickest. The breathless harrying of Lee Cattermole and Lorik Cana in central midfield was already in evidence when Sunderland took the lead, although it was brains rather than brawn that led to the game's opener. A neat interchange in attack culminated in Jones feeding Bent, who rifled a low 25-yard shot inside Ben Foster's post.

Although stung into action, United's intent was rarely underscored by the requisite quality in attack, and the first half passed without Black Cats goalkeeper Craig Gordon breaking sweat.

The half-time introduction of Anderson for Paul Scholes was designed to inject urgency into a hitherto lacklustre performance, and United quickly began to forge openings. Anton Ferdinand recovered well after a mistake to block Wayne Rooney's effort, before Berbatov superbly contorted to volley John O'Shea's cross into the far corner of Gordon's goal.

Galvanized by parity and the quality of the equalizer, United continued to bomb forward in search of victory, but were caught out just before the hour mark when Jones headed in a searching chip from

Andy Reid. The momentum was still with the champions, however, and both Welbeck and Rooney fired narrowly off-target from distance. The Reds' cause was further helped when ex-United winger Kieran Richardson was sent off for gathering two yellow cards. Cue another series of late surges towards the Stretford End and Sunderland's stubborn resistance finally wilted in the second of four added minutes.

After yet another goalmouth scramble, the ball broke to substitute Michael Carrick, who teed up Patrice Evra on the edge of the box. The Frenchman's low drive appeared to be heading wide, but clipped the helpless Ferdinand and spun into the Sunderland goal. Back on terms and backed by a strident home support, United piled forward for the remaining two minutes. Berbatov came close to snatching all three points but victory would have been undeserved after a display that only ignited in the second period.

Team: Foster; O'Shea, Vidić, Evans, Evra; Nani, Fletcher (Valencia 72), Scholes (Anderson 45), Welbeck (Carrick 72); Rooney, Berbatov

Scorers: Berbatov (51), A Ferdinand (90 (og))

Attendance: 75,114

Referee: Alan Wiley

'It was a big disappointment because it was a poor display,' conceded Patrice Evra, who took little consolation from his major role in the dramatic late leveller. 'We are very disappointed about the way we played. It was a bad game. We drew, and one point is a bonus. We are pleased to get a point, but I don't even know if we deserved it. We are very frustrated because it looked like we didn't have any energy or power. You have to say Sunderland played very well. We just didn't look sharp. Our game was slow, we lost a lot of challenges and in the first half we were very poor.

'After Berbatov scored the team pushed on, but then Sunderland scored again. It was difficult to come back after that. We did manage to in the last few minutes, but it's still not a good result for us.'

The Frenchman was similarly irritated by the latest concessions in a worrying spate of defensive lapses, especially coming mere months after United's record-breaking number of clean sheets during the 2008–09 campaign.

'We are worried,' Patrice admitted. 'We have conceded a lot of goals and I'm not happy with that because I am a defender. If you want to win the league, I think you need to keep clean sheets. Last season we conceded twenty-four goals and we don't want to concede more than that this season.'

Sir Alex Ferguson's mood mirrored Evra's and the United boss was particularly disappointed by the nature of Kenwyne Jones's strike, which put Sunderland ahead for the second time. But for the hulking striker's header, the manager felt his side would have built on Dimitar Berbatov's equalizer and gone on to take three much-needed points.

'Dimitar's goal was magnificent,' said the Scot. 'After that I thought, "We're back." I thought we were a certainty to go on and win it. The surge was there; the support was there; the momentum was there. Then we went and lost a really soft second goal. But credit to the players: they never give in. It's a good quality to have. We've got something out of the game on a day when we've played really badly.

'Our passing was just not what I expect of the team, right throughout the game. We tried to change it around by bringing Anderson on for the second half. But we continued to give the ball away repeatedly. It's always disappointing not to win your home games. We didn't make a lot of chances in the game and I didn't think our quality in the final third was good enough to create chances. We have to say it was an off day. You get them sometimes – we don't enjoy them but you do get them.'

There followed another international break, while nations settled the issue of World Cup qualification. After such an unexpected and uncharacteristic setback against Sunderland, the United squad craved another fixture to get back quickly on track. Instead, another fortnight would pass before Bolton arrived at Old Trafford. Not that it would be an uneventful lull ... FIFA instructed the Football Association they could authorize United's signing of Paul Pogba after an investigation deemed the midfielder had not entered into a contract with Le Havre.

A posse of players remained at Carrington while several squad members joined their respective nations. Nemanja Vidić and Zoran Tošić were part of the Serbia squad that qualified for South Africa, Frenchman Patrice Evra would go up against Irish club-mates John O'Shea and Darron Gibson in a play-off, and Nani's Portugal also qualified for a second shot at reaching the World Cup finals. At the same time, Dimitar Berbatov and Antonio Valencia's hopes of making the summer showpiece were dashed as Bulgaria and Ecuador failed to qualify. Already assured of a berth in the tournament proper were England, and Wayne Rooney, Rio Ferdinand and Michael Carrick all featured as Fabio Capello's side lost a dead-rubber match in Ukraine. Rooney picked up a slight calf injury during the defeat, leaving him with a race against time to make United's clashes with Bolton, CSKA Moscow and Liverpool. In another twist, the striker's wife, Colleen, was due to give birth at any time, casting constant doubt over his availability.

As Rooney returned to Manchester for treatment, so too did Northern Ireland defender Jonny Evans, who missed his country's clash with the Czech Republic owing to an ankle injury. Better injury news was provided by Gabriel Obertan, who had recovered sufficiently from his spinal trouble to make an eye-catching debut in the Reserves' Manchester Senior Cup win over Oldham Athletic.

While the Frenchman was delighted to be back on the field, long-term absentee Owen Hargreaves was just thankful to be at Carrington after spending several months in Colorado, recuperating from major double knee surgery. 'With an injury of this severity, both physically and mentally it's important you try and do everything you can and be really focused on your aims,' said the midfielder.

'At Carrington, the football and playing side of it is so important and I'd have been confronted with it on a daily basis [had I stayed in Manchester]. For someone like me, who can't play for an extended period of time, it would have been really tough. It was better being in an environment where I could focus on getting well, do my training and have no distractions.

'But being back has been great. That was one of the things I really missed, being with the guys in the dressing room. There is such a great energy around this club, and that's not just the players. It's everyone who works here. There are so many people who've been here a long time. It's a unique place, especially for such a competitive environment. The reception was great. It's fantastic being around the lads, the different characters and personalities. It helps.'

The midfielder's return to Manchester prompted eager forecasts that he could be back in action before the end of October. But the magnitude of double knee surgery – performed on cases of tendonitis which surgeon Dr Richard Steadman described as the worst he'd ever seen – meant Hargreaves would be given as long as necessary to ensure a successful comeback.

As United's squad members filtered back to Carrington from their international exertions, Sir Alex and his coaches swiftly gained a picture of who would be available to face Gary Megson's Bolton. Wayne Rooney was out, but Michael Owen had recovered from a groin injury and Edwin van der Sar was set to make his first outing of the season, having emerged unscathed from the Reserves' win at Everton.

'He came through that fine – it was the confidence booster he needed,' said Sir Alex. 'If Edwin comes through the Bolton game, he will have two very important away games against CSKA Moscow and then Liverpool. He couldn't come back at a better time. The calming influence he has on everyone around him is significant. Edwin's a fantastic goalkeeper. I think he and Peter Schmeichel have been the best two goalkeepers in the history of this club.'

The return of such an influential figure meant another enforced spell on the sidelines for Ben Foster, although the England international continued to earn plaudits from his club manager.

'Ben Foster's been outstanding in a lot of things,' Sir Alex told the press. 'He made a fantastic save at Wigan at an important time in the game, and the same at Stoke when it was nil–nil just after half time. These moments demonstrate the guy's ability, but he still hasn't had a lot of game time and experience because two cruciate knee injuries have curtailed his progress. Ben can only get better and he will be a fantastic goalkeeper. I still feel he's the best English goalkeeper around.'

Behind the scenes, however, Foster's confidence was further dented. Looking back, he concedes that Sir Alex had no choice but to withdraw him from the team. 'I didn't think I was playing great football at the time,' he says. 'The manager replaced me after the Sunderland game and I think he was fully justified. The manager always tells the player if you're going to be replaced in the team and he gave his reasons, which were pretty obvious really. I was low on confidence and Edwin was coming back to full fitness. I wasn't playing well and it grows through the team as well. When you're low on confidence, that's the way it is sometimes. I did get a bit of criticism, but that's the way it is. I think it made me a stronger person, though.'

While van der Sar was back and raring to go, also available for the Trotters' visit were Jonny Evans, sufficiently recovered from an ankle injury, and Rio Ferdinand, who had come in for waves of media criticism for an inconsistent run of form for club and country. Days after England manager Fabio Capello had backed the veteran defender to rediscover his A-game, Sir Alex echoed those sentiments.

'Maybe missing games has affected him,' proffered the manager. 'If he gets into a run of matches, I'm sure the rhythm will come back. I think all players worry about their form if they're making mistakes and getting criticism. They have to. They wouldn't be human if they didn't. So it's an unusual experience for him. But he will get through it, I'm sure of that.'

Evans, who was again set to deputize for Nemanja Vidić, was viewing the looming clash as an opportunity for United to make amends for a lacklustre display against Sunderland.

'We didn't really apply ourselves the way we can, especially at home, so we were disappointed with that,' said the defender. 'But we took a point out of the game, which probably wasn't a bad result given the way we played. The international break has meant we've been away from each other for a while. But we've all been looking forward to the chance to get out there against Bolton, get three points and rediscover the kind of form we were in before the Sunderland game.'

Barclays Premier League

Manchester United 2 Bolton Wanderers 1

Old Trafford, 17 October 2009

Once again Old Trafford witnessed a spirited performance from a visiting team, but this time United were able to ride out the storm and claim victory. Comfortably ahead through a Zat Knight own goal and Antonio Valencia's maiden competitive strike for the club, the Reds had to survive a late barrage from the Trotters, who had halved the deficit with 15 minutes remaining, through Matt Taylor.

Just five minutes in, Knight deflected in Michael Owen's errant effort and a leisurely afternoon appeared on the cards for the hosts, who could regain top spot with a win after Chelsea's shock defeat at Aston Villa. Only a stunning close-range stop from Jussi Jääskeläinen prevented Jonny Evans from breaking his duck and adding a quick-fire second goal, before Owen unwittingly deflected Dimitar Berbatov's volley wide of the mark. Kevin Davies missed the target with a free header at the Stretford End to serve timely notice of the visitors' dormant threat, but Edwin van der Sar – back in competitive action for the first time since the 2008–09 Champions League final – was untroubled throughout the first half.

The game was seemingly put to bed before half time, as a superb flowing move culminated in Valencia exchanging passes with Gary Neville and rifling the ball past the exposed Jääskeläinen. A procession of chances followed after the interval, with Owen twice denied, Berbatov thwarted by a superb save from Bolton's veteran Finnish goalkeeper and Valencia denied a strong shout for a penalty by referee Mark Clattenburg. The official's popularity quickly skyrocketed, however, when he chalked off Ricardo Gardner's goal on 70 minutes for a perceived foul on van der Sar.

The deficit was halved five minutes later when Taylor headed home Davies's back-post cross, prompting a sustained spell of pressure from the visitors and a white-knuckle climax for United. Aerial bombardments rained down on van der Sar and his defiant defenders, but Bolton couldn't muster an equalizer. There was a collective gasp inside Old Trafford when Gary Cahill powered a 94th-minute header straight at the Reds' goalkeeper, but it proved the last meaningful action of the game. A deserved three points took the Reds back to the top of the table and highlighted an invaluable blend of guile and graft.

Team: Van der Sar; Neville, Ferdinand, Evans, Evra (O'Shea 83); Valencia, Anderson (Scholes 86), Carrick, Giggs; Berbatov, Owen (Welbeck 84)
Scorers: Knight (5 (og)), Valencia (33)
Attendance: 75,103
Referee: Mark Clattenburg

'At the end we were hanging on a bit,' admitted Jonny Evans afterwards. 'We had a lot of chances, but full credit to Bolton: they got the goal and it gave them a chance towards the end of the game. You know you're going to be in for a long afternoon against Kevin Davies, and in the first half particularly I found it a bit tough, physically. In the second half, I thought I got to grips with the game a bit more, and his physical presence.

'It's a good day for us. But we were watching the Chelsea game in the changing room before the match and we know it's going to be quite an up-and-down season. A lot of teams in the Premier League are improving and they're getting closer and closer to the top. It's making it a really exciting league.'

Although he's been put through the wringer by his side on countless occasions down the years, Sir Alex Ferguson was left lamenting another nail-biting climax against unfancied visitors.

'We made it hard for ourselves when we should have been well in front,' the manager grimaced. 'When Bolton scored late on, the last ten minutes were nervous. We panicked at times, but we got through it. Just. Some of the football was very good. There was great speed to our game and we were a constant threat to them. It's a pity we didn't get our second goal earlier because we could have run up another good score.

'When Bolton came into the game a little bit before half time, we caught them on the break. That was a comfort zone for us – maybe too much, because the players were relaxed in terms of their play in the second half. We should have finished the game but didn't, and sometimes you can leave yourself regretting these things. But we got through it, and when you consider other results around today, it's a good day for us.'

In retrospect, skipper Gary Neville agrees that the Reds had landed in the comfort zone, but concedes that such pitfalls are no new thing. 'We've had those games over the years where you seem to be coasting and sometimes we can get a bit bored,' he admits. 'It sounds strange to say, but perhaps the crowd ease into thinking it's won, and so do we to an extent. You're two–nil up and coasting, but in the Premier League if a team gets a goal back, they can start causing you problems. Any team that comes back like that can put you under pressure. We always say that in any match you're going to come through a period of five to ten minutes where they will do better in the game, even at Old Trafford. It always happens, Bolton managed to do it and their period of pressure was right at the end and they finished in the ascendancy. You always get a few of those per season.'

Bolton's surprising late surge failed to take the shine off a win that sent the Reds back to the top of the table, as Sir Alex's men switched their attentions to European matters. A meeting with CSKA Moscow beckoned, and a return to the scene of one of the most dramatic chapters in the club's history: Moscow's Luzhniki Stadium. An unforgettable, epic penalty shoot-out win over Chelsea sealed the 2007–08 Premier League and Champions League double at the 80,000-capacity ground, and Sir Alex and his players were relishing the chance to return for a tricky-looking clash with Juande Ramos's side.

With an almighty trip to beleaguered Liverpool looming, Patrice Evra, Darren Fletcher, Ryan Giggs, Ji-sung Park and Wayne Rooney were all left in Manchester to nurse minor injuries in a bid to make the short trip to Anfield. Those who travelled to Russia were still airborne when news broke that the FA had charged Sir Alex with improper conduct for comments about referee Alan Wiley. The United manager had two weeks to respond to the charge.

Upon landing in Russia and scurrying over to the pre-match press conference, Sir Alex was soon faced with a more consuming issue: the Luzhniki pitch. Rather than the lush, rain-slicked turf on which John Terry tellingly slipped 18 months before, an artificial surface lay in wait.

'I watched CSKA's previous Champions League game and I didn't see any issue with it,' shrugged Sir Alex. 'It is a passing surface and we have good passers in our side. When Luton and QPR had them all those years ago we always played well. We had a great record at those artificial pitches and that was when the artificial pitches weren't as good. The one in Moscow has a far better covering on it.'

Despite a maximum six points from two games in Group B, the manager recognized his side would be hard-pushed to maintain that perfect record against a well-drilled CSKA side flying the flag for a notably stronger Russian league.

'For a few years now the Champions League has had a tremendous amount of quality in it,' he said. 'I think the Russian teams in particular have improved a lot in the last few years thanks to big investment. There are a lot of Brazilian players in Russia now. So we can expect a difficult game. We're in a strong position ourselves after winning our opening two games and, if we can navigate the back-to-back games against CSKA, we're through, I think. Nine points is an attractive number and that would almost get us into the next round with three games to spare. Winning is vital to me.'

Champions League Group B

CSKA Moscow 0 Manchester United 1
Luzhniki Stadium, 21 October 2009

While it lacked the drama of the Reds' last visit to the Luzhniki Stadium, United flew home from Moscow with mission firmly accomplished. Antonio Valencia's late winner put the Reds in control of Group B, with maximum points from three games, as a commanding performance made a mockery of the pre-match perception that CSKA Moscow would benefit from playing on their own plastic pitch.

Exuding all the maturity that had yielded two successive final appearances, the visitors controlled the vast majority of the encounter, despite a host of senior absentees. Livewire forward Miloš Krasić provided occasional moments of individual brilliance for the hosts, but his influence failed to inspire his colleagues. Even goalkeeper Igor Akinfeev, repeatedly linked with a transfer to Old Trafford, hardly covered himself in glory with a stumbling save from Paul Scholes on 25 minutes as United bossed matters.

Krasić drilled a low shot just past Edwin van der Sar's post in response, but it was Gary Neville who provided the half's final moment of quality by curling onto the roof of Akinfeev's net after Dimitar Berbatov's cut-back.

United's patient game-plan continued into the second period, and frequent forward forays posed problems for CSKA. Only a superb one-handed save from Akinfeev kept out Nani's diving header, while Valencia almost uprooted the goal with a blistering shot that smashed against the crossbar. Four minutes later, the Ecuadorian broke the deadlock with a powerful far-post effort after Berbatov's clever flick-on.

CSKA had no time to respond and Anderson almost added gloss to the scoreline with a curling effort that crept just past the post in injury time. With such a disciplined defensive set-up, however, one goal was always going to be enough to take United to the brink of yet another berth in the Champions League knockout stages.

Team: Van der Sar; Neville, Ferdinand (Brown 57), Vidić, Fabio (Carrick 88); Valencia, Anderson, O'Shea, Scholes (Owen 70), Nani; Berbatov
Scorer: Valencia (86)
Attendance: 51,250
Referee: Claus Bo Larsen

With two goals in as many games, Antonio Valencia's rapid development as a United player was yielding results and, in turn, plaudits from his increasingly appreciative team-mates. 'He's got a lot of quality, he's very strong and quick,' said Gary Neville. 'He's like an old-fashioned winger who likes to get crosses into the box. He's a constant threat to the defender – always on the shoulder – and tonight in the second half he was getting behind them all the time. We played quite a few balls in behind their left-back and Antonio made it very difficult for him.'

Rio Ferdinand was also full of praise for the Ecuadorian. Shy and retiring on and off the field, Valencia had been the antonym to the big presence of Cristiano Ronaldo, but Ferdinand could see a player rapidly adjusting to life in the spotlight. 'I think Antonio Valencia is in the Paul Scholes mould, in the way he approaches the game,' said the England international. 'He's a very humble lad. He comes in and does his work and then goes home. He's most comfortable out on the football pitch. He's been very impressive so far and I'm sure he'll keep improving. He's scoring goals now as well, which is great.'

The previous evening, Liverpool's home defeat to Lyon had condemned Rafael Benítez's side to their worst sequence of results in more than two decades. As United had equalled a Champions League record of 14 away games without defeat in Moscow, form dictated there would be only one winner when the sides met at Anfield. But Ferdinand, by now a veteran of English football's most-anticipated fixture, knew better.

'I think form goes out of the window in these games,' he said. 'We all know that when there's a big rivalry between two teams – whether it's a derby or a big cup clash – form doesn't come into it. It all comes down to who performs best on the day and that's what we're looking to do.'

So, despite United's encouraging form, nobody was expecting an easy day at the office when the Reds set off on the 33-mile trip to Anfield. It was widely acknowledged that the Merseysiders' patchy form would count for nothing in the crackling atmosphere of an invariably feisty derby. What's more, Ji-sung Park was out and doubts lingered over the availability of Wayne Rooney and Darren Fletcher, offsetting the good news that Ryan Giggs and Patrice Evra were fit.

If Rooney failed a fitness test, there was a very real chance Michael Owen would be asked to lead the line on his old stamping ground. 'Michael's got a chance of starting,' Sir Alex told his pre-match press conference. 'When he came on against CSKA, he did very well. His movement really started to trouble his opponents. I was pleased with that contribution, even though it was only thirty minutes. He has been doing very well and has been an excellent professional for us.'

While Owen had previously been afforded a warm reception at Anfield when returning with Newcastle United, it was widely expected that the Liverpool faithful would turn on their former idol for crossing into the enemy camp.

'He had some great years at Liverpool, so it's difficult to say what reception he'll get,' admitted Sir Alex. 'There are very few players who have played for both clubs. Paul Ince got a bad reception from our fans when he went to Liverpool, and Michael might get that again on Sunday. I don't think it'll bother him.'

Looking back, Owen admits he had few concerns about what lay in store. 'I'd blown away the cobwebs when I went to Anfield with Newcastle, so I wasn't worried about going back,' he says. 'Without wishing to distance myself from anyone, I'm not a Manc and I'm not a Scouser! I grew up pretty much equidistant between the two, in Chester, supporting Everton. I just don't think it matters, really. I'm a footballer, so I don't see it as your normal fan would see it. A fan would never change their colours. We've got a couple of players here at United who have played for just one club their whole career, but that's extremely rare these days. The vast majority of players will look at it as a job. If you ask fans whether they've been in their job since their teens throughout their working life, it rarely happens. I think fans see players as fans in some ways, but I just put my heart and soul into playing for whoever's employing me. I've been very fortunate to play for two of the biggest clubs around.'

With Owen's return providing yet another sub-plot to one of the season's most anticipated fixtures, the scene was set for another titanic encounter.

Liverpool 2 Manchester United 0
Anfield, 25 October 2009

For the third meeting in succession, Liverpool profited from an off-colour United display, as the Reds slipped to a tame defeat at Anfield. Second-half strikes from Fernando Torres and David Ngog sealed the points for Rafael Benítez's side, but a poor performance from the visitors – who lost Nemanja Vidić to a red card against the Merseyside men for the third time in as many matches – allowed the hosts to edge a game short on quality.

The hitherto on-song Reds had travelled to face a Liverpool side amid their poorest run of results in 22 years but, not for the first time, form counted for nothing in a local derby played in a powder-keg atmosphere. Pre-match, both sets of supporters had smattered the field with beach balls in reference to Liverpool's controversial defeat at Sunderland eight days earlier, in which Darren Bent's winning goal had tellingly deflected off another inflatable foe.

John O'Shea, Patrice Evra, Ryan Giggs and Wayne Rooney all returned from injury to bolster the side that had won in Moscow, and the England striker had a goal chalked off for offside after just three minutes. It was the hosts who took control, however, and Edwin van der Sar did superbly to make a double save to deny Fábio Aurélio and Dirk Kuyt. Moments later, the Dutch striker dragged a shot wide of his compatriot's post, before Aurélio prompted another smart save with a firm downward header.

Half time came with Liverpool on top, but United slowly began to threaten in the second period, with Michael Carrick and Giggs both marginally away from reaching deep crosses. Then, just as the visitors were starting to dictate play, came the key moment. Torres latched on to Yossi Benayoun's searching ball, raced into the area and fended off Rio Ferdinand before lashing a finish past van der Sar and into the roof of the Kop net. With something to cheer at last, Anfield erupted.

His hand forced, Sir Alex Ferguson introduced Michael Owen and Nani, with the former receiving a particularly vitriolic 'welcome' from his former club's supporters. Both were soon involved, with Nani firing a shot straight at Pepe Reina before Owen was hauled down by Jamie Carragher when he seemed certain to bear down on goal. Controversially, the defender escaped with only a caution.

United's closest brush with parity came when Antonio Valencia fired against the crossbar from a tight angle, but the odds were stacked in the home side's favour when Vidić picked up his second yellow card of the afternoon. As the Reds committed bodies to attack, Ngog strode through in the 96th minute to clinch the points for Liverpool and seal a miserable day for United.

Team: Van der Sar; O'Shea, Ferdinand, Vidić, Evra; Valencia, Carrick, Scholes (Owen 74), Giggs; Rooney, Berbatov (Nani 74)
Scorers: n/a
Attendance: 44,188
Referee: Andre Marriner

'We didn't deal with the wounded animal,' Sir Alex said at the final whistle. 'This is the most pain you can have when you play for United,' added Patrice Evra. Both were left dumbfounded by the performance of referee Andre Marriner, but conceded Liverpool were worthy winners.

'We never got any luck in terms of refereeing decisions, but we have to hold our hands up: we weren't good enough,' the boss said. 'The laws of the game were altered to prevent professional fouls of that nature,' he said of Jamie Carragher's challenge on Michael Owen. 'If Carragher goes off – their best player, their captain – it's a different game and Liverpool would have been under pressure. I'm not trying to take anything away from Liverpool – they were the better team – but there were so many controversial things that happened that we feel a bit aggrieved.'

Forthright full-back Evra shed light on the mood that consumed Anfield's away dressing room. 'I look more at the display of Manchester United and the display was poor today,' he said. 'Normally when United play, we create at least five or six clear chances, but we only had the one when Valencia hit the crossbar. It's not enough if you want to win against Liverpool. There was a big silence in the dressing room afterwards and we will need a few days to recover from this big disappointment.'

When it comes to defeat at Anfield, time neither forgets nor fully heals. 'We were shocking,' concedes John O'Shea. 'I don't think we could play that badly again. Nothing came off for us; it was just incredible. The game was so disappointing. Obviously you don't want to lose in any way, ever, but you can take some consolation if you come off beaten and you've created chances and you've been involved in the game. Then you can blame luck, but there was none of that.

The situation was extremely ramped up for Liverpool, after losing four in a row; it really was set up perfectly for them, but it was such a poor day for us. With Liverpool, the games are huge anyway, but because they'd been performing so poorly it was massive for them. We were devastated after the game because we know how much the game means to the fans. Never mind the derby games against the City, against Liverpool the intensity is hard to explain. You really can feel it on the pitch as well and it's great to be involved in those games, but when you lose it's devastating. It's one of those where you want the next game to come as quick as possible.'

Sure enough, the Reds were granted an opportunity to return to winning ways with a Carling Cup trip to Barnsley just 48 hours later.

Much of the pre-match coverage centred on a former United player managing a team against Sir Alex Ferguson. Not a new experience for the Scot, given his regular tête-à-têtes with the likes of Steve Bruce and Mark Hughes, but it was a first managerial meeting with Mark Robins. The ex-Red is widely credited with saving Sir Alex's job in 1990 with an FA Cup winner at Nottingham Forest, a goal many argue indirectly laid the foundations for United's modern dominance.

However, the United manager was keen to curtail the myth that he was set for the sack had it not been for Robins's intervention, saying: 'It was an important goal, don't get me wrong. And who's to say what would have happened without it? But I don't think it saved my job. One thing's for sure, Bobby Charlton would not have let it [my sacking] happen. He knows better than anyone the heartbeat of this football club. This football club needed the foundation of youth and we were doing some great work there. Bobby knew we were on the right road.'

That reliance on youth would again raise its head as, once more, Sir Alex shuffled his pack to make light of the hectic run of fixtures. Senior opportunities beckoned for the junior talents, including a debut for Gabriel Obertan.

Carling Cup Fourth Round

Barnsley 0 Manchester United 2

Oakwell, 27 October 2009

Danny Welbeck and Michael Owen struck as ten-man United overcame the dismissal of skipper Gary Neville to oust Barnsley and move into the Carling Cup quarter-finals. The spirited Championship side were chasing the game from the sixth minute, when Welbeck headed the opener, before a sublime strike from Owen effectively killed off their challenge early in the second half.

Barnsley passed up plenty of chances, but United's creativity in attack posed questions the hosts rarely had answers to. Full-debutant Gabriel Obertan was a particularly tricky thorn in their side, and it was the Frenchman who won the corner from which United opened the scoring. Anderson fizzed in a superb right-wing in-swinger, which dipped perfectly for Welbeck to glance past former United goalkeeper Luke Steele. Two Carling Cup starts, two goals for the young striker.

The Longsight-born teenager twice went close to doubling his tally, but Barnsley passed up three presentable headed chances from corners to remind their illustrious visitors that the tie was still in the balance.

There it hung until just before the hour mark when Owen, who'd earlier missed a presentable one-on-one chance, picked up Anderson's pass 35 yards from goal, sped through a cluster of defenders and steered a low shot around Steele's dive. It was a masterful finish from the arch poacher.

Just when it seemed United would stroll through to the last eight, Neville's high challenge on Tykes midfielder Adam Hammill prompted an immediate red card from referee Chris Foy. In the face of unexpected adversity, the Reds battened down the hatches. Ben Foster had scarcely been called into action, but was soon required to field Daniel Bogdanovic's low shot, before producing a wonderful one-handed save from substitute Jacob Butterfield.

The hosts' spurned opportunities ultimately haunted them, as the cup holders' clinical nature at key moments proved enough to secure safe passage into the quarter-finals.

Team: Foster; Neville, Brown, Evans, Fabio; Obertan, Anderson, Rafael, Welbeck (Tošić 53); Macheda, Owen (De Laet 65)
Scorers: Welbeck (6), Owen (59)
Attendance: 20,019
Referee: Chris Foy

Delighted to have progressed to the last eight, Sir Alex also took great joy from the education his young side gained in overcoming a spirited Barnsley outfit. 'Playing away from home in a cup tie is a completely different experience from playing at Old Trafford,' he said. 'Last year we had some good home draws, [so this] was good experience for the lads.'

For Rafael, the learning curve was steepened by a first senior appearance in the centre of midfield. It demonstrated his versatility, but his evening took a bizarre turn when he escaped a booking for fouling Jamal Campbell-Ryce. Instead, referee Chris Foy cautioned his twin brother Fabio, although the mistake was soon brought to light in the United dressing room and the caution later transferred to the correct offender.

Unmistakable was the razor-sharp finish from Michael Owen in scoring United's clinching goal, but the winding prelude to his unerring finish confounded press perceptions that the England striker is nothing more than a penalty-area predator. 'That's how people judge me, unfortunately,' he said. 'I started the recent game against Bolton, we won two–one and when I came off I was pleased. I thought I'd played really well but didn't score. When I looked in the papers the next day, I was given threes and fours! Tonight I played pretty average but I've scored so I'll probably get a six or a seven.'

Fellow goalscorer Danny Welbeck limped off early in the second period and joined a lengthy list of injury concerns in the Carrington treatment room. The striker was certainly out of contention to face Blackburn at Old Trafford, as were Darren Fletcher, Ji-sung Park and the suspended Gary Neville; Rio Ferdinand, Nemanja Vidić and Ryan Giggs were all touch-and-go.

Sir Alex confirmed at his pre-match press conference that the club had consulted a specialist to ascertain the root cause of Vidić's troublesome calf, while Ji-sung Park's recurring knee problem had flared up on a flight back from international duty with South Korea. Nevertheless, those who were fit were in confident mood, despite a run of inconsistent form.

'Without a doubt there's more to come,' said Paul Scholes. 'I wouldn't say we've been stuttering, but we haven't been as fluent as we know we can be. There's been the odd performance – like Tottenham away – where everything's come together, but I think the best is ahead of us. We're not too worried about our form because traditionally we're not great at the start of the season. The difference this time is that, more often than not, we've still been winning games. So I can't complain too much. But we would like to get back to the top of the league, and with style. Some teams might settle for getting results, but here at United we aim a little higher.'

Barclays Premier League

Manchester United 2 Blackburn Rovers 0
Old Trafford, 31 October 2009

Once again, Old Trafford was treated to a display of patience and resolve as United had to work hard to wear down a determined and defensive Blackburn Rovers side. The Reds were forced to wait until the second half to finally pierce the visitors' stubborn rearguard, as clinical finishes from Dimitar Berbatov and Wayne Rooney finally found a route past Rovers goalkeeper Paul Robinson.

The former Tottenham stopper was the star performer in a Blackburn side that turned up with the sole ambition of frustrating the Reds. Although the approach initially worked as chances proved few and far between, cautious visitors are a familiar foe at Old Trafford. United gradually turned the screw, with Berbatov forcing Robinson into action with a downward header and Valencia firing just off-target, before a linesman's flag correctly ruled Rooney had been offside in teeing up Berbatov to slide home.

Undeterred, the Bulgarian eventually broke the deadlock with a stunning piece of finishing early in the second half. Patrice Evra's speculative shot was heading wide, only for Berbatov to redirect it into the bottom corner with one touch to control and another to arrow a volley past Robinson.

Substitute Gabriel Obertan squandered two presentable chances to double United's lead, but the points were eventually safeguarded when Rooney met Anderson's delightful cross with a sumptuous half-volley that flew into Robinson's bottom left-hand corner.

The second goal shook Blackburn into life, as Nikola Kalinić was incorrectly flagged offside and deprived a consolation goal after Edwin van der Sar had done well to keep out Benni McCarthy's initial shot. An unlikely climax ensued, as the game descended into an end-to-end encounter, and Michael Owen came within inches of adding a third goal. But a comfortable win over stubborn opposition was more than satisfactory as Sir Alex's men continued their steady pursuit of league leaders Chelsea.

Team: Van der Sar; O'Shea, Brown, Evans, Evra; Valencia, Anderson, Carrick, Nani (Obertan 64); Rooney, Berbatov (Owen 79)
Scorers: Berbatov (55), Rooney (87)
Attendance: 74,658
Referee: Phil Dowd

Dimitar Berbatov characterized the Reds' patient approach, plugging away before finally getting his goal, and the Bulgarian was pleased to have negotiated a notoriously tricky opponent in Blackburn.

'It was difficult, but I think our defence did a magnificent job. We scored the goals and overall deserved to win,' he said. 'In the first half I had a couple of chances to score. You need to be patient and when another chance comes along, you have to score it, and I was very glad to score my chance. Then Wayne Rooney scored another and that was it finished for Blackburn. We were relieved because they are a difficult team to play against. Every time when you score a goal you are relieved because you feel you've done something special and that was the case for me.'

Although unable to match Berbatov's goalscoring contribution, winger Gabriel Obertan was delighted to make his Premier League bow for the Reds. 'It's been four months now that I have been injured, so it was a good debut,' smiled the Frenchman. 'I ran hard and tried to do my best. I think I need a bit of rhythm, a few games to be fully fit. It's going better and better and there's no reason to end it. I think I'll be better after a few games.'

Obertan conceded he was 'disappointed' to have fluffed a clear chance to slot home from six yards and cap a dream debut, and mid-fielder Michael Carrick sensed an opportunity for some gentle ribbing. 'It was great for him to finally play,' Carrick said. 'It was disappointing for him not to take his chance, but hopefully he'll get many more here. I think he might get a little bit of stick for his miss. We can't let him off for that!'

5

November

Talent will get you far, but fortune can make or break your ambitions. As November began, United were being gradually gripped by a spate of injuries. Crucially, persistent knocks undermined the involvement of two of the Reds' most influential players: central defenders Rio Ferdinand and Nemanja Vidić.

The pair had been cornerstones of 2008–09's miserly, record-breaking defensive displays, but their new season had been ravaged by spells on the sidelines. Ahead of United's home game against CSKA Moscow in the Champions League – a match that could assure the Reds of a berth in the knockout stages of the competition with two games to spare – both Ferdinand and Vidić were certain to miss out. The former had visited a specialist about his back injury, while the latter's persistent calf problem prompted a similar line of investigation.

Although concerned by the duo's ongoing problems, Sir Alex Ferguson took great solace from being able to call upon overtly able deputies. 'There was a lot made of Rio and Vida's absence in the papers, but when you've got Wes Brown and Jonny Evans as your back-up then it's not too bad,' he said. 'Take Ferdinand and Vidić out of the Premier League partnerships and there aren't many better than Brown and Evans. We've sent Vida to a specialist and hopefully he'll be OK. Rio's getting treatment . . . Ryan Giggs won't make Tuesday, neither will Rio. So we have a fight on our hands to get them ready for the Chelsea game.'

In addition to Ferdinand, Giggs and Vidić, Dimitar Berbatov and Danny Welbeck both missed training ahead of the CSKA match through injury, while Wayne Rooney was at Liverpool Women's Hospital with his wife Colleen, who had given birth to baby boy Kai. The striker's involvement was in doubt, but Michael Owen and Kiko Macheda were ready to deputize up front against a side whose preparations had been thrown into disarray.

Just six weeks into his role, CSKA coach Juande Ramos had been relieved of his duties and replaced by Leonid Slutsky. The former Krylia Sovetov manager would guide his new team into action at Old Trafford just a week after taking the post. No stranger to falling foul of the effect new managers often have on sides, Sir Alex was wary of Slutsky's appointment.

'You'd imagine the new coach will really want to win this game, obviously to strengthen his position in the job but also to enhance his reputation,' the United manager told his pre-match press conference. 'You have to be aware that football can throw clangers into the mix. We don't want that. I expect CSKA to play their strongest team. It's going to be a tough game, but we can consolidate our position at the top of the table. If we win, then we should finish top of the group and that's the right kind of incentive for me. We're at home and our home form is very good. Hopefully we can continue that way.'

Champions League Group B

Manchester United 3 CSKA Moscow 3

Old Trafford, 3 Nov 2009

Never simple, is it? The Reds qualified for the knockout stages of the Champions League with two group games to spare, but underdogs

CSKA Moscow almost sprung an almighty shock at Old Trafford. The Russians punished three instances of defensive slackness from United, who had equalized once in the first half, before Sir Alex's men required two goals in the final six minutes to salvage a point.

CSKA's intent was apparent from the first whistle, as Alan Dzagoev and Deividas Šemberas both fired narrowly off-target inside the first two minutes. Paul Scholes and Darren Fletcher gradually wrested control of midfield and the latter sent a powerful shot just past Igor Akinfeev's post just before the quarter-hour mark.

Michael Owen and Federico Macheda both came close to netting in a thrillingly open game, but Dzagoev broke the deadlock on 25 minutes when he latched on to Necid's chested pass and struck a powerful effort across Edwin van der Sar and into the far top corner. Although the shock sparked United into quickly levelling, as Owen swept home Nani's neat pass, parity lasted only a minute as the visitors sprung the hosts' offside trap and the impressive Miloš Krasić rounded van der Sar before slotting into the open goal.

A stunned silence gripped Old Trafford and was reprised three minutes after the interval as Vasili Berezutski took advantage of non-existent marking to head home Dzagoev's back-post free-kick. When Fletcher went to ground deep inside the CSKA area it appeared United had earned an immediate route back into the game, but Portuguese referee Olegário Benquerença surprised everyone by instead brandishing a yellow card in the Scotsman's direction.

Wayne Rooney, a sleep-deprived substitute following the birth of his first child, was soon introduced, and his presence lifted United. Unfortunately, Akinfeev merely upped his own game and provided repeated validation of pre-match praise from the United boss.

Scholes, Owen and Rooney were all denied and Macheda headed against the post before Neville flighted in a perfect free-kick from the right for Scholes to nod in a powerful header. Old Trafford cranked up the volume and the roof almost came off in the first of four added minutes when Antonio Valencia bagged the sixth goal of the night. The Ecuadorian's powerful 25-yard strike was heading wide until it struck the chest of Georgi Schennikov and spun past the committed Akinfeev and into the unguarded goal.

Having saved face at the death, United almost completed the unlikeliest of turnarounds when Neville sprung the offside trap in the 94th minute, only for the visitors to clear. Despite losing Deividas Šemberas to a second booking in injury time, the Russians held on to bag a vital point, the least they deserved for pushing United all the way. The Reds, meanwhile, could reflect on unexpectedly hard-fought progress through to the last 16.

Team: Van der Sar; Neville, Brown, Evans, Fabio (Evra 59); Valencia, Fletcher, Scholes, Nani (Rooney 58); Owen, Macheda (Obertan 82)
Scorers: Owen (29), Scholes (84), Valencia (90)
Attendance: 73,718
Referee: Olegário Benquerença

'We were absolutely fantastic in terms of our desire to win the match and were unlucky at times,' a breathless Sir Alex said afterwards. 'Their goalkeeper made some fantastic saves; we hit the post and missed a lot of other chances. And we also had a stonewall penalty turned down. I can't believe that decision. It's one of the worst I've seen in my lifetime.

'But we didn't make it easy for ourselves and it became an uphill fight. That's maybe not a bad thing, though, because it's a reminder that when you leave yourself open in European football it can be very dangerous. Their first two goals were soft ones to lose and the third was unbelievable – a free header at the back post on a set piece. That's the first goal we've lost on a set piece for a year. It's a good reminder for us about how we need to defend those situations, especially as we'll face a lot of set pieces on Sunday at Chelsea.'

United's rousing fightback could be traced to the introduction of Rooney, not least for the panicking effect his presence had on the visiting defenders. Just a day after becoming a father, the striker had been thrown on in a state of emergency. Incredibly, he admits he'd rather have started.

'I was a bit tired before the game,' he recalls. 'The day before, Colleen had given birth and I'd been up all night without any sleep. I got a phone call to say I was in the squad and then when I got to Old Trafford I found out I was sub, so I was gutted with that. But I got on and I think adrenalin, more than anything, got me through the game.'

United's collective cause had benefited from a more familiar circumstance: chasing the game at the Stretford End. 'We didn't expect to find ourselves in that situation,' recalls Paul Scholes. 'We rested a few players, but it was a shock to go three–one down, especially as we hadn't lost at home in Europe for a long while. It was important to get the result because we needed a point to qualify. Chasing games at the Stretford End seems to work for us. There have been loads of games over the years where we've been up against it, either being behind, or drawing when we need to win and we're attacking the Stretford End. Time and again in that situation we've managed to create chances and goals.'

By hook or by crook, United were in the last 16 with two games to spare. With a gargantuan top-of-the-table clash at Stamford Bridge looming large, however, there would need to be an improvement across all areas of the team.

'We've definitely got to play better at Stamford Bridge and keep it tight at the back,' admitted Wes Brown. 'Some people thought it would be an easy game for us at home, but CSKA proved what a good side they are. It was very frustrating to go three–one down. We didn't play particularly well in the first half – they kept the ball well, scored early and generally made things hard for us. But in the second half we managed to put some pressure on them, the crowd got behind us and we were lucky to get the draw. Qualification was the most important thing. It would have been nice to win, but now we've qualified we can concentrate on the league.'

'Chelsea are playing very well at the moment. They're a strong side who are well organized and scoring a lot of goals. We're going to have to go there and play really well if we're to come away with any points.'

Buoyed by the potential return of Nemanja Vidić, Ryan Giggs and Dimitar Berbatov, Sir Alex was aiming for a return to winning ways at Stamford Bridge. United and Chelsea games had previously been famed for the unlikely amount of away successes, but that quirk had been quelled somewhat in recent seasons. Indeed, the Reds' last win at the home of the Blues had come in 2002, and the United manager began his pre-match press conference by admitting: 'We would like to improve our record there. It's not been great in the last few years. We've had a couple of draws, but nothing more than that. We used to have a terrific record at Stamford Bridge, but in the last few years we've let it slip. We have to get our act together. But the players realize it's a big game and their performance is going to be important.'

The victors would end the afternoon atop the Premier League table – either Chelsea by five points or United by one – but Sir Alex was quick to dismiss talk of the game proving pivotal in the race for the title.

'It doesn't come into my thinking that this could be a league decider,' he said. 'But it could be an important game. Towards the end of the season, you might think, "I'm glad we got a result at Chelsea." But it's difficult to pinpoint the importance of Sunday in relation to where we'll be in May.' Hindsight would offer that insight.

Barclays Premier League

Chelsea 1 Manchester United 0

Stamford Bridge, 8 November 2009

There are some things you just cannot legislate for. An almost flawless display of defensive solidity and midfield pressing, built on a sound game-plan from Sir Alex and his coaching staff, counted for nothing after John Terry's controversial late winner. The Chelsea skipper, part of Old Trafford folklore for his role in United's 2008 Champions League triumph, headed home 14 minutes from time at Stamford Bridge, although legitimate doubt was cast on both the validity of the goal and the free-kick from which it arrived.

The result was incredibly harsh on a United side who carried the greater threat and dictated the tempo of the game in a masterful fashion. Darren Fletcher stood out for an incredible all-action display, while lone striker Wayne Rooney wasn't far behind after a manful shift of hold-up play that kept both Terry and Ricardo Carvalho on their toes throughout.

Chelsea's formidable home record established them as favourites ahead of the game, especially as United lined up without Rio Ferdinand and Nemanja Vidić in the centre of defence. Nevertheless, Jonny Evans and Wes Brown were more than equal to the powerful challenge of Didier Drogba and Nicolas Anelka.

In an absorbing tactical battle, seldom was either goalkeeper employed. Edwin van der Sar made a routine early stop from Branislav Ivanović and the Blues applied moderate pressure towards the end of the first half. But Ryan Giggs's volley over Petr Čech's bar was the outstanding attacking moment of the opening period.

Instead, a midfield battle royal dominated matters. Against the unyielding home triumvirate of Frank Lampard, Michael Essien and Michael Ballack, United's Fletcher, Michael Carrick and Anderson shone in a display of breathless harrying, crisp passing and gritty desire. On the flanks, Ryan Giggs and Antonio Valencia shielded their full-backs dutifully, while Rooney provided an eye-catching reference point when the Reds gained possession.

It was Rooney's growing influence that had seemed set to give United victory. As Sir Alex's men answered the home side's every question, the ball was increasingly ferried to the England striker, and midway through the half he flashed one shot just past the upright, then drew a superb fingertip save from Čech with a curling 25-yard effort that was bound for the top corner.

Just as United cranked up the pressure, disaster struck. Not only did Darren Fletcher clearly win the ball from Ashley Cole, only to be penalized on the left flank, but, as Terry glanced Frank Lampard's in-swinging set piece towards goal, Drogba hauled Brown out of the way and waved a boot at the ball as it passed Edwin van der Sar. All from an offside position.

Somehow, the goal stood. United's disbelieving players were incandescent, but nevertheless pressed for a route back into the game. A point was the least the Reds' efforts deserved but, despite five added minutes, the closest call came when Valencia flashed a shot wide of Čech's post.

Instead, it was Chelsea who could celebrate three points at full time, with United left to bemoan the injustice of it all. Certainly, any satisfaction gained from an impressive performance couldn't mask the disappointment at the five-point gap by which the champions now trailed the challengers.

Team: Van der Sar; O'Shea, Brown, Evans, Evra; Valencia, Anderson (Owen 85), Carrick, Fletcher, Giggs (Obertan 85); Rooney
Scorers: n/a
Attendance: 41,836
Referee: Martin Atkinson

'Clearly Darren has won the ball,' Sir Alex Ferguson complained afterwards. 'He never touched Cole, who has jumped up in the air. Then Drogba pulled Brown to the ground for the goal. The referee's position for the free-kick was absolutely ridiculous. He can't see anything. He's got a Chelsea player standing right in front of him and he doesn't even move. It was a bad decision, but what can you do? There's nothing we can do about it. You lose faith in referees sometimes – that's the way the players are talking in the dressing room. It was a bad one.

'That goal should not have been allowed, but we dominated the game and had some chances to win the match. We had great opportunities in terms of the football we played to get to the edge of the box, and some good chances in and around the box. But we should be finishing them off. We only have ourselves to blame in that respect. Sometimes you need a bit of a break and we never got the break we needed.'

'We've been let down by that goal,' echoed Wes Brown. 'The decision to award the free-kick was harsh. Then Drogba was holding me and pulling me down, obstructing me from challenging for the ball when the free-kick came in the box. The ref didn't see that, either.

'It's very hard to take. I thought we played really well and passed the ball brilliantly. We were the better team and had more chances. We should have done better with our chances, but we definitely didn't deserve this result and it's tough because we go home with no points.

'I thought we played well as a back four, and I thought we limited them to very few chances. In that sense, we felt like we did our jobs, which makes it worse when they score a goal like that. It's disappointing. We just have to keep going and try to put this behind us. We need to carry on playing as we did today, but just add goals to the performance.'

Another member of the resolute back four, John O'Shea, sought positives from the display, but was left to lament the five-point gap between the two sides, and the enforced fortnight's wait until the Reds could set about whittling away the lead.

'We hate losing games and we know that we now have to go on a great run,' said the Irishman. 'The international break comes at a bit of a bad time – you'd prefer to have another game a few days later to help put the defeat out of your mind. There's a bit of a sour taste left, but hopefully we'll get over that.

'Not many teams come to Stamford Bridge and dominate games. We had great spells where we had Chelsea really pinned back and we caused them problems on the counter-attack, but our final ball or shot just didn't go for us. We stuck to our game-plan very well and were the better team. Unfortunately, we didn't get what we deserved.'

For O'Shea, attentions would quickly switch to Ireland's World Cup play-off with Patrice Evra's France. With Darron Gibson also in the Eire camp, United's French left-back was convinced the Irish were trying to subliminally irk him.

'I've had the impression for days that certain people have been wearing green on purpose,' he said. 'Maybe that's just my imagination. But the other day I opened a can of Sprite, took a good look at it and decided I had to swap it for another drink. The moment I see anything green, I think about the Republic of Ireland.

'These last few days at United have been difficult. John O'Shea has promised me it will be hell at Croke Park. I have had the mickey taken out of me a lot. It's normal, though. When England failed to make Euro 2008, I asked my English team-mates if they wanted a remote control to switch between games on TV. Now it's started once more. Darren Fletcher, who plays for Scotland, tells me we'll spend the summer together. The joking has to stop now. We have to qualify. It has become an obsession. I have never given such priority to the national team as I have done over the last few months.'

Nani was also involved in the play-offs, as his Portugal side faced a tricky two-legged tie against Bosnia & Herzegovina, while 16 other squad members were either contesting friendlies or UEFA European U21 Championship qualifiers.

In the first half of the play-offs, both France and Portugal won 1–0. Evra, O'Shea and Nani all started, while Gibson was an unused substitute at Croke Park. After a relatively uneventful first leg in Dublin, the second instalment in Paris soon achieved infamy. Ireland's shock 1–0 lead took the game to extra time, only for Thierry Henry to blatantly handle the ball and tee up William Gallas's decisive equalizer for the French. Despite long, loud protests from the Irish, including an appeal to FIFA to have the game replayed, France progressed to the World Cup.

'We played really well in the game and deserved to win before it could go to extra time,' recalls Gibson, a second-half substitute in the Stade de France. 'We had the chances but didn't take them. Obviously, it was disappointing to go out in the manner we did, but if you look at it in hindsight, if one of our strikers had done the same thing and we had gone through, we wouldn't have been complaining. That's just the way football goes. I was on the pitch, ten yards away from the goal when it went in, and I didn't see the handball, so you can see how the referee missed it. It happens. People might not like it, but that's the way it goes.'

From a United perspective, the evening was tainted when John O'Shea limped off with what he assumed to be a dead leg. 'It came from a clearance over the top,' recalls the defender. 'Henry was chasing it, Shay Given came out and we both tried to shepherd the ball out. I don't know how it happened, but as me and Shay both slid, his knee went into the middle of my quad muscle. I knew it was a bad dead leg because I couldn't carry on, so I told the physios and they treated it as a dead leg. I expected to maybe be out for a week or ten days. How wrong I was!'

Having flown back from Paris straight after the game, O'Shea reported to Carrington the following morning and consulted the club's medical staff. They were cautious, having recently treated Reserves defender Reece Brown for a similar complaint. He'd suffered a dead leg and then taken another knock, which had worsened the injury.

It was obvious O'Shea would miss Everton's impending visit to Old Trafford. Meanwhile, Sir Alex Ferguson's own involvement would be limited to watching from the stands after the FA handed him a £20,000 fine and a four-match touchline ban (two games suspended until the end of the 2010–11 season) for his October comments about referee Alan Wiley.

Not that United's players were perturbed. 'I hope we show the character to win the games without him,' said Nemanja Vidić. 'But we know what is waiting for us and what he expects of us. Nothing changes. In that respect, I don't think there will be a big difference. He sees everything.'

The Serbian's 70-minute outing for the national team thrust him into contention to face David Moyes's injury-hit side, while Jonny Evans was another potential fit defender, an increasing luxury, with Rio Ferdinand and Fabio injured and Gary Neville still suspended. As for Owen Hargreaves, his forecasted speedy return was yet to materialize, prompting the media to grill Sir Alex at the manager's pre-Everton press conference.

'He's doing his training very well,' said the boss. 'I think it's more a confidence thing for the lad to come back into full training. He's doing good work with the physios and some football-related training, although not at a competitive level at the moment. I think that's down to being out for a year and two months. We're of the mind that we'll take our time and not rush it.'

For United, five points behind Chelsea, bedevilled by injury and still reeling from that controversial defeat at Stamford Bridge, confidence would stem from three vital points against Everton.

Barclays Premier League

Manchester United 3 Everton 0
Old Trafford, 21 November 2009

Having waited patiently for the chance to chip away at Chelsea's lead, United quickly and confidently got down to business by dismantling Everton at Old Trafford. A Darren Fletcher blockbuster opened the scoring, before second-half strikes from Michael Carrick and Antonio Valencia secured a routine victory over David Moyes's out-of-sorts side.

Usually so assured of posing a stern challenge to any team, the Toffeemen's stuttering start to the season continued with a limp display in M16. It seemed only a matter of time before their limited ambition was overcome. It took a magnificent challenge from Leighton Baines to deny Valencia a clear goalscoring opportunity early on, and the central defensive pairing of Sylvain Distin and Joseph Yobo just about managed to repel further efforts from the Ecuadorian and ex-Everton-starlet Wayne Rooney.

Ten minutes before the interval, the visitors' resistance was broken. Patrice Evra's deep cross reached Valencia, who could only head downwards towards the edge of the area. Fletcher steamed in and smashed the loose ball into Tim Howard's top corner, making a mockery of the ball's high bounce with textbook technique. Boyhood Everton fan Michael Owen almost added a second moments before the interval, only for Howard to rush from his line and further narrow an already tight angle for the United striker.

Although Everton upped their involvement after the break, with substitute Yakubu firing just wide and Marouane Fellaini having a goal disallowed for offside, United's threat was almost constant. Owen rounded Howard but shot wide from an awkward position before Rooney clipped the crossbar with a 20-yard effort. The Reds were knocking on the door and the Old Trafford faithful weren't kept waiting very long for a second goal.

From a Ryan Giggs corner, Rooney's errant shot flashed across a packed area and landed back at the taker's feet. Giggs kept the ball in play, shaped to cross towards goal and instead slid an enticing ball across the box for Carrick to fire through a ruck of players.

Valencia deservedly got in on the scoring shortly afterwards after another United attack easily punctured the visitors' backline and allowed Scholes to tee up the Ecuadorian. His low shot cleared Howard and nestled in the far corner after nicking Baines *en route* to goal. A routine return to winning ways and a quick climb up to second spot after Arsenal's defeat at Sunderland made for a highly satisfactory day's work.

Team: Van der Sar; Rafael (Scholes 63), Brown, Vidić, Evra; Valencia, Carrick (Gibson 83), Fletcher, Giggs; Rooney (Obertan 74), Owen

Scorers: Fletcher (35), Carrick (67), Valencia (76)

Attendance: 75,169

Referee: Steve Bennett

With international commitments fulfilled and Champions League qualification secured, United's victory over Everton marked the beginning of a spell of sustained concentration on the quest to win a fourth successive Premier League title.

'It's a busy period now and it's all club, club, club,' said Darren Fletcher, fresh from opening the scoring against David Moyes's side with a stunning volley. 'The Champions League is important for us, but we've done our job in the tournament now so we can look forward. We need to kick on and put a run of league wins together. Beating Everton was a good start. They came and made it difficult for us, but we kept the ball and we were patient and took our chances when they came.'

'It was a controlled performance,' added Sir Alex. 'We showed a lot of patience, particularly in the first half when we were trying to open them up. Fortunately we got the first goal at the right time. The name of the game for us is to kick on now. I stand by the view that if we get to New Year within a point, in front or round about the leaders, we have a big chance in the second half of the season.'

The Reds' cause had a new supporter: Kai Rooney, who had sampled his first United match aged just 20 days, perched in one of Old Trafford's private boxes. 'We weren't going to take him along, but Colleen and I decided it would be nice for his first game to be between United and Everton, given that I'm an Everton fan as well, so it's a game he can always look back on now,' reveals Wayne Rooney. 'He's got United, England and Everton kits now. He's got a Barcelona kit as well – my dad got it for him, so he's got a good choice of teams there!'

Youth promotion would be high on the agenda for Sir Alex Ferguson, too. Regardless of the Reds' domestic focus, there were still two remaining Champions League group games in which ideally to seal top spot in Group B and blood a number of youngsters and fringe players, and the first of these was against Beşiktaş.

Edwin van der Sar, Gary Neville, Rio Ferdinand, Jonny Evans, John O'Shea and Fabio all missed training ahead of the Turks' visit, while the likes of Gibson, Macheda, Obertan and Welbeck took part with genuine hopes of starting the game.

'This is a good fixture,' Sir Alex told his pre-match press conference. 'I can try one or two things. We did that in the last game and we were far too open. But it ended up being a fantastic game.

'In the situation we're in, we could have an absolute non-event if we wanted to. But it's not the way we want it. We want an exciting game and we'll do our best to challenge the younger players that will play. It's difficult to say whether it's more important to finish first or second in the group stages these days. But we will try to win it because that's the best thing to do. You always want to finish first.

'We've analysed Beşiktaş and their domestic form has been transformed in the last six matches. They've won them all, beating the top-of-the-league team Fenerbahçe three–nil on Saturday. So they're in very good form and we will need to deal with that.'

Champions League Group B

Manchester United 0 Beşiktaş 1
Old Trafford, 25 November 2009

There are few steeper learning curves than Champions League football. For United's youngsters, the unforgiving environment of Europe's premier competition dealt a harsh lesson as Beşiktaş staged a shock smash-and-grab raid at Old Trafford.

The Reds' 24-game unbeaten home run in Europe was ended by

Rodrigo Tello's deflected first-half strike, but the hosts were left to rue spurned chances and wasted possession.

Sir Alex Ferguson blooded his youngsters, with Danny Welbeck, Kiko Macheda, Gabriel Obertan, Darron Gibson and Anderson injecting vigour into the starting line-up. Ji-sung Park also returned after a niggling knee injury, making his first appearance in two months.

While the pressure was off United, already assured a berth in the last 16, Beşiktaş had just two matches to salvage a campaign that had yielded only one point from their first four fixtures. Little surprise, then, that the Turkish champions flung themselves into challenges from the first whistle. The opening 20 minutes were spent with both sides encamped in the Beşiktaş half, save for two rare forays from Michael Fink and Bobo, who both came close to snatching the lead against the run of play. United, meanwhile, almost opened the scoring through Welbeck and Gibson before Nemanja Vidić headed over.

Then Old Trafford was stunned. Chilean winger Tello advanced on goal from the right and struck a powerful effort goalwards. Ben Foster may have had it covered, but a telling deflection off Rafael took the shot past the England international and into the bottom corner.

Chips down, United responded positively, continuing to commit numbers to attack and dictate the game's tempo. Beşiktaş's own game-plan – defend, defend, defend – also held firm. Macheda and Obertan were both frustrated by heroic blocks as the Turks put everything on the line in the name of a famous upset.

Visiting goalkeeper Rüştü Reçber had little to do in the first period, but his contribution after the break proved decisive. The veteran stopper, who shipped six goals on his previous OT outing, with Fenerbahçe in 2004, smartly tipped Obertan's low shot around the post before producing two stunning saves in the dying stages.

Patrice Evra was denied what seemed a clear penalty after two defenders converged to halt his run into the area before Rüştü tipped over Macheda's point-blank header to preserve his side's lead. With virtually the game's final act, he acrobatically leapt to keep out Wes Brown's header. Full time prompted wild scenes of celebration from the visitors. The result was of little genuine consequence for either side, but nevertheless prompted a thorough post-match inquest both inside and outside Old Trafford.

Team: Foster; Neville, Brown, Vidić, Rafael (Evra 74); Park (Owen 68), Anderson, Gibson (Carrick 74), Obertan; Welbeck, Macheda
Scorers: n/a
Attendance: 74,242
Referee: Stephane Lannoy

'I'm disappointed, of course,' said Sir Alex Ferguson, having left behind a predictably deflated dressing room. 'But it was an opportunity to play some younger players and I'm not disappointed in them. Gabriel Obertan is twenty, Danny Welbeck is nineteen tomorrow and Federico Macheda is eighteen. They all showed potential and playing in these games gives them incentive to improve themselves. They know they'll get that opportunity at this club. The club's history is based on producing young players who can excite, and these players can all excite. They were anxious to do well and sometimes young players don't know how to slow down, and maybe we played too quickly at times. But that's not their fault – that's a natural part of improving and developing a young player. In the main, they showed great ability.'

Nemanja Vidić, meanwhile, was happy to see United's youngsters given a chance, and fully expected them to be back in the future, all the wiser for the experience. 'It's important for young players to get chances,' said the Serbian. 'They're still young, but they're growing up a lot and we will see a lot more from them.'

The press did not entirely agree, as the Reds' vanquished fledglings were handed a savaging for their shock defeat. 'To be honest, I don't think the media affects the players too much,' says Darron

Gibson. 'It doesn't really get into the dressing room because not too many players read the papers in the morning. It didn't really affect the lads in the way you might have thought.' Nevertheless, coming under the media microscope is par for the course for those coming through the Old Trafford ranks. So says Gary Neville, a member of the team so famously criticized by Alan Hansen in 1995 *en route* to winning the Double.

'The manager picks young players or brings them on in games where he knows he can get away with it,' says Neville. 'What he's exposing them to is not just the glory of playing for Manchester United, but also the harsh schooling of it. If you don't play well you're going to get absolutely ripped apart by the newspapers and the broadcasters. You're at the top, there to be shot at, and what it'll have done for those lads is give them the education of the other side of the coin and show them it's not all roses in the garden. It's hard work playing for Manchester United and you've got to get through moments of difficulty, criticism and mistakes.

'Young players who are going to last here have to experience those things. You're not going to play five, ten, fifteen years here without going through lows. And can you handle the highs? The success, the fame, the increased money that comes into your life? Can you also handle the criticism, the bad performances, being dropped? If you don't handle both sides of the coin well, you won't be here very long.'

While the external examinations of United's squad continued, attentions inside the camp switched to facing struggling Portsmouth with a familiar face at the helm. Avram Grant's first and last games in charge of Chelsea had come against United, and the Israeli was installed as the new manager at Fratton Park in advance of the Reds' visit, prompting wariness from Sir Alex.

'It's not easy to go to Portsmouth,' he told his pre-match press conference. 'Obviously they have a new manager, so you would imagine there will be a response, as you always get from a team with a new manager. We know Avram very well from his time at Chelsea. He's very experienced and I'm sure he will get the right reaction from his players. We've kept in touch quite a lot and he will be glad to get back into management. But he has got a challenge, because when your team is bottom of the league you've got a real task on your hands. But hopefully he can manage that.

'They have some very good players. I've watched videos of their games and they might be in a false position. But being bottom of the league often causes a reaction from owners of clubs. They don't like to see their team at the bottom – that's the danger position. And that often leads to a change of manager.'

Sir Alex would not be given the chance to pit his managerial wits against Grant on the Fratton Park touchline by virtue of being banished to the stands, but the United boss was confident that being out of sight would not put him out of his players' minds.

'It shouldn't really affect us,' he said. 'We've got our communication lines in place for the game. The only problem you've got is that it's a very noisy place, Fratton Park. It's one of these old stadiums where the stands are a bit rickety and the directors' box is towards the home end, where all the drums and noise is going on. It's a good racket and a terrific ground. But we should be OK.'

Barclays Premier League

Portsmouth 1 Manchester United 4

Fratton Park, 28 November 2009

Ryan Giggs finally bagged his 100th Premier League goal for the Reds at Fratton Park, but not before Wayne Rooney's third United hat-trick sealed victory in an entertaining clash. The England striker struck twice from the penalty spot and once to cap a sweeping move, before Giggs completed the scoring with a late free-kick. It wasn't all plain sailing down at a rain-swept south coast, however.

Kevin-Prince Boateng levelled for beleaguered Pompey during the first half, again from the penalty spot, while Tomasz Kuszczak was required to make a string of impressive saves, including a world-class stop in each half. The Pole was called into action early on as United struggled to get out of first gear, rushing from his line to make a close-range stop from Aruna Dindane. Shortly afterwards, Kuszczak produced a stunning fingertip save from Jamie O'Hara's dipping volley.

Despite conceding ground and chances with alarming regularity, it was United who struck first when Rooney tumbled under Michael Brown's challenge before firing the resultant spot-kick clinically inside Asmir Begović's post. Pompey's raucous support bemoaned their misfortune, a common theme hitherto, but referee Mike Dean soon presented them with unlikely compensation. Bowing to the say-so of his assistant, Dean awarded the hosts a perplexing penalty for Nemanja Vidić's minimal tug on Frederic Piquionne's shirt. Controversial, perhaps, but Pompey were worthy of their equalizer and their equality at the interval. It didn't last.

Three minutes of the second period had elapsed when Darren Fletcher sprung the hosts' offside trap with a lovely chipped pass to Giggs, whose centre for Rooney gave the striker the simple task of slotting a left-footed finish past Begović. Two soon became three for United and Rooney, with Giggs again central to proceedings. The veteran winger lost possession to Piquionne before quickly winning it back, and the Frenchman fouled his opponent just inside the area for the most glaring of the three penalties awarded. Rooney went the same way, with the same outcome, and sealed his hat-trick.

Far from sated, United continued to press. Valencia and Giggs both came close, before Giggs was seemingly tripped again in the Pompey box. Another penalty award was never on the cards, as Giggs's knowing smile towards Dean suggested. The Welshman did have the final say, however, by curling home a low, 20-yard free-kick to cap another magnificent personal performance. Time remained for Kuszczak to do likewise, somehow turning John Utaka's close-range scissor-kick up and onto the crossbar, and ensure a record win for the Reds at Fratton Park.

Team: Kuszczak; Neville, Brown, Vidić, Evra; Carrick (Anderson 76), Fletcher, Scholes, Valencia, Giggs; Rooney
Scorers: Rooney (25 (pen), 48, 54 (pen)), Giggs (87)
Attendance: 20,482
Referee: Mike Dean

When it rains, it pours goals, according to Ryan Giggs. The veteran winger felt a half-time downpour at Fratton Park gave United a priceless advantage, as Portsmouth were swept away in a one-sided second period.

'The rain helped,' he said. 'It made the pitch a lot quicker and we were much slicker with our passing. Just after half time we created chances and soon after that Wayne managed to score. It was the perfect start. After that, the goals came at good times – two quick goals and then we were able to be more confident on the ball.'

Giggs also reserved special praise for hat-trick hero Rooney, saying: 'He was brilliant; he was up there on his own. He tied down the two centre-halves and was brilliant all game. He took his goals well and he could have had more.'

Rooney was quick to return the compliment, paying tribute to Giggs's achievement of reaching 100 Premier League goals and saluting his enduring excellence. 'Giggsy's amazing,' said the striker. 'His energy, his work-rate, his passing and his movement are unbelievable. It's a privilege to play with him. He's thirty-six but plays more like a twenty-six-year-old; he's up and down, he's everywhere. It's great for him to get his hundredth Premier League goal. I didn't know about the record until after the game, but I'm delighted for him.'

For Giggs, Rooney et al., the following day brought news of a potential engagement with an old foe: a mouth-watering FA Cup third-round draw with either Kettering Town or Leeds United. First, however, there was December to negotiate. Although Champions League qualification had been secured, the new month would begin with the Reds hosting on-song Spurs in the Carling Cup, while

Chelsea's thumping win at Arsenal had given them a five-point lead in the Premier League. And with fixtures coming thick and fast and a glut of injuries to contend with, it wasn't going to be easy. Make no mistake: Sir Alex's men faced stern examinations of both immediate and long-term ambitions.

6

December

Youth has always been given the chance to flourish at United. But the opportunity to shine on the biggest stage brings with it added pressure and increased scrutiny from a headline-hungry press pack. So it was after November's defeat to Beşiktaş. The youngsters on display that night may not have covered themselves in glory, but they couldn't have imagined the stinging series of rebukes that would compound their embarrassment over the following days.

Ever keen to protect his players, Sir Alex Ferguson insisted he would stand by them as December began, thrusting them into a tricky Carling Cup quarter-final against Harry Redknapp's resurgent Tottenham at Old Trafford. While the United manager was calm and patient with his young charges, he was quick to vent his ire at the media's knee-jerk condemnation after the Beşiktaş defeat.

'One journalist wrote: "There's no future for these players, no tomorrow for them",' Sir Alex said. 'What an idiot! I can't believe that. It's unbelievable. When Beckham, Butt, Scholes and all those lads played [in 1996], they were twenty-two years of age – three years ahead of these players. So that kind of reaction is amazing, isn't it?

'Of course they will grow from that experience [losing to

Beşiktaş]. I was confident of playing them and they had every right to play. They will play on Tuesday, too. Against Beşiktaş they got anxious. They'd made good chances but hurried things – that's not the biggest crime in the world. We're not talking about ability here, we're talking about experience. That's why we have to play them. Games are the one thing we have to give them. We can't just provide them with that old head that helps you deal with situations like on Wednesday in the final third of the field.

'The number of young players we have is stacking up and they need to be challenged. I thought they did OK and I didn't think they deserved that kind of criticism. But the same journalists will be wanting articles from them when they are stars, going cap-in-hand, begging them for interviews in a few years' time. Mark my words on that. They'll be hypocritical and say: "I've always said you were going to be a wonderful player." What a world we live in. The thing is, Alan Hansen made comments in front of millions of people on TV and gets slaughtered for it, while the journalist I mentioned writes that and it gets buried in the middle of a newspaper article and he gets off with it. He should be sacked!'

Gary Neville, one of those subjected to *Match of the Day* pundit Hansen's withering assertion that 'you'll never win anything with kids', wasn't surprised to see his manager persisting with youth.

'I think he'll always give players a second chance and an opportunity,' said the club captain. 'There can't be many players who leave this club, thinking, "I can't believe he got rid of me." To be honest, if you've had your chance, then you haven't taken it, or if you haven't had your chance, then you weren't good enough. It's as simple as that. He's not in the habit of getting rid of players who are good enough to play for United. There haven't been many young players who have left and come back and bitten us. He gets it right.

'Those players had a bad experience against Beşiktaş and you want to see how they handle the setback. It's a continual test in those early games. Eric Harrison [Youth coach] always used to say to us that you've not been through the education period at United until you've played a hundred games. You can't say you've made it until you've passed that marker.'

The visit of Spurs provided the Reds' latest batch of highly monitored youngsters the opportunity to show they'd learned lessons from the chastening experience a week before.

Carling Cup Fifth Round

Manchester United 2 Tottenham Hotspur 0

Old Trafford, 1 December 2009

Darron Gibson's eye-catching double capped a solid display from United's young side, as a strong Spurs team were brushed aside by the Carling Cup holders. A repeat of the 2008–09 final was expected to be just as tight and tense as the goalless draw at Wembley nine months earlier. Instead, the Reds secured a spot in the semi-finals before half time, as Gibson twice struck from distance to end the challenge of a visiting side that failed to live up to their growing reputation.

True to his word, Sir Alex Ferguson, perched in the directors' box as he completed a two-game touchline ban, made just three changes to the side that had come under fire after defeat to Beşiktaş. Tomasz Kuszczak replaced Ben Foster in goal, Ritchie De Laet started at left-back and Dimitar Berbatov returned from a knee injury to boost his match fitness.

A virtually full-strength Tottenham team began with plenty of intent and it took a smart save from Kuszczak to field a powerful effort from on-song striker Jermain Defoe, while plenty of last-ditch challenges inside the United area kept the visitors at bay. Just after the 15-minute mark, United moved into the lead and would never look back. Anderson's run infield was curtailed by a David Bentley challenge, but the ball ran to Gibson and the Irish midfielder drilled a low, measured shot past Heurelho Gomes and into the far corner.

Although it took heroic blocks from De Laet and Nemanja Vidić to deny Defoe and Robbie Keane respectively, it was Berbatov who shone as the outstanding attacker on the field. Having already teed up Park for one close call, the Bulgarian fed Gibson, who swapped passes with Danny Welbeck and curled a sumptuous second goal into the top corner.

Left with a mountain to climb in the second period, Spurs' appetite for the game disappeared. Kuszczak made a superb reaction stop from Bentley's close-range effort, but the visitors offered nothing more to trouble a back four superbly marshalled by Vidić and Wes Brown in the centre of defence. Substitute Kiko Macheda drilled into the side netting in injury time, but United's course to the semi-finals had long since been plotted. The holders were into the last four and the flak-smattered youngsters had proven a point against one of the Premier League's top sides.

Team: Kuszczak; Neville, Brown, Vidić, De Laet; Park, Anderson (Tošić 82), Gibson, Obertan (Carrick 62); Welbeck, Berbatov (Macheda 62)
Scorer: Gibson (16, 38)
Attendance: 57,212
Referee: Mark Clattenburg

'I'm not shy of shooting,' admits Darron Gibson. 'I'm basically under instruction to shoot. I'm told: "If you get a chance, hit it." For the first goal against Spurs, it broke to me and I just decided to have a go. I shoot from everywhere, so I thought I might as well hit it. It wasn't the cleanest hit, but fortunately it went in the bottom corner. The second one was better. Berba played it across, I played a one-two with Welbeck and stroked it into the top corner instead of the usual power strike. Obviously I was delighted to get two and it's a nice reward because I've been working on my shooting over the last three years.'

Gibson's pair of classy long-distance strikes took United through to the Carling Cup semi-finals, but Sir Alex admitted his side had ridden their luck in the opening exchanges against Harry Redknapp's visitors.

'I thought we were fortunate in the first half,' said the United manager. 'Tottenham dominated the first half an hour or so and could have been two or three up. We had to defend really well: Tomasz made a good save from Defoe, and Vidić had a couple of great tackles that kept us in it. We took time to get going, but when we got the first goal we improved. We played much more controlled football in the second half and Anderson and Gibson really started to impose themselves on the game. We've ended up comfortable winners in the end, but we can't dismiss the fact we were playing a very good team. We're very pleased to be in the semi-finals.'

In the space of a week, United's youngsters had experienced the sapping lows and dizzying highs of life at the club. The good news kept coming for Kiko Macheda, who penned a four-year contract extension, tying him to the Reds until at least 2014.

In a surprise twist, it was then revealed Serbian prodigy Adem Ljajić would not be joining the club from Partizan Belgrade. The tricky playmaker had been part of a deal agreed in principle 11 months earlier, and was expected to move to England in January. Instead, a club statement revealed: 'We had an option to buy the player but, having closely monitored his development over the past twelve months and taken into consideration the young players emerging through the ranks, we have chosen not to pursue the transfer.'

Taking the place of Sir Alex, who had a prior engagement, assistant manager Mike Phelan expanded on United's decision at the pre-West Ham press conference. 'We went down the road of trying to obtain a work permit,' he said. 'We made a tentative approach to get one and what we got back from the Home Office is that we couldn't get it through in time for when we had to make a decision on Adem in January.

'The question then is: do you lay out the money for Adem when there is the possibility you could or couldn't get the work permit? We decided it wasn't the time to do it. As you can see, we've got young players and we're a team that requires young players to develop and come through into the first team. We've looked at Adem and he has the potential to do that, but you can't fight these things sometimes. Some people you can get work permits for, some you can't. Adem fell into the category of being hard to get a work permit for, so we made the decision.'

The shock collapse of the Ljajić transfer was one of several issues touched upon in a busy press conference. Another was the Carling Cup semi-final draw, which had thrown United together with Manchester City. 'It's a great draw. I think it will get things buzzing around town,' chuckled Phelan.

More pressing was the series of injuries hampering United ahead of the ever-tricky trip to Upton Park, as Rio Ferdinand, John O'Shea and Jonny Evans remained sidelined. For Paul Scholes, absentees mattered not – victory was imperative. 'It's a tough place to go,' he admitted. 'But it's vital we go on a long run now. Chelsea are five points clear and a strong outfit, as they proved at Arsenal last weekend. They look a little bit more determined than they have done over the last few years. 'It's up to us to put pressure on them and the only way we can do that is by going on a long run of wins, while hoping our rivals slip up here and there. The belief is always there at this club. We believe we can win every game.'

Barclays Premier League

West Ham United 0 Manchester United 4

Upton Park, 5 December 2009

The rough and the smooth are seldom far apart when United are involved, but the rollercoaster nature of the Reds' storming win at Upton Park beggared belief. A four-goal win and Chelsea's subsequent defeat at Manchester City provided the day's good news, but injuries to Gary Neville and Wes Brown compounded an unfathomable run of misfortune that also claimed Nemanja Vidić in training before the match.

Their collective absence meant United's back four at the end of the game comprised Darren Fletcher (who started at right-back), Michael Carrick, Patrice Evra and Ryan Giggs. Fortunately, West Ham had long since been vanquished by a devastating burst of goalscoring either side of half time.

A scrappy opening to the game did little to betray the drama that would follow. Few chances were created in the opening half-hour, with Giggs's hurried clearance to keep Jack Collison at bay providing the only real scare for the visitors, who had Sir Alex Ferguson back on the touchline after his suspension.

The manager's patched-up defence was further hampered when Neville sustained a groin injury. Already operating out of position in the centre of defence, the skipper was replaced by midfielder Michael Carrick as the Reds sought to hammer a round peg into a square hole. By half time, the unlikely defence had something worth protecting. Paul Scholes, outstanding throughout, chested a clearance into space and hammered a left-footed rocket into Rob Green's top corner, even though the England goalkeeper did get a strong hand to the ball.

There was no hint of blame attached to United's second soon after the interval. A flowing move down the Reds' left culminated in the ball reaching Gibson infield and his scorching right-footed effort arced away from Green's dive and tore into the back of the net. Game over, but United weren't done. Two more goals followed, little more than a minute apart and strikingly similar in construction and execution. Two neat passing moves, two balls slid across the area, two no-nonsense finishes: one apiece for Antonio Valencia and Wayne Rooney.

The late removal of Brown, again through injury, cast a shadow over the victory, but the quartet that finished up defending Tomasz

Kuszczak's goal held on for an unlikely clean sheet, demonstrating the champions' inherent character.

Team: Kuszczak; Fletcher, Neville (Carrick 34), Brown, Evra; Valencia, Anderson, Gibson (Berbatov 67), Scholes, Giggs; Rooney (Owen 73)
Scorers: Scholes (45), Gibson (61), Valencia (70), Rooney (72)
Attendance: 34,980
Referee: Peter Walton

'Losing defenders the way we are doing at the moment is a bit of a headache to us,' admitted Sir Alex Ferguson afterwards. 'Nemanja Vidić was out with flu, meaning we had to put Gary Neville at centre-back and then he goes off after half an hour. Then Wes Brown came off at the end.

'Michael Carrick came in and did very well. We were very pleased with that. The reason we put him on the bench this afternoon was to cover us in the event of anything happening to the back four. He has the height, the composure, the pace and the experience to play there. There was an option to play Ritchie De Laet, but away from home against West Ham . . . it's a difficult place to go to. I felt an experienced player was important. I would actually like to have played Michael in midfield from the start because he's in good form. But I felt like I had to err on the side of caution, and I'm glad I did.'

Carrick's absence from the United engine room was hardly detrimental, thanks largely to the timeless excellence of Paul Scholes. Not only did the little master open the scoring at a vital time, but his dictation of the game's tempo underlined his enduring value. Meanwhile, Darron Gibson and Anderson both benefited from playing alongside the on-song veteran.

'Paul is an incredible player and he is conducting our play so well at the moment,' enthused Sir Alex. 'He's making it look good for us. Darron and Anderson are both only young boys of twenty-two and twenty-one years of age. They are going to be great players and they accept Paul Scholes is the finished article. They see a man who has been doing it for fifteen years at the highest level. He's a great example to them and it will rub off, I'm sure.

'As I've always said about Darron, he has this ability and power to score from outside the box, which he proved again today with a marvellous strike. I was pleased that we did try to shoot on a number of occasions, and it does give us an extra dimension to our game because we don't normally have midfield players who can do that.'

For all the midfield talents young and old, it was the scarcity of fit defenders that threatened to have a telling impact on United's season and, most notably, the bid to reach a third successive Champions League final.

With a final group game against Wolfsburg to negotiate and less than two days until the travelling party departed, the club's medical staff faced a race against time to have any extra bodies fit for the trip. For John O'Shea, by now a near-fixture in the treatment room as he continued his recuperation, the situation was unfathomable.

'I was looking around the treatment room, thinking, "Oh my God. How's your luck?" It was ridiculous,' says the Irishman. 'Younger players were having operations, when it was just the kind of situation you need for young lads to get an opening at a club like United. Then the boss can call on them and they can show how good they are, but it was just unfortunate they were all injured. As it was, Michael Carrick ended up being used as the main man in the centre of defence. Because he's a central player who's quite tall and with a general idea of how to play the game, it was a case of "You'll do".'

Although O'Shea was able to appreciate the comedic undertones that came with watching his colleagues retrain for defensive duties, his own battle with a complicated dead leg was proving a major struggle.

'It was worrying for a little while, because I'd never had a serious injury before,' he says. 'The blood and bone cells grow and once they mix together it forms the calcification, like a new bone has grown right in the middle of your muscle, which you don't want because you can't bend your leg! You lose the muscle in your leg and, like I say, you get a bit fearful.'

O'Shea remained at Carrington as Sir Alex's squad jetted to Germany. So too did every previously injured defender and, in an unlikely twist, Ritchie De Laet. The Belgian seemed certain to play in some capacity across the back line, but he had not been at the club for two years, a requisite of UEFA rules on the inclusion of additional players. In his place, along went Oliver Gill, who was one of just two fit defenders in the squad. Of the 19-man group that flew to Wolfsburg, 13 were midfielders.

Gill was joined by fellow Reserves regulars Cameron Stewart, Oliver Norwood, Matty James and Magnus Eikrem. Their presence lent a cherubic appearance to the travelling party, especially with Wayne Rooney and Dimitar Berbatov all staying in Manchester with their own injury concerns and Ryan Giggs rested for the following weekend's visit of Aston Villa.

'I felt like one of the older players in the squad,' smiles Darron Gibson, still relatively fresh from his teenage years. 'Obviously I'm still young, but when the younger lads come in you do feel like you can help them out a bit and take them under your wing. You've been there before and you know what happens.'

At the Reds' pre-match press conference, Sir Alex tried to make light of the grim selection problems hampering his bid to win Group B. 'There's no good news with all these injured players,' he said. 'We have a lot of thinking to do about team selection. Maybe it's worth trying one defender! Manchester United are always first at doing something, so we will try and do that again on Tuesday by playing with just one defender!

'Considering we don't have natural centre-backs, we have a difficult task picking a back four that can unite together and give me good organization and good passing ability. These are the decisions we are addressing and hopefully we get the answer.'

Having already qualified for the competition's knockout phase,

United's primary concern revolved around fielding a balanced starting XI. For Wolfsburg, however, the final group encounter was a watershed in their maiden Champions League campaign. The Germans needed to win, having allowed CSKA Moscow to move level on points in second spot. 'Wolfsburg will be delighted that we have so many injuries because it's a big game for them,' said Sir Alex. 'I have to look at the bigger picture and that means looking to Saturday and future league games. We've qualified for the last sixteen, and looking at the groups I'm not sure whether first or second really matters. So that is a major boost to us. If we are second, I don't know if it does matter.'

Champions League Group B

VFL Wolfsburg 1 Manchester United 3

Volkswagen Arena, 8 December 2009

A patched-up, ragtag United side provided one of the season's highlights with a heroic victory over the reigning Bundesliga champions, courtesy of Michael Owen's first hat-trick for the club. The striker stunned Wolfsburg with a clinical treble, while a shock formational switch to 3–5–2, with a central defence of Patrice Evra, Michael Carrick and Darren Fletcher, outfoxed the dangerous, motivated hosts.

Goalkeeper Tomasz Kuszczak was well protected by his makeshift shield as the game wore on, but the home team could have been out of sight in the early stages. Carrick survived a strong penalty shout for a challenge on Makoto Hasebe, before Andrea Barzagli and Zvjezdan Misimović both powered free headers wastefully off-target.

As United grew into the game, however, only a marginal offside decision prevented Danny Welbeck from celebrating his first Champions League goal. Instead, the teenager's confident, slotted finish counted for nothing but a sign of the Reds' growing ambition.

Soon after, the Longsight striker dragged wide after a neat exchange with Owen.

Kuszczak was forced into an eye-catching fingertip save from Hasebe's effort, but the opening goal finally arrived just before the interval. It was worth the wait. Paul Scholes sent a magnificent pass wide to Nani, whose superb in-swinging cross was emphatically nodded home by Owen.

Sparked by the growing threat of missing out on the knockout stages, Wolfsburg began the second half with greater intent and soon drew level. Marcel Schafer escaped Ji-sung Park and clipped in a superb cross for Edin Džeko to power home from close range.

Although Kuszczak was helpless to prevent the Bosnian's goal, he soon resumed his repelling efforts, with smart stops from Brazilian striker Grafite and Ricardo Costa. Just as the pressure seemed to be building on United's unfamiliar line-up, Owen struck again. Substitute Gabriel Obertan, on for Nani, demonstrated his array of trickery with silky skills and fleet feet down the left flank, before crossing for Owen to tap into the unguarded goal with just seven minutes remaining.

There was time for one more scare, as Christian Gentner some-how contrived to miss a simple chance in injury time. To compound the midfielder's misery, the same passage of play concluded with Owen latching on to Obertan's through-ball, racing clear and clip-ping a beautiful finish over goalkeeper Diego Benaglio. The full-time whistle prompted jubilant scenes of celebration both on and off the field. The vocal travelling support paid tribute to their heroic, injury-ravaged team, while the players could bask in the glory of securing top spot.

Team: Kuszczak; Fletcher, Carrick, Evra; Park, Anderson, Gibson, Scholes, Nani (Valencia 74); Owen, Welbeck (Obertan 74)
Scorer: Owen (44, 83, 90)
Attendance: 26,490
Referee: Bjorn Kuipers

Having hammered square pegs into round holes pre-match, Sir Alex Ferguson was elated with his side's unlikely victory in Germany. 'It was an experimental system, but the good thing is there was still enough quality there,' he said. 'You have to trust the players are good at their job. They are, and they've proved it again tonight. I thought our control in the first half was very good. It was the same in the second half. Our threat towards the end and our speed on the counter-attack were great.'

At the sharp end of United's counter-attacking incision was hat-trick hero Michael Owen. Famously the scourge of Germany's defence on home soil for England in 2001, the striker had once again hogged the limelight. 'It was a fantastic hat-trick,' said Sir Alex. 'You know how good he is in that penalty box. He's on the shoulder, he makes runs across defenders, and his timing with his runs is fantastic. I'm really pleased for him.

'His performance tonight, as he's proved many times, shows he is one of the best strikers in the last third of the field in terms of positioning, movement and clinical finishing. The evidence is always on the football field and Michael has given plenty of evidence of what he can do tonight.

'I made the point some weeks ago that his training performances have improved steadily and I would never have a problem with him starting any game. We've recently chosen to play one central striker – normally Wayne Rooney – with three central midfield players. Tonight, we had a different system with Danny Welbeck and Michael. He's proved his worth and we're delighted with his contribution.'

Owen was predictably pleased to have plundered all three goals, but was swift to pay tribute to his fruitful supply line. 'Obviously I've scored a few hat-tricks in my time, but it's nice to get one that caps off a great team display,' he said. 'Me getting the three goals will probably grab the headlines, but I thought it was an excellent team performance.

'I was playing a bit deeper than normal, because with us having

Despite the best efforts of goalkeeper Tomasz Kuszczak, United's injury-hit side is roundly thrashed at Craven Cottage by Fulham.

Dimitar Berbatov celebrates sliding home United's late clincher against Hull City, as United return to winning ways at the KC Stadium.

Rafael da Silva roars with delight after hitting his first goal of the season against Wigan, as the Reds end 2009 with a resounding 5-0 victory.

Michael Owen is thwarted in an almighty goalmouth scramble as United suffer an embarrassing FA Cup third round defeat to Leeds.

Ji-sung Park and Darren Fletcher celebrate an own-goal from Birmingham's Scott Dann, but the Reds can only draw at St Andrew's.

As the lights go down at Eastlands, United's travelling supporters add a dash of colour to proceedings.

Rio Ferdinand returns from injury, but a clash with Hull City's Craig Fagan lands the defender back on the sidelines.

Wayne Rooney prepares to go head over heels after nodding home a dramatic injury-time winner against City to book a place in the Carling Cup final.

Nani is mobbed by his jubilant team-mates after his mesmerising run and chip puts United into the lead at the Emirates Stadium.

Michael Carrick takes the plaudits for his goal against Portsmouth, as the Reds put on a five-star show on the anniversary of the Munich air disaster.

Wayne Rooney salutes United's travelling fans in the San Siro, having assured the Reds of a first away win over AC Milan.

Back to reality: Everton's fans rejoice as a listless United display ends in defeat at Goodison Park.

Michael Owen demonstrates his enduring predatory instincts with a clinical finish against West Ham.

Wayne Rooney's second-half header against Aston Villa seals a comeback victory in the Carling Cup final.

Darren Fletcher holds aloft the trophy, as United's players join the travelling Red Army to celebrate.

The winning habit continues, as the players clutch a ninth major honour in just five seasons.

Paul Scholes bellows in delight after slamming home a vital late winner against a stubborn Wolves side at Molineux in early March.

Seven years after leaving United, David Beckham says an emotional farewell to Old Trafford after AC Milan's 4-0 drubbing.

so many players out we had to protect our back three. Me and Danny Welbeck were dropping in and trying to pick up their central midfielders where possible, while hopefully getting into the Wolfsburg box when there were chances to do so. European football is a different type of football to the domestic game. If you get a chance you've got to stick it away.'

And the match ball? 'I gave it to the masseur,' smiled the striker. 'I get a bit shy when I'm holding it as it draws attention to me! Hopefully he'll get it signed by the lads and then pop it in my bag when we get back to Manchester.'

In the squad's absence, work was already under way at Carrington to get more bodies back for the impending visit of Aston Villa. Nemanja Vidić was expected to recover from a bout of flu, Wayne Rooney and Dimitar Berbatov were winning battles with hamstring and knee injuries respectively, while Ryan Giggs was assured of involvement after being excused the trip to Germany.

For Michael Carrick, it was a case of waiting to see who could drag themselves from the treatment room to the training pitch in order to relieve him of his moonlighting duties in defence. Despite being out of his comfort zone, however, the midfield playmaker was prepared to extend his stint if required.

'We will have to see who is back for Villa,' he said. 'That might be the end for me at centre-back. We'll have to see what the body count is like. It is a lot different playing centre-half to midfield. It's not the physical side that's hard about playing centre-half – it's the mental aspect. Concentration and focus are vital . . . and hoping for the best!'

There was no prospect of Rio Ferdinand, Jonny Evans or John O'Shea featuring again before 2009 was out, so Carrick's role against Villa would be determined by the availability of Wes Brown, who was edging closer to full fitness.

While Villa's visit loomed large, so too did the BBC Sports Personality of the Year award. At his pre-match press conference, Sir Alex tipped Ryan Giggs to take the gong. He also poured scorn on suggestions that another veteran, Paul Scholes, had decided to retire at the end of the season.

'I don't think Paul actually said that,' insisted the manager. 'When I read it and spoke to him he said he never said that. When you get into your thirties, everyone starts to wonder what the next year holds for you. But we're sure about him and his qualities and we'll offer him a contract. When you see his performances at West Ham and Wolfsburg, there's no reason to think he can't do it again next year.

'The same goes for Ryan. He's an example to young people. He's never changed and I think he's producing his best form now. He's retained that amazing quality in his game and enthusiasm to play. Longevity should be rewarded, and we reward it. He will be offered a new contract next season and that's an indication of what we think of him at thirty-six, going on thirty-seven next year. Consistency and longevity isn't always rewarded, but sometimes a young sportsman can come on the scene and shine. That's the competition Ryan's had to face all his life, but he has shown a consistency that has brought him to this level. And we hope Ryan gets the reward he deserves on Sunday.'

While the two old stagers were tipped for umpteenth contract extensions, there was also talk of a newcomer rubber-stamping his very first deal with the club. Senegalese youngster Mame Biram Diouf, who had spent more than four months on loan at his Norwegian club Molde since agreeing to join the Reds, had caught the eye in training at Carrington. 'He's looking very exciting,' said Sir Alex, before adding that the club would be pushing for the striker's work permit.

But the short-term focus remained the early evening clash with Martin O'Neill's Aston Villa. The Midlanders had beaten Liverpool and Chelsea in the early months of 2009–10 and were heading north full of confidence, despite a wretched run of 26 years without a win at Old Trafford. For Ji-sung Park, there was no solace in that statistic. 'We have a good record against them but we have to look at the present. Our past results won't help us this time,' said the Korean. 'Villa have been strong for the last few years and they're more determined than ever to break into the top four. This season they have performed very well.'

Barclays Premier League

Manchester United 0 Aston Villa 1

Old Trafford, 12 December 2009

All good things must come to an end. United, so accustomed to vanquishing Villa on home turf, were overcome by Gabriel Agbonlahor's early header and a magnificent defensive display from Martin O'Neill's side. Despite the return of Wes Brown and Nemanja Vidić in the centre of the Reds' beleaguered defence, Agbonlahor nipped in to convert a superb Ashley Young cross at the Stretford End before handing over to his colleagues to keep United at bay thereafter.

Wayne Rooney thundered a shot against the crossbar in United's closest brush with an equalizer, but Villa, marshalled impeccably throughout by Richard Dunne, turned in 90 minutes of graft and discipline to earn three points and notch their first victory at Old Trafford in 26 years.

Initially, it had been the thronging home support that buzzed with anticipation, buoyed by the chance to go level with table-topping Chelsea, who had twice surrendered the lead to draw 3–3 with Everton at Stamford Bridge. United were soon knocking the ball about with purpose and poise, but too often the final pass was rendered wasted by a Villa interception, often from Stephen Warnock, who did superbly to cope with a lively start from Antonio Valencia.

Villa's grit in midfield and defence was supplemented by guile in attack. The deadlock was broken on 21 minutes when Young, on song throughout the first half of the season, sent in a magnificent left-wing cross for Agbonlahor to nip between Vidić and Tomasz Kuszczak and glance home a header.

Wayne Rooney characterized United's response: namely, redoubled efforts. The firebrand striker came closest to hauling the Reds level when he demonstrated breathtaking control to kill Patrice Evra's fizzed cross with his instep before side-footing against the underside of Brad Friedel's crossbar.

The American goalkeeper was rarely called upon in the first half, so impressive were his defenders, but he reserved his customary Old Trafford heroics for the dying stages. Shortly after Stewart Downing had cleared Vidić's header off the line, Friedel produced a magnificent fingertip save to turn substitute Dimitar Berbatov's low shot past the post. Michael Carrick, back in his familiar midfield role, dragged a shot wide in injury time as the Reds' final chance came and went. As Villa deservedly milked their post-match celebrations, United were left to reflect on missed opportunities . . . both in the match and the title race.

Team: Kuszczak; Fletcher, Brown, Vidić, Evra; Valencia, Anderson (Gibson 68), Carrick, Giggs (Owen 46), Park (Berbatov 63); Rooney
Scorers: n/a
Attendance: 75,130
Referee: Martin Atkinson

The home dressing room was a sullen scene afterwards. 'We are very disappointed. We had a game at home and the chance to share the first position with Chelsea but we didn't take it,' said Nemanja Vidić, dragging himself before the media.

Sir Alex Ferguson was similarly frustrated, but magnanimously paid tribute to the way Martin O'Neill's defenders had succeeded in blunting United's attack. 'We were camped in their box for a lot of the second half and had some really good chances,' he said. 'We only needed to take one to get us back in the game and it might have changed then; it was just one of those days when it wouldn't go in.

'Their defenders worked their socks off and they deserve full credit for that. They were closing down players, blocking shots and doing everything they could. It was a strong effort by them. Hopefully, we can put the game behind us and get the result we need on Tuesday against Wolves.'

The next three days could not pass quickly enough. But before Mick McCarthy arrived at Old Trafford with his Wolverhampton Wanderers side, Ryan Giggs would need to travel to Sheffield to attend the BBC Sports Personality of the Year awards. Despite being the most decorated player in British football history, reigning PFA Player of the Year and in form that stood comparison with any point in his epic career, the winger wasn't exactly hopeful of winning the award.

'I remember when the shortlist of ten contenders first came out,' recalls the winger. 'A member of staff told me I was on it and I immediately thought it was a joke. But they insisted it was genuine so I just thought, "Well, I'm not going to win it, there's not really any point going." That was my attitude at the time of being nominated. Then, as the ceremony got closer I was in the top three, so in that situation you've really got to go along. So I was sat there on the night, and it wasn't until [Formula One driver] Jenson Button's name was called out that I paused and thought, "My God, I've won this!" So I literally had five seconds to prepare what to say and do, but up until then I honestly thought Jenson Button was going to win it. It really was a tremendous honour, though.'

Among those who voted for the veteran Welshman was Wolves boss Mick McCarthy. 'I never usually vote on those things but I thought he deserved the accolade for what he has achieved in his career,' revealed the former Republic of Ireland manager. 'I don't think anyone needs to talk about how difficult it is to play at the top level for twenty-odd years – just look at how few players have done it. There have been some really good players come and go during Sir Alex's reign but Ryan has stayed the course.'

Fortunately for McCarthy, Giggs would be given the night off when Wolves arrived at Old Trafford. However, it was the visitors' squad rotation that would set tongues wagging.

Barclays Premier League

Manchester United 3 Wolverhampton Wanderers 0

Old Trafford, 15 December 2009

Goals from Wayne Rooney, Nemanja Vidić and Antonio Valencia gave United the most routine of victories over Wolves, but Mick McCarthy's controversial team selection never allowed a fair contest. The visitors' starting line-up contained just one player that had been in the side that stunned Tottenham at White Hart Lane three days earlier. A curious move on the face of it, but McCarthy clearly felt he should focus more on Wolves' next test, a home game against Burnley.

Despite Sir Alex Ferguson's relatively minor rotations – Ritchie De Laet, Darron Gibson and Gabriel Obertan all started, while Michael Carrick reverted to defence in Wes Brown's injury-enforced absence – United dominated proceedings from the off.

Rooney had already drawn a smart stop from Marcus Hahnemann and fired another shot just past the post when he was given the chance to open the scoring from the penalty spot. Ronald Zubar's needless handball provided the opening; Rooney thundered home the finish. Zubar's nightmare evening continued when, just before half time, he lost United skipper-for-the-night Vidić at a corner, allowing the Serbian to nod home an effort that squirmed under Hahnemann and inside the post.

'Forty quid to watch reserves,' bellowed the disenchanted travelling support, as their side struggled to muster any play to trouble United, injuries and all. The game's one remaining flash of class came when Valencia completed the scoring. Paul Scholes released Dimitar Berbatov, who required only two touches to control then hook a pass over his head for Valencia to thump a half-volley into the roof of the Stretford End goal.

The evening's sole negative came when Vidić limped off with a recurrence of his troublesome calf injury but, from there, the game meandered to a close with United barely breaking sweat. Seldom have three points been procured with such minimal fuss.

Team: Kuszczak; De Laet, Vidić (Fletcher 60), Carrick, Evra; Valencia, Gibson, Scholes, Obertan (Welbeck 71); Berbatov, Rooney (Owen 76)
Scorers: Rooney (30 (pen)), Vidić (43), Valencia (66)
Attendance: 73,709
Referee: Steve Bennett

Even though he was scarcely tested by Wolves, goalkeeper Tomasz Kuszczak conceded that organizing the merry-go-round of defenders – makeshift and orthodox – had been a dizzying experience. 'It's confusing, of course,' said the Pole. 'We don't always have enough time to find composure, but we played well enough. Michael Carrick, Fletch and Ritchie did really well. It's difficult for them, but we didn't concede and that's most important. We have to be happy that even with so many injuries we still have players who can do the job properly.'

Kuszczak had impressed since replacing out-of-form Ben Foster as the second-in-command to Edwin van der Sar, but he remained keen to hone his game. 'I still make some small mistakes, which I'm not happy with,' he admitted. 'I'll stay honest about my performance. OK, I didn't concede, but I made some mistakes that could have cost us a goal.

'They didn't, but I'll try to play better next time and have more composure. Every single game for me is like a lesson. I need games to get better, but I'm enjoying playing regularly because you can do something with your performance. To play at Old Trafford – and just to play for Manchester United – is always nice. I've had some hard times in the past when I didn't play and my goal is to play. Now it is my turn when I'm playing regularly and I want to do everything to keep doing this for a long time.'

Anderson, who had hit a sustained run of impressive form, was unhappy to spend the entire Wolves game on the bench. The Brazilian's slow start to the season was long forgotten and his infectious enthusiasm for the game had all parties looking to the future.

'Midfield is the hardest area for our young players to progress because we have some excellent players operating there,' said Sir Alex. 'But Anderson has certainly cranked up the contest for places after hitting great form. He took his time – he's only twenty-one, remember – but he has settled and matured. The competition has not dimmed his self-belief, which is important. He has a Brazilian belief in his own ability and he is going to become a top player. He is flying at the moment and he certainly wants to play. In fact, he has a face on him like a bag of tripe when I don't play him.'

The Brazilian was itching to be involved in the Reds' next outing, a tricky trip to Craven Cottage to face Roy Hodgson's Fulham. But first there was the small matter of the draw for the knockout stages of the Champions League. Fresh from confirming that Old Trafford had been accepted as a venue in the Football Association's bid to bring the 2018 World Cup to England, chief executive David Gill represented the Reds in Nyon.

With Bayern Munich, AC Milan, Porto, Internazionale, Lyon, Stuttgart and Olympiakos on offer, United were eventually paired with Leonardo's San Siro giants AC Milan, a draw that immediately prompted a press frenzy around the prospect of on-loan David Beckham clashing with his former team.

'I am happy for David Beckham because he did a lot for United and I know he wanted to play again at Old Trafford,' said Patrice Evra upon learning the draw. 'I will say, "Welcome home" to him, but I will make sure he doesn't have an easy game! I like him because I have met him and he is a good person, a real gentleman. He's a professional and that is why Milan wanted him. I like that type of player and he has one of the best right feet in the world. I'm sure all his old team-mates who are still here are looking forward to welcoming him back.'

As talk turned to a United youth product who had left the Reds in his prime, so another demonstrated the benefits of staying put. Ryan Giggs agreed a new contract that would tie him to United until at least June 2011, prompting Sir Alex to speculate: 'I am sure he will play for another two years. His form is fantastic at the moment and he is playing some of his best football.'

Giggs would miss the Fulham clash with a minor niggle, putting him on a long list of players poised to return to action after the Reds had travelled to Craven Cottage. Wes Brown, Rafael and Gary Neville were all tipped to play again before 2009 ended, while January was earmarked as the month for Rio Ferdinand, Jonny Evans, John O'Shea and Owen Hargreaves to return. Edwin van der Sar travelled to Holland for a consultation with the Netherlands' team doctor over a knee injury, while Nemanja Vidić's calf problem marked him as a major doubt for Fulham, with Ritchie De Laet poised to cover if required.

The Belgian's rapid ascent from Stoke City second string to first-team duties at Old Trafford was a remarkable tale, albeit hastened somewhat by circumstance. 'Ritchie's been fantastic,' Sir Alex told his pre-match press conference. 'We gave him a new contract about six weeks ago because we see there is good potential there. He's developed in training, he's only twenty, he's very quick and powerful, and he's now in the Belgian squad, so it's been a remarkable turnaround for him.' With Vidić struggling to shake off his injury, De Laet's football education was set to continue at Craven Cottage.

Barclays Premier League

Fulham 3 Manchester United 0
Craven Cottage, 19 December 2009

The visit to Craven Cottage to face Roy Hodgson's wily, well-drilled Fulham side proved one step too far for United's injury-hit defence.

Roy Hodgson's cunning Cottagers identified weaknesses in the Reds' makeshift backline and ruthlessly exploited them, posting a second successive home win over United.

Danny Murphy opened the scoring, Bobby Zamora killed the game in the first minute of the second half and Damien Duff put the icing on the cake to seal the Reds' fifth league defeat of the season and plunge the champions' title defence into serious jeopardy.

Shorn of Nemanja Vidić and Wes Brown, Sir Alex Ferguson reverted to the 3–5–2 formation that had succeeded against the odds in Wolfsburg, with Michael Carrick flanked by Darren Fletcher and Ritchie De Laet. From the first whistle, the trio struggled to answer the questions posed by Zamora's rugged forward play and Zoltán Gera's craft.

United did enjoy possession, but without penetration, and it took a breathtaking reflex save from Tomasz Kuszczak to turn Gera's rocketing volley over the bar. Fulham were turning the screw, but it took a rare moment of lax play from Paul Scholes to prompt the hosts' opener. The 35-year-old was caught in possession by Murphy, who nicked the ball, advanced on goal and drilled a low shot into Kuszczak's bottom corner from just outside the area. Confronted with an uphill task, United were in for a tough afternoon.

Zamora headed a presentable chance wide before the interval, but he required just 19 seconds of the second period to double his side's advantage, lashing in from close range after Clint Dempsey's nod-back. With all half-time advice rendered redundant, Sir Alex switched to a 4–4–2, pairing Fletcher and Carrick in the centre of defence, with Patrice Evra at left-back and bringing on Fabio for De Laet on the right. Dimitar Berbatov also replaced Darron Gibson and joined Michael Owen up front, with Wayne Rooney moved to the left flank.

Berbatov's impact was instant and he quickly teed up Rooney and Scholes to fire off-target. But, just as the seeds of an unlikely comeback were being sown, Duff killed the game, smashing a low volley past Kuszczak from the edge of the United area. The flickering flames of United's revival had been emphatically doused. Now, could the Reds rise from the ashes?

Team: Kuszczak; Fletcher, Carrick, De Laet (Fabio 58); Valencia, Anderson, Gibson (Berbatov 58), Scholes, Evra; Rooney, Owen (Welbeck 72)
Scorers: n/a
Attendance: 25,700
Referee: Howard Webb

'I hope that loss doesn't prove too damaging,' said a rueful Sir Alex, addressing the club's television station by the Craven Cottage pitch afterwards. 'In other words, I hope it doesn't cost us the league. There was a fragility at the back today, but we couldn't do anything about that. I have sympathy for my players, because it's difficult for midfielders to play as centre-backs and Ritchie De Laet's only twenty, so he's not yet got the experience you need for these type of matches.

'The players are feeling a little bit sorry for themselves at the moment because of the situation they find themselves in. But I think it's obvious that if we get our defenders back we'll be OK. We need them back to give us a proper chance of challenging for the league.'

For Darren Fletcher, one of those used in emergency deployment for much of December, the Fulham defeat capped a run of games that couldn't pass quickly enough.

'If I'm honest, there was no enjoyment in it at all,' he says, looking back. 'It was very difficult. I've said before that playing at Manchester United, in the best league in the world, and in the Champions League, is tough enough as it is, but to play in positions you've never played in is so difficult. I've found it hard on the right wing, but what we had in December was me getting pushed back to centre-half or right-back. Centre-half was the more difficult one because you're there in the Premier League against top-class strikers and you don't know where you are yourself half the time. It was really difficult.

'The longer we had to play there, the more it was going to become a problem. You can get away with it for one or two games, but after that teams can study you and know how to punish you. If it's a one-off game they don't know how to prepare for you, but Fulham would have watched us play that way a few times and they knew how to exploit it.

'Craven Cottage is one of the toughest places to go, and when you're going there with one fit defender, you know you'll be in for a tough time. It's a tight pitch, they kept playing the ball into the channels and just kept us under pressure. It was like having a target on you, but you've got to battle on as best you can. They didn't have loads of chances, but they seemed to take every one they had.'

Fortunately for Fletcher, Sir Alex had already set his medical staff the task of 'working overtime' in the run-up to Christmas in a bid to have recognized defenders available for the trip to Hull City's KC Stadium. Gary Neville and Rafael were both in the running to feature, while Wes Brown was close to regaining full fitness. With those (and more) due back to swell the ranks, there was never a question of United moving into the transfer market for a short-term solution, despite wild tabloid rumours suggesting Sol Campbell might have been a target.

Without any such tabloid fantasy or fanfare, a major internal appointment took place at Carrington, when it was announced that John Alexander would replace Ken Ramsden as the Reds' new club secretary at the end of the campaign. After ten years in the equivalent position at Tottenham, Alexander was excited by the prospect of becoming just the fifth incumbent of the role since its inception in 1926. 'I have a series of very hard acts to follow,' he said, 'but I am looking forward to working with Sir Alex, David Gill and the team.'

The club received another pre-Christmas boost when both

Patrice Evra and Nemanja Vidić were named in the FIFPro World XI for 2009. For the former, however, all that mattered was taking six points from looming encounters with Hull and Wigan. 'It's a crucial time,' said the Frenchman. 'We lost against Aston Villa and Fulham, but the target is to win our other games before January. We usually do well during this period and we want to again. It would be great to be in first place before January.'

As the trip to the KC Stadium approached, United's chances of ending 2009 on a high were boosted by Sir Alex's confirmation that he would have both Da Silva twins available. Wes Brown and Nemanja Vidić were also likely to feature. Given the rare luxury of no fixture until 27 December, United's players were handed Christmas Day off for the first time in years.

Further festive cheer arrived on Boxing Day, when Chelsea were held to a goalless draw by in-form Birmingham City. Poor form forgotten, United could move to within two points of the table's summit with victory over the Tigers.

Barclays Premier League

Hull City 1 Manchester United 3
KC Stadium, 27 December 2009

Wayne Rooney's influence was unremitting throughout 2009–10. As United bagged a vital victory at the KC Stadium, the on-song striker had a hand in all four goals of an error-strewn but absorbing encounter. Having opened the scoring, Rooney inadvertently contributed to Hull's equalizer from the penalty spot. But he atoned with two late assists – one for an Andy Dawson own-goal, one for Dimitar Berbatov's tap-in – to keep United within touching distance of Chelsea.

Neither side could reflect on a classic performance, but the unpredictability of the passing and defending made for an enthralling, end-to-end affair. A recognizable back four of Rafael, Nemanja Vidić,

Wes Brown and Patrice Evra took to the field, allowing Michael Carrick and Darren Fletcher to shift their partnership back to the familiar territory of midfield.

Clearly more balanced from the off, United were soon forging openings. Ryan Giggs had the game's first two chances, volleying onto the roof of Boaz Myhill's goal before curling a free-kick just past the stopper's upright. There was plenty of pluck about the hosts, however, and Tomasz Kuszczak made a tidy low stop from Seyi Olofinjana's 30-yard drive.

Kuszczak and Myhill then traded saves, tipping away efforts from Olofinjana and Rooney respectively, before Stephen Hunt and Berbatov fired off-target. Rafael forced the save of the game from Myhill with a left-foot blockbuster before United took the lead on the stroke of half time.

Fletcher retrieved an errant Berbatov cross and curled in a superb right-wing cross that was missed by Giggs but slotted home by the onrushing Rooney. Rather than galvanize United, however, the goal took the edge off both sides in the early stages of the second half. In keeping with an odd lull in the game, Rooney's short back-pass to Kuszczak was intercepted by Craig Fagan, who rounded the Pole and crossed for Jozy Altidore. The American was stretching to reach the ball, but Rafael's indiscreet nudge on the striker prompted referee Alan Wiley to award a penalty, which Fagan duly slipped home.

Rooney was mortified and set out on a one-man rescue mission. Inevitably, he was involved as United moved ahead once more, sliding an inch-perfect ball across the six-yard box that evaded Myhill and was turned into his own net by Dawson. In truth, the defender had only hastened the inevitable, as Ji-sung Park was lurking behind him.

Far from sated, Rooney killed the game off with another sublime assist eight minutes from time. Breaking in from the left, the striker spotted a chink of daylight between two Hull defenders and slid in a pass that required Berbatov merely to tap home. Out of sorts but back to winning ways, United were tiptoeing back into contention for honours.

Team: Kuszczak; Rafael, Brown, Vidić, Evra; Valencia (Park 63), Carrick, Fletcher, Giggs (Obertan 78); Rooney, Berbatov
Scorers: Rooney (45), Dawson (73 (og)), Berbatov (82)
Attendance: 24,627
Referee: Alan Wiley

'I was worried about what the manager would say,' admitted Wayne Rooney, recalling his rare lapse in gifting Hull the chance to equalize. 'Obviously it was a mistake by myself, but thankfully we got the win. I don't think the manager would've been too pleased if we hadn't! It's the first time it's ever happened to me. It wasn't a nice feeling. I didn't want to let the lads down and at the time it looked like I had.'

It was largely down to Rooney's breathless efforts that United did recover from the heavy blow of conceding, but that didn't prevent his team-mates giving him some gentle ribbing for his uncharacteristic slip.

'Wayne did fantastic for us, although we were joking in the dressing room that he had three assists to his name!' revealed Dimitar Berbatov. 'But he bounced back after their goal and made both the second and third ones, which was great. If he can keep playing the way we know he can, then I don't think anyone can stop him. He's still young and the future is ahead of him.'

For Rooney, just being in touch with Chelsea after such an unpredictable first half of the season was a major boon. For the second instalment, consistency would be key in what the striker termed 'a mad league'.

'A lot of teams are dropping points and it's really close,' he continued. 'It's an exciting league to be part of and hopefully we can be more consistent in the second half of the season than we have in the first and retain our title.'

Once again, there would be mixed team news for Sir Alex Ferguson to digest and divulge at his pre-Wigan press conference. While Gary Neville and Anderson were fit, Edwin van der Sar had been told to remain in the Netherlands to tend to his wife, Annemarie, who had suffered a brain haemorrhage. 'There is no point in him being here,' said Sir Alex. 'The best thing is for him to be with his wife.' Fortunately, Annemarie would soon be on the road to a full recovery.

Sir Alex also took time to dismiss tabloid talk that Dimitar Berbatov would miss up to three months of action because he required knee surgery. 'It's not the case,' he stated. 'He's had a niggle but he's improved and he came through the full game at Hull. We've been treating him quite carefully in terms of the number of games he's been playing, because we know we need him in the second half of the season. But on Sunday he was fine and hopefully it's gone now.'

A fit and firing Berbatov would provide a massive fillip for United's aspirations to silverware, but Sir Alex was delighted to be two points from the summit as he prepared to take his squad into 2010.

'I'm definitely quite happy, considering all the defenders I've had out injured,' he said. 'It was a key period for us to try and get through, and if we win tomorrow then hopefully we've gotten through it. As we get our players back (and hopefully they stay back), the important thing now is that we find the consistency we usually do during the second half of the season. That will be key.'

Barclays Premier League

Manchester United 5 Wigan Athletic 0
Old Trafford, 30 December 2009

The Reds rounded off a successful 2009 with a five-star show against Wigan, fuelling hopes that 2010 could be another silver-lined year.

Wayne Rooney, Michael Carrick, Rafael, Dimitar Berbatov and Antonio Valencia all netted in a dominant United display that mirrored August's win at the DW Stadium in scoreline. In truth, the Reds could easily have reached double figures, so woeful was the visitors' display.

Latics goalkeeper Chris Kirkland was called into action as early as the fourth minute when he made a smart stop from Valencia. Berbatov and Rooney were then both thwarted as, in a rare change, United attacked the Stretford End in the first period. Kirkland was eventually beaten by Nemanja Vidić's shot, only for Paul Scharner to hook the ball to safety and spare his side.

When Rooney cut in from the left flank, beat two players and drilled a magnificent shot against the inside of Kirkland's post, the game seemed crucially poised: either it would be 'one of those days' or there was a rout on the cards. Fortunately for United, the latter transpired.

The deadlock was broken just before the half-hour, as the magnificent Rafael bombed down the right flank and drilled in a fine cross, which Rooney steered past Kirkland. Shortly afterwards, Valencia's sprint down the right was capped by a pull-back of great vision for Carrick, who slotted home clinically.

Dam cracked, the goals kept flowing. Before half time United had a third, as Rafael cut in from the touchline, skipped past two challenges, briefly lost control of the ball but recovered before catching Kirkland off-guard with a low, left-footed effort into the bottom corner. He then raced towards the home bench to celebrate with twin brother Fabio.

The bedraggled Kirkland was replaced at half time by Mike Pollitt, and the former United trainee picked up the baton of bailing out his hapless colleagues with a smart stop from Rooney. He was soon beaten, though, as Valencia's cross teed up Berbatov for a classy poked finish. Rooney then headed against the bar as United continued to press mercilessly for more.

The only surprise of the evening was that the fifth goal took so long to arrive. But when it came, with 15 minutes remaining, it was worth the wait. A beautiful, incisive ball from Rooney gave Valencia time and space, and the Ecuadorian heaped more misery on his former side with an impish, outside-of-the-boot finish.

Team: Kuszczak; Rafael, Brown, Vidić (Anderson 68), Evra (Fabio 69); Valencia, Carrick, Fletcher, Park; Rooney, Berbatov (Welbeck 68)

Scorers: Rooney (28), Carrick (32), Rafael (45), Berbatov (50), Valencia (75)

Attendance: 74,560

Referee: Lee Mason

'It was an excellent performance,' said Sir Alex, who had seen his team demolish their opponents on the eve of his 68th birthday. 'Wayne was absolutely fantastic. The energy he shows and his desire to win is marvellous. I was pleased to see Valencia get another goal for us, too. He'll get more goals. It was also brilliant seeing Rafael celebrate his goal by running over to his brother. They love playing football and it's terrific to see that enthusiasm. It's an underestimated quality at times. But those two boys are a pair of aces.

'But I don't really want to pick individuals out at this important part of the season because every man has to play his part, and they all did tonight. There was fluid movement, a good tempo and we created a lot of chances. Goal difference, you never know, could be important come the end of the season. We're now two points behind Chelsea and our goal difference is up there. We're in with a great chance. I can have a happy birthday now!'

The New Year promised plenty of intrigue and excitement. The Reds remained firmly in the running in what was rapidly becoming a familiar three-horse title race with Chelsea and Arsenal. There was also a stellar Champions League tie with AC

Milan to look forward to, and the small matter of a Carling Cup semi-final and a fresh assault on the FA Cup. If 2009 had brought highs and lows at unpredictable intervals, 2010 promised to be just as captivating.

7

January

New years bring new starts, but two old rivalries lay in wait as 2010 began. Leeds United and Manchester City would test the Reds in the domestic cups, lending an intriguing edge to a month of frosty fixtures. The City double-header would be another barometer of the Blues' progress, but Leeds' visit to Old Trafford in the FA Cup third round was their first clash with United since February 2004. Although the Whites had sunk to the third tier of English football, Sir Alex Ferguson was in no doubt about the magnitude of the rivalry.

'I don't need to spell out to Manchester United fans and players what Leeds games have meant over the years,' Sir Alex told his pre-match press conference. 'They were fantastic, feisty occasions every time we met. There was always a tinge of hostility hovering around the game and we always told the players to behave themselves on the pitch.

'I used to enjoy the games because they made us perform. We had some great games at Leeds because the atmosphere was always electric and our record was good – I think we only lost once there. They were two competitive teams then, but it's a different United team now and we just have to make sure we play our normal game. They're bringing nine thousand fans, so it will be a brilliant atmosphere and a fantastic cup tie.'

Simon Grayson, one of many linked with Sir Alex's vacant assistant-manager position after the departure of Carlos Queiroz in 2008, had taken Leeds to a runaway lead in League One as they attempted to rescale English football's ladder. Against an in-form team with a promising young manager, United weren't about to take this test lightly.

'Simon Grayson has done a fantastic job,' said Sir Alex. 'He's a former Leeds player and I think he's reached his target in managing them. He has great motivation and his team are not letting him down – they're playing really well at the moment. But I don't think they'll be too far from the Premier League in the next couple of years. It looks like they're certain to be promoted to the Championship next season and, with their manager's drive and motivation, they have a great chance.'

Maybe so. But surely facing England's reigning champions in their own backyard would be too tough a task, even for the fantasists and romantics?

FA Cup Third Round

Manchester United 0 Leeds United 1

Old Trafford, 3 January 2010

The term 'upset' doesn't even do it justice. For everybody associated with Manchester United, this was a dark, embarrassing day. Jermaine Beckford's clinical first-half finish gave Leeds a stunning victory at Old Trafford, but Simon Grayson's men deserved to progress, having outfought United for long periods and passed up several chances to put the game out of sight. The Reds could reflect on scores of missed opportunities, but were ultimately left to rue a failure to match the visitors' dogged determination.

Sir Alex Ferguson blended youth and experience with his team selection, most notably deploying an inexperienced midfield four in which Darron Gibson, 22, was the elder statesman. The Irish international had the game's first opening, curling just off-target, before Danny Welbeck's cross evaded the stretching Dimitar Berbatov. Home hopes of embarrassing the visitors were stoked by the Reds' promising start, but Leeds' approach had also betrayed an ambition to attack whenever possible.

After 19 minutes one such attack, albeit unsubtle, brought the game's only goal. A speculative punt forward fell for Beckford, who held off the attentions of Wes Brown and flicked a neat finish past Tomasz Kuszczak.

Old Trafford would have been engulfed by a stunned silence were it not for the bellowing, 9,000-strong army of travelling supporters who could scarcely believe what was happening. And things almost got worse for United when, two minutes after Beckford's strike, Luciano Becchio headed a simple chance over the bar.

Wayne Rooney's determined response characterized the grit required to haul United back into the match. Twice in five minutes the striker was agonizingly close to levelling, as one shot was cleared off the line by Jason Crowe and another curled inches wide of the post from 20 yards. Welbeck was denied a strong penalty claim in the second half when he was body-checked, before Casper Ankergren produced a wonderful one-on-one save from the tricky youngster.

Mindful of the situation's gravity, Sir Alex Ferguson threw Ryan Giggs, Antonio Valencia and Michael Owen into the fray for the final 20 minutes. That prompted sustained United pressure, but it was Leeds who twice went within a whisker of finding the game's second goal when Robert Snodgrass hit the bar with a free-kick and Beckford fired wastefully off-target.

Andy Hughes was fortunate to escape without censure for fouling Owen in the area before the England striker headed wide and Fabio shot off-target in a final goalmouth scramble. Sir Alex's men had fought until the end, but Leeds could not be denied their day in the spotlight.

Team: Kuszczak; Neville, Brown, Evans, Fabio; Obertan (Valencia 57), Anderson (Owen 69), Gibson, Welbeck (Giggs 57); Berbatov, Rooney
Scorers: n/a
Attendance: 74,526
Referee: Chris Foy

'The preparation for the game was very good, but I'm shocked by the performance,' said a crestfallen Sir Alex. 'We didn't start right and Leeds did. They got their goal and had something to hold on to. They fought like tigers, and we expect that with any team coming to Old Trafford for an FA Cup tie. It's a disappointment.

'We did speak about Beckford's pace up front. We were caught napping, really. It was a bad goal for us to lose. The whole performance in the first half was bad. We never got going and the quality of the passing . . . the whole performance was just bad. It's one of these things. We're only human and sometimes you have performances that surprise you. I don't think any of the players can say they had a good day. But we didn't expect that today.

'We have to get this result out of our system as quickly as possible,' added Sir Alex. 'We have a Carling Cup semi-final on Wednesday and a lot of these players won't be playing. You have to view this performance in the right light. We'll make sure we're ready for Wednesday now. We had a team in mind, but there will be a few changes for that.'

Even once the dust has settled on 2009–10, defeat to Leeds stings. It was a first FA Cup third-round exit and a first defeat to lower-league opposition under Sir Alex. What's more, it was sustained against disbelieving, euphoric rivals who could instantly draw on their victory as a piece of club history. It hurt then, and still does.

'It was so tough to take,' says Wes Brown. 'We didn't play

141

particularly well and I admit I didn't. Leeds came at a time when they were playing well in the league and they were confident. I thought in general they wanted it more than us. It's one of those disappointing defeats you don't like to look back on.'

'It was a massive disappointment for us to go out of the FA Cup and a huge disappointment for the fans to lose to Leeds,' echoes Darron Gibson. 'It was a real low point in the season to lose to them. They made it a cup tie, the tackles were flying in and, looking back, you can see they were more up for it than we were.'

A short trip to Eastlands three days later provided a conflicting prospect: on one hand it was tailor-made for United to vent rage and embarrassment; on the other it represented another potential hammer blow against familiar, fired-up foes. Fate postponed the verdict, however, as plummeting temperatures and snowfall conspired to bring Britain to a standstill. Carrington was a ghost town as staff and players were unable to navigate the dangerous conditions, and Sir Alex Ferguson's pre-match press conference was cancelled. The weather forecast for the night of the first leg was minus six degrees. Unsurprisingly, the decision was taken that both Carling Cup semi-finals – City v United and Blackburn Rovers v Aston Villa – would be postponed.

The first leg would be shunted back 13 days, with the second due at Old Trafford the following week. That weekend's Under-18s clash with Wolves also fell foul of the weather, but Birmingham City quickly issued a statement boldly declaring that they saw no reason why the Reds' senior clash at St Andrew's could not go ahead.

Either way, Nemanja Vidić would not be involved, having sustained a problem with a nerve in his right leg during the warm-up before United's defeat to Leeds. Joining Rio Ferdinand and Edwin van der Sar on the sidelines, Vidić's absence rendered a tricky match even tougher. Sir Alex was still scrambling around for fit defenders – even though the entire squad was now able to reach Carrington and train indoors in the Academy building – and he was quick to scotch suggestions that Gary Neville had decided to call time on his epic career.

'I don't know where these kinds of rumours come from,' the

manager told his pre-match press conference. 'Gary hasn't made any decision and we haven't made any decision. I always say to my players: "When you're going to make a decision about your future, make sure you do it in the summer." You don't make decisions like these in the middle of the season. That's nonsense.'

Another veteran star whose contract had less than six months to run was Paul Scholes, but his focus was entirely on bouncing back from the shock of defeat to Leeds.

'We've been written off so many times before and come back and proved people wrong, so hopefully we can do that again,' said the midfielder. 'We're only two points behind Chelsea in the league, in the last sixteen of the Champions League and the semi-finals of the Carling Cup. So there's no disaster yet. We're still in the hunt for three major trophies and hopefully we can win at least one of them.'

Up against a Birmingham side unbeaten in 12 games, however, Scholes conceded United's bid to return to winning ways would not be straightforward. 'They're having a fantastic season and playing really well,' he said. 'They appear to be a very hard-working team who defend very well and St Andrew's is always a difficult place to go, whatever form Birmingham are in.'

Barclays Premier League

Birmingham City 1 Manchester United 1

St Andrew's, 9 January 2010

The chance to snatch top spot was passed up as United were held to a frustrating draw by in-form Birmingham at St Andrew's. The Reds dominated the first half, only to fall behind to Cameron Jerome's effort just before the break. United did force an own goal from Scott Dann after the interval, although few chances followed and the visitors' irritation was compounded by the dismissal of Darren Fletcher.

On an unfathomably cold afternoon, Sir Alex Ferguson made seven changes to the team humbled by Leeds United, as Paul Scholes,

Rafael, Patrice Evra, Antonio Valencia, Michael Carrick, Ji-sung Park and Fletcher all returned. They were faced by a Birmingham side fast establishing itself as a Premier League force built on strong defensive foundations. When Darren Fletcher's stinging early effort was deflected wide off Sebastian Larsson, the tone was set for heroic, life-on-the-line stuff from the hosts.

It took 25 minutes for United to get a clear sight of Joe Hart's goal. Wayne Rooney latched on to Valencia's neat through-ball, but was thwarted by a fine sprawling save from the on-loan Manchester City goalkeeper. Rooney then headed just wide and Carrick had a brace of efforts blocked before Birmingham opened the scoring with their first attempt on goal. James McFadden's corner descended into penalty-box pinball and the ball eventually fell for Jerome to slot home from three yards. It was a sickening blow for the dominant champions, who visibly slumped either side of the interval.

As falling snow began to settle, so did the Reds. Scores were level just after the hour mark when stand-in skipper Evra's drilled cross was emphatically rammed home by Dann. Despite the frantic waving of a linesman's flag for a perceived offside, referee Mark Clattenburg consulted his assistant and confirmed the goal would stand.

Both sides were full of endeavour in pursuit of victory, but neither could muster the guile or wit to find another route past their opposing defence, even though debutant Mame Biram Diouf was introduced in search of an instant impact. When Fletcher was dismissed for a second booking, awarded for a routine clip on Jerome, United's job changed to withstanding the hosts' late pressure. That was achieved, but the missed opportunity of going to the table's summit left the Reds rankled after a freezing, frustrating 90 minutes.

Team: Kuszczak; Rafael, Brown, Evans, Evra; Valencia, Carrick, Fletcher, Scholes (Diouf 81), Park (Giggs 66); Rooney
Scorer: Dann (63 (og))
Attendance: 28,907
Referee: Mark Clattenburg

Disappointment hung heavy in the United camp at full time, even though the Reds had taken a point from an on-song Birmingham side in sub-zero conditions.

'We're disappointed, of course,' said goalkeeper Tomasz Kuszczak. 'We came here for three points. We know what we have to do to keep up our challenge for the title and we want to win every match, no matter who we play. If we lose some points we are disappointed.' The Polish international also labelled the conditions 'the coldest I have ever played in', a sentiment echoed by Patrice Evra.

'Oh my God, I have never felt so cold at a game before,' recalls the Frenchman. 'It was virtually the only Premier League game played that weekend and I remember in the warm-up it was impossible to get warm! Honestly, I thought the game was going to be suspended because it was not possible to play in that weather.'

Being first into the hot shower was some semblance of a silver lining for the harshly dismissed Darren Fletcher, who was backed to the hilt by his manager after the match. 'You won't see a softer sending-off,' insisted the boss. 'Darren's not that kind of player. It's a simple clip on the boy [Cameron Jerome], who actually stumbled. I think it was a terrible decision and it gave them some momentum.'

The press soon had plenty else to feast on, as Red Football Ltd – the holding company of Manchester United Ltd – published its summary for the financial year ended 30 June 2009. The document declared pre-tax profits of £48.2 million, before the club announced it would aim to raise £500 million through the sale of bonds. The announcement provoked a colourful backlash from sections of supporters unhappy with the club's ownership; they clad themselves in green and gold, a symbol of their discontent and a nod to the club's original Newton Heath colours.

'The green-and-gold campaign clearly had great momentum during the season, from their perspective,' says chief executive David Gill. 'It was born out of an event – the bond issue – which, as I tried to articulate, has improved the financial structure of the club. It's replaced bank debt with a more flexible financing instrument with greater public reporting. We issued a document associated with that and, like a lot of financial documents issued in the City, it betrays a lot of risks for prospective investors to understand. That has to be done, and a lot of those risks have been there for donkey's years, so they weren't new. One was that there is a risk when Alex Ferguson retires. Now, everyone's aware of that, but when you put it in black and white, everyone majors on it.

'So the green-and-gold campaign was born out of that and it gained momentum. There's a minority of fans who want to change things, and in a very visible way. I think the majority of fans want to support the team, watch the game in a safe, comfortable stadium with lots of modern amenities, watching attractive football and have the team challenging for honours under stable ownership. I think the Glazers have provided just that. They've let Alex get on with the football side of things and have been very supportive of him in terms of investment. But no matter how much you tell the world there is money to invest, if they don't want to believe it, then they're not going to believe it. But the money is there from the sale of Cristiano Ronaldo, plus we've delivered on the commercial side of the business.

'A lot of people don't like the Glazers, but they wouldn't like whoever owns Manchester United. They didn't like it when we were a quoted company, or when Martin Edwards was chairman, although he delivered great success. We have to accept that. Do I like seeing the green and gold in the stadium? No, I don't. We're red and white and I'd much prefer to have a stadium full of red and white – all for one and one for all – but that hasn't happened. We'll see what transpires over the course of the next few months and next season. It's clear the Glazers aren't sellers. They enjoy owning the asset and they believe there's good potential in the club. They understand the importance of what happens on the pitch to their plans off the pitch, and there's no desire to sell.'

For Sir Alex Ferguson and his players, the issue was best left alone. 'It doesn't really matter what colours the fans wear, so long as they get behind the team,' says Darren Fletcher. 'It's a really sensitive subject but we're all of the opinion that as long as the fans are there supporting the team, that's all that matters. In that respect, I think the fans have been great. There's no animosity towards the players; that's when it would become a problem. But it's not going to be like that and the fans are fully behind the team.'

The focus in the dressing room – shooting for silverware – never changed. With Britain still stuck in the icy grip of winter, however, the Reds jetted out to the ASPIRE Academy for Sports Excellence in Doha. First-team coach René Meulensteen, a former manager in Qatar with Al-Ittihad and Al-Sadd, as well as the country's Under-18 national team, played a major role in securing the training facility.

'I had heard a lot about the fantastic facilities at ASPIRE from my coaching staff,' said Sir Alex, while basking in the 20-degree heat. 'With the weather being so good at this time of the year in Qatar, it was the perfect opportunity to test them out. The welcome we have received has been superb and we have already done an excellent training session that just would not have been possible in the conditions in the UK.'

'I think it was a great idea to get away for a few days,' admitted Patrice Evra on the Reds' return. 'It's better sometimes when you wake up and you see the sun out of your window! But it was more about making sure everyone understands that now we have a chance not to throw the league away. It made everyone unite for the same target: to win the title for a fourth time in a row and do something nobody else has done.

'We enjoyed staying together and had a good time, but we worked hard as well and talked about what we needed to achieve before the end of the season. It was about both training and talking among ourselves. The facilities were unbelievable and it's nice to train in good weather. But we talked a lot as well. I think we will see the effect of this against Burnley.'

The trip had already had a positive impact on Dimitar Berbatov, who had previously been operating beyond the pain barrier with a niggling knee injury. Keyhole surgery and a three-month lay-off was one option, but after training without discomfort in Qatar he was ready to play on. The Bulgarian and his colleagues would be joined by Edwin van der Sar for the first time in 12 games after the goalkeeper's wife, Annemarie, recovered sufficiently from her brain haemorrhage. With Rio Ferdinand close to returning and Owen Hargreaves taking part in sections of first-team training again, there was light at the end of the tunnel. Three points against Burnley, managed for the first time by Brian Laws, could be the springboard for a customary upturn in fortunes going into the second half of the season.

Barclays Premier League

Manchester United 3 Burnley 0

Old Trafford, 16 January 2010

Despite an opening 45 minutes of frustration, United saw off a spirited challenge from Burnley with a second-half goals salvo. Dimitar Berbatov, Wayne Rooney and Mame Biram Diouf secured the Reds' first victory of 2010 and ensured no reward for a sweat-soaked shift from a visiting side galvanized by new manager Brian Laws.

Edwin van der Sar returned between the posts and kept a clean sheet, but the Dutchman was called into action far more regularly than he would have envisaged against a side with the Premier League's worst away record. Indeed, both Steven Fletcher and David Nugent passed up glorious openings for the visitors when the scoreline was frozen at 0–0. With United committed to attack from the off, Burnley broke in numbers after seven minutes and should have forged ahead, only for Fletcher to drive past van der Sar's far post.

Burnley's primary aim was containment, however. At ease with letting United enjoy the majority of possession, a deep-seated midfield and a penalty area packed with defenders made for long periods of frustration, although United did experience plenty of joy down the flanks. As a result, visiting goalkeeper Brian Jensen had little involvement of note during the first period, only really stretching himself to plunge to his right and turn Nani's spectacular overhead kick past the post.

United's second-half start carried enhanced purpose, however, and Jensen was called into action by Scholes and Nani within two minutes. Then Berbatov displayed mind-blowing touch and dexterity to control Antonio Valencia's pass and fire against the outside of the post. That miss almost proved costly when ex-Red Chris Eagles fed Nugent, again with United outnumbered, but the on-loan Portsmouth striker stabbed wastefully wide.

Burnley were soon made to pay for their profligacy. Wayne Rooney's threaded pass found Berbatov, who shrugged off Michael Duff before firing a left-footed shot past Jensen, via a slight nick off the Clarets defender. Just four minutes later, the game was effectively won. Berbatov's shot was parried out by Jensen as far as Rooney, who displayed remarkable calm in a packed area to control, shimmy and slip a low shot inside Jensen's post.

Job done, the strike partnership made way for home debutant Diouf and Michael Owen. Burnley's Steven Thompson headed against van der Sar's far post, but Diouf had the final word, reaching Neville's long-range pass just before the hesitant Jensen to head into the untended goal. There was elation for the Senegalese striker, but relief was the over-riding emotion as the Reds swerved another potential shock against the Clarets.

Team: Van der Sar; Neville, Brown, Evans, Evra; Valencia, Carrick (Anderson 65), Scholes, Nani; Rooney (Owen 73), Berbatov (Diouf 73)
Scorers: Berbatov (64), Rooney (69), Diouf (90)
Attendance: 75,120
Referee: Lee Probert

'It's good to be back,' said Edwin van der Sar afterwards. 'I felt pretty good out there, although I was a bit nervous before the game. It's

been a good week for myself and the team. We had some good training sessions in Qatar and now we've topped it off with a win. Burnley
are a resilient side and they've shown that all season. They were a big
challenge for us and I had to make a couple of saves, but we hung on.
It was important to win and stay close to the leaders. That's what we
did so hopefully now we can go from strength to strength. We've got
a few players coming back from injury as we come to the business
end of the season.'

Sir Alex Ferguson's tone was also laced with relief. 'It was a funny
game,' said the manager. 'We were frivolous with our chances and
they had chances themselves. It could have been embarrassing. We
were maybe just a bit nervous and anxious about our game. You need
that goal to break open teams like that, particularly teams who are
settling in at Old Trafford with men behind the ball.'

The hard-fought win was capped by Mame Biram Diouf's home-
debut strike – a 20-yard header, no less – but the forward was realistic
about his chances of regular involvement so soon after arriving at Old
Trafford.

'It feels good to score in my first game here,' he said. 'I was nervous for the first two or three minutes, but then you forget about all
the people in the stands and you do your job. Now I'm just going to
work hard and do my best and we'll see when the manager needs me.

'I'm sure I can learn from Wayne Rooney, Michael Owen and
Dimitar Berbatov. They are top players, some of the best in the
world. They've done so much in football and in this league so I'm
going to try and learn a lot. I want to give my best for my new team
and be ready when I'm needed. I'll work hard in training, never give
up and be ready for the next chance that comes along.'

Diouf's reward was inclusion in United's next squad, which made
the short trip across town to Eastlands. Once more, the derby enraptured supporters and media alike in the build-up. With a chance for
City to elbow past United *en route* to a first trophy in 34 years, the
scene was set for a public power shift across Manchester. Not that
such talk was being entertained at Carrington, of course.

'We need to win at Manchester United,' said Patrice Evra. 'It's an important game against City, a big game, but I only talk about it because I want to win this game and have a chance to win a trophy. Maybe that's the difference between Manchester United and Manchester City: we play the game to win and to win the Carling Cup, whereas they play to win against Manchester United.'

For the Frenchman, the chance to wind up close friend and former team-mate Carlos Tévez was proving irresistible. 'Every day I have been texting Carlitos,' said Evra. 'I congratulated him for the hat-trick he scored against Blackburn. He said, "It's just the warm-up for United" because he wants to reach the final. I told him, "No chance!" I don't want him to score against us. It still hurts to see him in the Manchester City shirt. He was a good player here, and now he's showing that at City. I just hope he doesn't show it in these games.'

For all Evra's pre-match goading of the Blues and his cross-city comrade, it was a relatively innocuous passage from Gary Neville's column in the *Times of Malta* that fanned the hottest pre-match flames.

'The manager over the years has made many decisions with regard to players coming and going, and he has almost always been proved correct,' wrote United's club captain. 'I can't disagree with his decision on Tévez. He was a good player for us, but if the financial demands are too big then that's just the way it goes.' When those quotes were seized upon by the English media, they attracted the attention of Tévez and his team-mates at City's training facility. The fallout would begin at the sounding of the first whistle.

Carling Cup Semi-final First Leg

Manchester City 2 Manchester United 1

Eastlands, 19 January 2010

Inevitably, Carlos Tévez proved the central figure as goals either side of half time gave City a 2–1 first-leg lead over the Carling Cup holders. The Argentinian smashed home a controversial penalty and nodded in from close range as the Blues recovered from conceding an early opener to Ryan Giggs. The result was harsh on a United side that dominated possession and chances for long periods. But the visitors couldn't draw level once Tévez had struck his double, despite a spate of close calls in the late stages of the game.

Mindful of the occasion and the opposition, Sir Alex Ferguson fielded a strong side at Eastlands. The home support was clearly geared up to manufacture a rousing atmosphere, dimming the lights for a rendition of 'Blue Moon' as the players took to the field. Over in the away section, a handful of red flares lit up the gloom: United fans were never going to be content to sit in City's shadow.

Sir Alex's men were similarly unmoved by City's pre-match antics and set about dictating play from the first whistle. Antonio Valencia was central to the Reds' best play and played a major role in the opener with a superb cross. Wayne Rooney's poked effort was saved by Shay Given, but Giggs was on hand to tap in from virtually underneath the crossbar.

The goal was the only clear chance of the first period, although there were hearts in mouths when Tévez failed to connect properly with a presentable header. He would soon have his goal, though.

Referee Mike Dean was central to the City equalizer, deeming Rafael's tug on Craig Bellamy worthy of a penalty, even though the first contact had occurred well outside the area. There was no such ambiguity from Tévez, who laced the penalty high into the roof of van der Sar's net to give the hosts an undeserved leveller. As he raced away in celebration, the former Old Trafford hero exchanged gestures with Gary Neville, who was warming up on the touchline.

Regardless, United almost opened the scoring in the second period when Given bravely blocked Rooney's close-range effort. That let-off sparked City into life and, after two penalty area mêlées, Tévez struck again. Slipshod United defending failed to clear a Bellamy corner and when the ball was eventually hooked into the six-yard box it was Tévez who nodded home to send Eastlands into delirium.

While City's dander was up, Shaun Wright-Phillips drew a solid save from van der Sar. United's response was the introduction of Michael Owen. The substitute quickly released Rooney, but Given produced another excellent save. From the rebound, Owen's shot was cleared off the line by Nedum Onuoha. The tone had been set for a breathless final ten minutes. Rooney's mesmerizing run and poked shot forced Given into a fine reaction stop before a stretching Valencia only just failed to stab home at the far post. When Given again tipped wide from Rooney in injury time, United were beaten. Eastlands resounded with giddiness as City moved into pole position. But the tie was far from over.

Team: Van der Sar; Rafael (Diouf 90), Brown, Evans, Evra; Valencia (Scholes 88), Anderson (Owen 73), Carrick, Fletcher, Giggs; Rooney
Scorer: Giggs (17)
Attendance: 46,067
Referee: Mike Dean

A rueful yet positive Sir Alex Ferguson was keen to iterate that at least 90 minutes of the tie remained, and that outplaying City once again should spawn confidence. 'I think we dominated the game. We just let it slip for two minutes in the first half,' he said. 'We had a mad two minutes where we lost a bit of our composure and they got into the game. There was some good football; I was pleased. The performance was good. The important thing is to win at Old Trafford. Forget the scoreline here: win our match and we have a great chance.'

As well as the shock of losing a game United had largely controlled, bewilderment and confusion surrounded the pre-match festival at Eastlands, where dimmed lights and dramatic music provided an unlikely preamble for the first leg of a semi-final. 'We weren't expecting all the shenanigans to be going on at the stadium,' says Ryan Giggs. 'We thought it was the Superbowl or something! It was carnival time for them, so it was great for us to look over and see the Reds with flares behind the goal in the away end. It was really impressive.'

There was plenty more to be said by the City camp, not least by home hero Carlos Tévez, who sounded off about his celebration in an interview with an Argentinian radio station. 'My celebration was directed at Gary Neville,' he said. 'He said I wasn't worth twenty-five million pounds . . . I think he did the wrong thing because I was his team-mate and I never said anything bad about him. I always respected Neville.'

The incident provoked widespread media coverage but was met with mirth rather than sensationalism inside the confines of Carrington. 'It's one of those things where the press make more of it than it probably deserves,' says Michael Carrick. 'We just had a laugh about it. Carlos has gone to another club and he's got his own agenda. He wants to do well for them and obviously we want to do well for United, no one more so than Gaz.'

'Carlos has a lot of respect in the United team,' adds Darren Fletcher. 'Even his little spat with Gary, if you look back at it, was just harmless. It wasn't aggressive; there was no real anger shown. It's a bit of fun and the lads just laughed it off. Carlos is a great player and was a great player here. The fact he's joined our local rivals makes for an interesting story and you can understand the media buying into it.'

Although United had a vital game against Hull that could precipitate a return to the top of the Premier League, almost each day brought a new headline about the simmering rivalry between Reds and Blues. Perhaps most eyebrow-raising were quotes from City chief executive Garry Cook, delivered at the Mad Hatter pub in New York. Addressing City supporters at a private event (but filmed for television), Cook insisted his club were on course to become 'without doubt the biggest and best football club in the world'. A major step towards this would apparently be taken 'not *if* but *when* we are at Wembley having beaten Manchester United yet again'.

That issue would soon be settled, but first there was the visit of Phil Brown's Hull. United's early FA Cup exit gave Sir Alex's men the chance to steal a march on Chelsea and Arsenal and put some points on the board, leaving the rest to play catch-up.

'We're the only game tomorrow so it's an opportunity for us and hopefully we can take it,' the United manager told his pre-match press conference. 'If you can go on a consistent run, then you'll have a great chance. Arsenal proved that: they've won their games recently and they're now top after they were previously written off. That's the nature of the league this season.

'I think you've got to win your games now. We're seeing some light at the end of the tunnel in terms of defenders being back and van der Sar being back – that's really crucial to us – so hopefully we're on the way. It's an opportunity for us to go top tomorrow and then we've got Arsenal next Sunday. It'll be a massive game and then Arsenal play Chelsea the next week. It's an interesting time.'

Intriguing, even, and an ideal juncture for Rio Ferdinand to make his long-awaited return from injury. Although Nemanja Vidić was still a fortnight away from action, having Ferdinand and Edwin van der Sar available proved a huge boon for United's title aspirations.

'It's a big boost,' said the manager. 'It's been the weakest part of our game this season, the defence. Van der Sar, Vidić, Ferdinand, Gary Neville, John O'Shea, Wes Brown and Jonny Evans have all been injured at various times. We've had a rough time, so to get them all back can only be good for us.'

Barclays Premier League

Manchester United 4 Hull City 0

Old Trafford, 23 January 2010

Wayne Rooney's form shot from prolific to devastating as he plundered the first four-goal haul of his professional career against Hull City. The Tigers were left mauled by Rooney's virtuoso performance, which took the Reds to the top of the table despite long periods of frustration against Phil Brown's team.

Rio Ferdinand's welcome return marked a sizeable fringe benefit to the afternoon's events, but Rooney hogged centre-stage almost from the first minute. The striker had already had one effort deflected wide before he opened the scoring on eight minutes. Paul Scholes's booming long-range effort was only parried by Boaz Myhill; Rooney took a touch and drilled the rebound home.

Hull's early concession, allied to their miserable away form, made for an uncertain, nervy display from the visitors. United tried in vain to press home the advantage, with Nani firing over and Ji-sung Park close to turning in Darren Fletcher's cross, while Rooney's long-range free-kick curled just past Myhill's upright. On the right wing, Nani was enjoying an impressive afternoon, and he delivered a series of tantalizing crosses early in the second half.

The longer the scoreline remained so close, the more the Old Trafford crowd grew baffled by their side's inability to kill off the visitors. Widespread nerves were only heightened when substitute Darron Gibson spurned a clear breakaway, opting to go for a long-range chip that narrowly missed the target. On merit it was a good effort, but under the circumstances, passing up such an inviting opportunity to stride through on goal and seal the game only cranked up the pressure.

The Irish midfielder atoned for his rash choice, however, and helped safeguard the points by teeing up Rooney's killer second goal. The striker smashed home after a goalmouth scramble, although Hull half-heartedly protested that play had continued with Andy Dawson grounded.

Those qualms were rendered pointless four minutes later when Nani produced a sublime right-wing cross for Rooney to nod home and complete his hat-trick. Three became four in injury time when Rooney latched on to substitute Dimitar Berbatov's pass, worked his way into the area and slid home a low finish.

Then, as had been the case for much of the game, the name of 'Rooney' boomed and resounded around Old Trafford. Top of the table was secured and now the red-hot striker and his colleagues could look forward to a mouth-watering second-leg cup meeting with Manchester City.

Team: Van der Sar; Rafael, Ferdinand, Evans, Evra (Fabio 88); Park, Fletcher, Scholes (Gibson 72), Nani; Rooney, Owen (Berbatov 72)
Scorer: Rooney (8, 82, 86, 90)
Attendance: 73,933
Referee: Steve Bennett

For all the pre-match talk about United's dilapidated defence, it was the devastation wreaked by Wayne Rooney that stole the headlines. 'The last time I scored four goals was probably when I was about twelve!' he joked afterwards. 'It's my first time in professional football so I'm obviously delighted. It's a great feeling to score one goal in the Premier League, so to score four makes me very proud.'

Rooney's eye-catching quartet was the day's standout performance, but there was also a noteworthy contribution from Nani, who shone throughout and, in only his second appearance in six weeks, harmonized ingenuity and end product to great effect. 'I thought Nani was excellent today,' said Sir Alex. 'In the second half he hit some fantastic crosses into the box. On another day he might have made four or five goals.'

'It was very frustrating to be out injured, but it happens in football,' added the winger. 'I'm back now and I feel very good. I was happy with my performance and I just want to keep improving every week so I can help the team be successful.'

Like each of his team-mates, Nani was itching to be involved in the decisive visit of Manchester City. A bitter taste remained from the first-leg defeat, while post-match comments from Messrs Tévez and Cook had merely added fuel to the fire lit by Roberto Mancini's insistence that he and his players would be tearing down the Stretford End ticker that traces City's years of trophy atrophy.

'It wasn't your average Carling Cup semi-final, was it?' smiles Michael Carrick. 'There were so many different ingredients in the build-up to the game. In the first leg we played well and couldn't believe we'd lost. We were still pretty confident we could do the job at Old Trafford. Obviously there were a lot of things in the press – Garry Cook said what he had to say and that type of thing gives you a little lift and a boost more than anything else.'

'There was a lot said between the games,' agrees Darren Fletcher. 'I think a lot of people forgot it was only half time. There was a lot to play for, and that's when comments you make can come back to haunt you sometimes. But those comments weren't significant to our motivation. We were up against City in the second leg of a cup semi-final at Old Trafford with the chance to get to a final, having lost the first leg. The United players don't need any more motivation than that. I think we just had to go out and perform.'

Paul Scholes, succinct as ever, perhaps put it best: 'It's not your main motivation, to stop them winning a trophy, but you'd never hear the end of it if they did.'

Fortunately, Sir Alex Ferguson was able to draw upon a strong squad for the seismic clash, having reported no new injuries from the victory over Hull. A potential problem arose, however, when Rio Ferdinand was charged by the Football Association for an off-the-ball clash with Tigers attacker Craig Fagan. United had a choice: start a three-game ban against City or risk an extension by appealing. The Reds took the latter option.

Coincidentally, that same day United announced the capture of a defender aiming to follow Ferdinand's career path to the very pinnacle of the game. Chris Smalling agreed terms to transfer from Fulham, but would spend the remainder of the campaign on loan at Craven Cottage. His prospective capture was the major move in a busy month of activity for the Reds, in which Danny Simpson permanently joined Newcastle United, while Danny Welbeck and Zoran Tošić embarked on loan deals with Preston North End and FC Köln respectively.

Smalling's arrival demonstrated yet again that the Reds always have one eye on the future. But never mind that: it was the present everybody was talking about.

Carling Cup Semi-final Second Leg

Manchester United 3 Manchester City 1

Old Trafford, 27 January 2010

Sometimes, it's best to do your talking on the field. For all the pre-match mudslinging and self-championing from across Manchester, United simply went out, overturned City's first-leg lead and booked a trip to Wembley.

It was Wayne Rooney who provided the tie's dramatic denouement, heading home Ryan Giggs's sublime cross in injury time at the Stretford End. Earlier, Carlos Tévez's third goal of the tie had halved City's deficit on the evening and levelled the aggregate scores, after Paul Scholes and Michael Carrick had struck early in the second half. The ground-shaking din that greeted Rooney's winner was merely the climax of an electrifying atmosphere that had soundtracked a game that lulled for the first 45 minutes before lurching into overdrive after the break.

Rio Ferdinand was available by virtue of his appeal against his FA misconduct charge, leading to an unchanged team from that which had thumped Hull City. Rooney, four-goal hero against the Tigers, had the first noteworthy effort of the evening, but Shay Given fielded his 25-yarder with little fuss.

Tévez forced a more impressive save from Edwin van der Sar with a diving header on 20 minutes before Given turned away Giggs's low effort. That aside, there were few scares for the visitors as they were roared into the interval by their 9,000 supporters. City fans would have been celebrating a stunning opening goal in the early stages of the second half were it not for van der Sar's fingertip save from Micah Richards's corner-bound effort. Instead, United drew first blood.

Seven minutes into the half, Nani was caught in possession in the City area. As Carrick poked the ball loose from the subsequent scrum, Scholes raced onto it and rammed a low, deflected shot inside Given's right-hand post. Bedlam gripped Old Trafford.

Roared on by a vocal support eager to see the tie turned on its head inside 90 minutes, the Reds established a vital lead with 20 minutes to play. Fine approach work from Nani fed Fletcher inside the area and the Scot kept his cool under pressure to slip a pass to Carrick, who displayed incredible poise to sidefoot a finish inside the far post and put United on the brink of the final. Two minutes later, Rooney somehow contrived to slot wide as the cup holders threatened to bury Roberto Mancini's teetering side.

Out of the blue, however, City drew level on aggregate. There seemed little danger as Craig Bellamy's cross dipped towards the near post, but Tévez nipped in ahead of Ferdinand and flicked a superb finish past van der Sar.

United were stunned, but City made the mistake of retreating rather than trying to further their foothold in the game. Carrick fired wide at the second attempt and Fletcher's header was magnificently turned away by Given. But with such a big prize at stake, the Reds would not be denied. From a short corner, Giggs whipped a magnificent ball into the six-yard box and there, criminally unmarked, was Rooney to thump home his header, take United to Wembley and break Blues hearts. Again.

Team: Van der Sar; Rafael (Brown 74), Ferdinand, Evans, Evra; Nani (Valencia 89), Carrick, Fletcher, Scholes, Giggs; Rooney
Scorers: Scholes (52), Carrick (71), Rooney (90)
Attendance: 74,576
Referee: Howard Webb

Given the rare thrill of a floodlit Manchester derby, plus a happy ending, it was little wonder United's supporters were so strident throughout the match. 'I thought our fans were unbelievable tonight,' Sir Alex grinned. 'When Old Trafford is like that, the players really respond. The fans dragged us home. I have to pay special tribute to them. They were wonderful.'

'We could have finished it off earlier when we were in a commanding position but to win it like we did in injury time makes for a very special night,' added Michael Carrick, emerging from the crossfire of champagne corks in the home dressing room. 'The place was bouncing and we've sent everyone home happy on the red side.'

The midfielder also heaped praise on match-winner Wayne Rooney, indisputably the country's in-form marksman. 'He is awesome,' said Carrick. 'He just keeps improving. When I first came to the club, I thought he was a great player. But three years on he's improved again. He just gets better and better. All credit to him because he's taken on more responsibility up top and not only is he scoring goals, he's creating them for others. He's doing everything you could possibly ask of him. Let's hope it continues until May.'

For Rooney et al., thoughts of a Wembley date with Aston Villa, conquerors of Blackburn Rovers in the other semi-final a week earlier, could wait. 'We'll assess the final when we get to it,' said Sir Alex. 'We've got some important games in the league and the Champions League to look forward to now. Arsenal on Sunday at the Emirates is a big game for us – we need to win.'

The Gunners' goalless draw with Villa had kept them below United in the table, but Chelsea had retaken top spot with a 3–0 win over Birmingham. With virtually no demarcation between the title-chasing trio, the Reds' trip to the Emirates would carry immense magnitude. 'It's a huge game again, one we love playing in,' said Michael Carrick. 'It's tight at the top now and we're well aware we need to go and get a good result.'

'It was good Wayne popped up with the winner against City – extra time wouldn't have been the ideal preparation,' admitted Darren Fletcher. 'That was a bit of a relief. But it's a big game and our attention now swings back to the Premier League. That's what it's about, being at Manchester United: you have a semi-final in mid-week and then you have to win an important league game at the weekend. We're looking forward to a game against a team in good form. But we'll recover and get ready for it.'

Rio Ferdinand would not be able to participate at the Emirates after his appeal against an FA charge was deemed frivolous and the prospective ban extended to four games. Nevertheless, he would be the only guaranteed personnel change from a game that had galvanized United's patchy start to 2010. And just in time, according to Sir Alex.

'Looking at how the league is shaping up, the Arsenal game is, to my mind, the biggest game of the season,' said the manager. 'With Arsenal going on a consistent run, it's amazing how this league has changed. The team that is the most consistent will win the league now. Arsenal's current form has been very good, so it's a massive game for us. If Chelsea win their game in hand, they can go four points in front. We're playing catch-up with that part of it, but Sunday's game is of most relevance to us because both teams have a real chance of winning the league.'

The Reds had already stolen a march on the Gunners with the signing of Chris Smalling and the England youth international would be at the game as a guest of United, much to the pleasure of Sir Alex and chief executive David Gill.

'There had been a lot of interest in Chris. Arsenal were particularly interested so we had to beat off competition from them,' says David Gill. 'He was there with us at the Emirates and I read later that his mother's an Arsenal fan, so that was a nice touch for us!' For Smalling, the game would provide glaring affirmation of his choice.

Barclays Premier League

Arsenal 1 Manchester United 3

Emirates Stadium, 31 January 2010

United produced a masterclass in incisive, counter-attacking football as Arsenal were left humiliated at the Emirates Stadium. The Reds moved ahead through a goal from Nani that was sublime in approach but fortuitous in finish, before sensational breakaway goals from Wayne Rooney and Ji-sung Park rendered Thomas Vermaelen's late strike mere consolation.

Just as in the Champions League semi-finals nine months earlier, United's tactics of stifling the Gunners and exposing their over-commitment worked almost flawlessly. Andrei Arshavin did curl the first chance of the game just wide for the hosts, but United then dominated matters.

William Gallas's last-ditch block denied Wayne Rooney, while Samir Nasri cleared off the line from Denílson's errant header as the Gunners clung on until just after the half-hour. Then, building on a series of improved recent performances, Nani showed jaw-dropping skill to evade two challenges and work his way into the box. Once there, his clipped, drifting cross was flapped into the back of the net by the back-pedalling Almunia. An own goal on first impression, but the mass flock of United players towards Nani betrayed the goal's inception. Five months later, the Premier League's Dubious Goals Panel would award it to the winger.

The Portuguese was soon involved in doubling United's lead. In little more than ten seconds, the ball was ferried from the visitors' area to the back of the hosts' net in devastating fashion. Park chipped to Rooney, who cut inside and spread the play to Nani before haring towards goal. Nani advanced, carried and slipped a perfect pass between defenders for Rooney to sweep emphatically into Almunia's corner. He could hardly have brought up 100 Premier League goals in more stylish fashion.

A blip in United's control allowed Arshavin an opening, which he thankfully skewed wide, before half time came and went. The Reds began the second period brightest and Rooney's unexpected snapshot required decent fielding from Almunia. The Spanish stopper was left horribly exposed shortly afterwards, allowing United to secure the points. Michael Carrick's insightful pass released Park, who strode towards goal, took advantage of criminally slack defending from the visitors and slipped a neat finish home.

Done and dusted. Plenty of time remained, but Arsenal's efforts only carried genuine intent after Vermaelen's deflected strike had beaten van der Sar. By then it was too late, and Rooney almost had the last word, only to steer his injury-time shot just past the upright.

It was a convincing, swaggering victory at the home of a major title rival and it confirmed beyond doubt that the champions were clicking ominously into gear.

Team: Van der Sar; Rafael, Brown, Evans, Evra; Nani (Berbatov 89), Carrick, Fletcher, Scholes (Giggs 71), Park (Valencia 87); Rooney
Scorers: Nani (33), Rooney (37), Park (52)
Attendance: 60,091
Referee: Chris Foy

According to Sir Alex, United's cut-throat victory was inspired not only by superb individual displays from Wayne Rooney and Nani – labelled 'world-class' and 'absolutely outstanding' respectively – but by the manner of victory over Manchester City four days earlier.

'I think Wednesday's result and performance has galvanized us again,' said Sir Alex. 'You could see today that the players were really ready for the game. They were sharp and good in their passing. And they made a lot of chances. It was a great performance by us, there's no doubt about that, and I was really pleased. At this time of year, you really need to kick on.

'Counter-attacking has always been part of our game anyway, particularly away from home. We capitalized on the opportunities today because Arsenal play a lot of good football and get to the edge of your box regularly. If you can win the ball there and counter-attack quickly, you've got a good chance.'

It was also a highly satisfying, if slightly odd, day for Wes Brown, who played through a sudden bout of flu owing to the absence of Nemanja Vidić and Rio Ferdinand. 'I was properly blowing,' laughs the Longsight-born defender. 'It was a weird game for me, but the way we went and approached the game was fantastic. To come away from there with that result at that point in the season was great. It was a difficult game – we didn't have all our players again – and we scored some fantastic goals.

'Those are games you really enjoy winning. When we play teams like Arsenal and Chelsea we always try to limit them to very few shots. Arsenal like to play a lot of football and make a lot of short passes, so if you stop them doing that it messes up their game and allows us to play ours. We like to counter-attack and score goals, and in that game we pulled it off.'

With a cup final booked, a glittering Champions League resumption to come and an enthralling title race meandering through its capricious course, there was much to anticipate as the season edged towards its nitty-gritty phase.

'There's still a long time to go in the league – three months – so we just have to concentrate on our own performances,' said Ji-sung Park. 'We can deal with the pressure. We'll see whether Chelsea can. We just have to keep winning and putting them under pressure.'

8

February

As February began, plaudits were raining down on Wayne Rooney. The English media, buoyed by seeing their country's star man at the peak of his powers in a World Cup year, could barely contain themselves. Rooney's face adorned back pages and his exploits filled countless column inches as superlatives for his form ran dry.

'My favourite position is playing forward,' he said. 'I've been used out wide or in midfield now and again, but as a forward I feel I can influence the game a lot more. Thankfully the manager has played me there all season. I've started scoring more goals inside the six-yard box, which I've not really done a lot in previous years. I've been working on trying to improve my movement in the box and creating space to get my shot off. It's all starting to pay off.

'We do shooting practice with the team, but then after the session I'll go and work on things myself. Sometimes people don't realize how hard it is to practise every day. It's hard to constantly put the work in to improve your game. But if you want to get the rewards from it, you have to do it. The best players always practise to get better. That's what I've done since as far back as I can remember. I've played football every day for most of my life.'

Practice was yielding near-perfection for the on-song striker, and one of his most potent supply lines, winger Antonio Valencia, was also catching the eye after rapidly assimilating to life at Old Trafford.

'I thought I'd be used sparingly at first and then more as I settled in at the club, but as a footballer you train hard so that you're always prepared to play,' said the Ecuadorian. 'Then it's down to the manager to make the decisions, and he has given me lots of opportunities. I'm really enjoying my United career so far, and this is just the start.

'We want to win as much as we can. You could see our determination in the Carling Cup semi-final, and I'd really like to play at Wembley. It would be great for me to sample any kind of silverware in my first season. We want to win trophies at all costs and to retain the Premier League title and make it four in a row. That is very, very important to us.'

Of even greater significance was the Reds' enduring recognition of the Munich air disaster. For only the eighth time in the 52 years since the crash, United would play on the 6 February anniversary, against Avram Grant's bottom-of-the-table Portsmouth. 'Every anniversary is important – that doesn't change, and never will,' said outgoing club secretary Ken Ramsden. 'If you look at the defining moments in United's history, then I think you'd be hard-pressed to find a more defining moment than the Munich air crash. We will continue to embrace the significance of the tragedy.'

Wayne Rooney was prepared for an extraordinary circumstance surrounding Pompey's visit, and insisted that paying a fitting tribute with three vital points would be the players' aim.

'It's always an emotional day when you play on the anniversary,' he said. 'You see how emotional the fans get and all the old players are back in the stadium. Of course we'll still remember everyone from the disaster, but we have to try and do the job the best we can to show how much it means to the club and how much the history means to the club.'

Barclays Premier League

Manchester United 5 Portsmouth 0

Old Trafford, 6 February 2010

United heaped more misery on struggling Pompey with a crushing victory, although Avram Grant's side were left to reflect on the price of charity, having scored two of the Reds' five goals themselves. Wayne Rooney, Dimitar Berbatov and Michael Carrick struck for the Reds, while own goals from visiting defenders Anthony Vanden Borre and Marc Wilson assured the champions of a healthy goal-difference boost and a temporary return to top spot.

An immaculately observed minute's silence preceded the match to honour the memory of those who perished in Munich. Then, almost as soon as the first whistle had sounded, the visitors seemed content to cede possession and concentrate entirely on defending. To a point, the tactic worked, as it took 12 minutes for a first opening to materialize. Jonny Evans headed Gary Neville's cross just wide before Pompey even mustered two quickfire efforts on the break. Fortunately, Edwin van der Sar was equal to stinging shots from Vanden Borre and Nadir Belhadj.

The Algerian then came within a whisker of opening the scoring after a lightning break from the visitors. The quick thinking and foresight of Evans prevented it, however, as he sprinted behind van der Sar and cleared Belhadj's shot off the line.

Immediately, Berbatov somehow contrived to fire wide after a surging run from Neville, but the Bulgarian's blushes were spared shortly before the interval when Darren Fletcher's superb cross gave Rooney a gimme to nod home from six yards. It was soon two, as Nani's cross deflected off Vanden Borre and trickled over the line, despite a comedic flail from goalkeeper David James.

Keen to make the visitors pay for their unyielding first-half efforts, United began the second period with unmasked intent. Carrick belted home a 25-yard effort via the underside of the crossbar – again having taken a sizeable deflection off Richard Hughes – before Berbatov collected and kept the ball inside the area, worked his way outside the box and drilled a superb low shot into James's far corner.

Although Sir Alex shuffled his pack, introducing Mame Biram Diouf, Michael Owen and Darron Gibson, United's dominance never wavered. When the fifth goal arrived, however, it was another calamity for the visiting defence. Nani touched on Patrice Evra's cross, only to see Wilson slam an unstoppable volley high into his own goal. Diouf fired over from a promising position as United continued to press, but a five-star show was enough to confirm once more that the champions were in metronomic, silverware-snaring form.

Team: Van der Sar; Neville, Brown, Evans, Evra; Valencia, Carrick, Fletcher (Gibson 66), Nani; Berbatov (Owen 67), Rooney (Diouf 66)
Scorers: Rooney (40), Vanden Borre (45 (og)), Carrick (59), Berbatov (62), Wilson (69 (og))
Attendance: 74,684
Referee: Lee Mason

'It took us a while to get the first goal, but we had a lot of pressure, a lot of possession and we were patient enough,' said Sir Alex Ferguson afterwards. 'I think that's important, especially when teams come and sit there, like Portsmouth did today. They were there to make it difficult and eventually we got the goal just before half time. We were fortunate with the second one, but that was important. It opened the game for us and in the second half we had a good performance. It makes it difficult for your opponents because they have to come out in order to win the game, but it galvanized us in the sense that we could then chase goals ourselves, and fortunately we got three more.'

Some post-match reports suggested Michael Carrick's long-range strike should be credited as a Richard Hughes own goal, and the United midfielder concedes he was stunned to hear the news at full time.

'I couldn't believe it as we came off the pitch, being told it was down as an own goal on the telly,' he smiles. 'It's just one of those things that was out of my hands. If there hadn't been any other own goals it probably wouldn't have been an issue – they would have just given it to me. But I guess it's not as good a headline as three own goals. It killed me a bit, but it doesn't matter, to be honest, because we played well and won.' The Reds midfielder would eventually have the last laugh: five months later the goal was confirmed as Carrick's by the Premier League's Dubious Goals Panel.

Rio Ferdinand missed the canter against Portsmouth through suspension, but found himself a hot topic of post-match debate. Following alleged high-profile personal indiscretions by John Terry, the Chelsea defender was stripped of the England captaincy by Fabio Capello. Ferdinand was quickly installed as the new incumbent.

'We're pleased for him,' said Sir Alex. 'We think it's great for Manchester United to have one of our players captaining their country. Over the years we've had Gary Neville, Bobby Charlton and Bryan Robson, of course, who was England captain for something like sixty games. So we're very proud.'

'It's a great honour to captain your country,' added Neville. 'Rio's done very well for England over a long time and he's vice-captain so he was the natural successor. It's great for the club to have an England captain.'

Ferdinand's decision to drop an appeal against his four-match Premier League ban meant he would miss the tricky away trips to Aston Villa and Everton, although he could feature in the trip to AC Milan in between, before eventually coming back into contention for the visit of West Ham and the Carling Cup final.

A daunting glut of fixtures beckoned, but Sir Alex was confident in his squad's ability to absorb the pressure and deliver the right results. 'We've got an important period coming up and we've got to keep the momentum going,' he said. 'We've got a big few weeks where consistency and form are going to be very important. Historically we've always grasped the nettle at this time of year and the players realize there is a lot at stake and they can't afford inconsistency.'

United's record at Villa Park in recent years has been a study in consistency. However, the Villans' first win at Old Trafford for 26 years had provided a startling realization that Martin O'Neill's side were now more than capable of upsetting the Reds.

'Maybe there is a sense of revenge from December,' admitted Wes Brown. 'Villa are playing well at the moment. They have some really good players. But, when we met them before, we weren't playing too well. We are playing really well now. Once we get to this stage of the season it's no longer about wanting to win. You have to win.'

Barclays Premier League

Aston Villa 1 Manchester United 1

Villa Park, 10 February 2010

No victory for the Reds, and a total of five points dropped against Villa over the course of the season. But the manner with which United procured a point with just ten men was nothing short of heroic. With the score locked at 1–1, Nani's dismissal after half an hour for a high challenge on Stiliyan Petrov appeared to put the Reds up against the odds. Instead, the visitors' magnificent efforts had the hosts chasing shadows and should have yielded victory.

From the off, United were in charge. Brad Friedel was forced into a smart save from Nani's 25-yard free-kick and Ryan Giggs had an effort deflected over as the hosts were penned inside their own half. Then, against the run of play, Villa took the lead. Stewart Downing's right-wing cross was only half-cleared by Rafael. The ball fell for Carlos Cuéllar to guide a drifting header over Edwin van der Sar and into the far corner. Another Villa defender would add the game's second goal four minutes later; fortunately for United, it was at the wrong end.

Nani stormed down the right wing and picked out Giggs at the back post. The veteran winger shanked his volley somewhat, only to see it ricochet off the shins of fellow Welshman James Collins and spin into the net.

Nani's menace was curtailed shortly afterwards when he flew into a challenge with Petrov and was promptly dismissed by referee Peter Walton. Nevertheless, United continued to dictate the game's tempo and combated Villa's numerical supremacy by reverting to a 4–4–1 formation, sacrificing Paul Scholes for Antonio Valencia to retain vital width.

It was a move that almost paid instant dividends, as the Ecuadorian reached Giggs's cross, took a touch and fired narrowly over Friedel's crossbar. Valencia constantly looked to link with Rooney, and the pair terrorized the home side, whose only effort of note was a low James Milner shot.

United's cause was further hampered when Steve Sidwell clattered into Ryan Giggs, leaving the veteran winger with a suspected broken arm. Regardless, Rooney continued to try to win the game almost single-handedly, giving Collins and Richard Dunne a torrid time in the Villa back four. Only a magnificent tip-over from Friedel denied Rooney a late winner. At full time, news of Chelsea's defeat at Everton rendered United's point both valuable and frustrating, given victory would have taken the champions back to the Premier League's summit.

Team: Van der Sar; Rafael, Brown, Evans, Evra; Nani, Carrick, Fletcher, Scholes (Valencia 46), Giggs (Berbatov 75); Rooney
Scorer: Collins (23 (og))
Attendance: 42,778
Referee: Peter Walton

Despite missing the chance to go top, Sir Alex Ferguson was in proud, forthright mood afterwards. 'It was a magnificent perform-ance from us and the players were absolutely brilliant,' he said. 'If there was a team who deserved to win the game it was us. We had plenty of chances but just couldn't get the ball in the net in the second half. I'm very proud of the players and can't praise them enough, especially as we only had ten men. We thought it might be an important night, and Everton's win over Chelsea has allowed us to gain one point and one goal and, who knows, that could turn out to be important.'

The match also provided the latest addition to a long list of own goals in United's favour. It was a discussion point that dominated post-match headlines, although Darren Fletcher quickly insisted there was no evidence to support the theory that the Reds had Lady Luck on the payroll.

'It comes from putting teams under pressure,' he said. 'If you put the ball into the right area it's difficult to defend. If you can whip the ball in between the goalkeeper and the defence there's a chance one of your players can get onto the end of it. If not, it also causes problems for defenders and fortunately they've been knocking them into their own net. But if you look at the own goals this season there's always a United player coming in behind who can easily tap into the net.'

If there was any fortune about Ryan Giggs's mis-hit shot leading to United's equalizer at Villa Park, it was quickly overturned by the news that he had suffered a broken arm.

'It was just an innocuous challenge,' recalls the winger. 'I think Patrice played it to me, I've stretched for it and put my arm up, and Sidwell's kneed me right in the arm. I heard it crack straight away and there was a big dent right in my arm. It didn't hurt but I said to the ref, "I think I've broken my arm", and he said, "Yeah, I heard it." I've fractured my cheekbone before, but that was the first time I've broken my arm. I had to have a plate put in it.'

Six weeks on the sidelines was the diagnosis, robbing Sir Alex of the club's most experienced player just at a time when his know-how could prove vital. However, with no weekend commitments and a mouth-watering trip to Milan to consider, the United manager allowed his players to recuperate over a couple of days without training.

'Of course we'd like to still be in the FA Cup, but after playing the majority of the Villa game with ten men, this weekend will be a welcome break,' admitted Darren Fletcher. 'If we had to play at the weekend and then play AC Milan it would have been tough, although we've got the squad to deal with that and the manager would have made changes. Nevertheless, it's a nice break and the lads will be delighted to get a rest before a massive game against Milan.'

For two of the Reds' more recent arrivals, the trip to the San Siro would be the next stop on their polarized agendas. For Antonio Valencia, in his maiden Champions League campaign, the Milan clash represented 'the biggest games I've played in club football', while Dimitar Berbatov, twice a losing finalist, admitted, 'I want to be in a final again.'

'The Champions League is a huge competition and Milan are one of the biggest clubs around,' continued Valencia. 'They've won so much in their history and they've won the Champions League and European Cup a lot, so it will be a big test for us. Every game is important, but the lads are definitely looking forward to both matches.'

'It'll be a great game,' added Berbatov. 'Some people say Milan aren't in the best shape, but it's deceiving. In the Champions League everybody is different. They'll prepare very well for us. There's no favourite; it's fifty–fifty.'

The record books may have disagreed. In four previous two-legged meetings, the Rossoneri had knocked the Reds out of Europe on each occasion, so Sir Alex's back-to-back finalists would have to overcome history in order to book a quarter-final berth.

With Ryan Giggs already sidelined through injury, he was joined on the absentee list by Nemanja Vidić and Anderson as United's 22-man party made the trip to Milan. In the San Siro, a citadel of sound and intimidation, the big-game experience of Giggs and Vidić would be missed. However, their absence was offset by the return of Rio Ferdinand, who was free of suspension and, crucially, injury.

'We have to consider whether Rio will start tomorrow but I think he probably will,' said Sir Alex at his pre-match press conference. 'We feel we've got to the bottom of the back problem. We certainly hope he'll be OK for the rest of the season. He's not missed a training session in the last six or seven weeks. We've worked really hard with him and he's worked very hard himself. He's now doing really well with his core work and we feel that will help him in the future.'

While United would undoubtedly benefit from Ferdinand's know-how, a number of questions in the press conference centred on a perceived surfeit of experience in the Milan ranks. Leonardo, a young manager, was portrayed as controlling a team with too many ageing stars to seriously challenge United.

Nevertheless, Edwin van der Sar – ironically just shy of 40 himself – was preaching caution as he addressed the media's pointed questions. 'The moment you start to underestimate a team it sends out the wrong signal to the players,' said the Dutchman. 'It's the last sixteen of the Champions League and Milan have quality players who have already achieved so much. You can't take anything for granted. We have to be careful at the back and make sure we take at least one of the opportunities we get on the night so we can take a good result back to Old Trafford.'

There was a sumptuous game of football lying in wait, although much of the pre-match discussion centred on the reunion of United and David Beckham, on loan at the San Siro from LA Galaxy. The former Reds winger had admitted: 'I don't usually get nervous, but I think there will be a few butterflies before kick-off at both games.'

Sir Alex, meanwhile, was keen to shift focus from a former United great to a player seemingly fast-tracked to similar legendary status. 'Manchester United builds up heroes very quickly,' said the boss. 'We are peculiar because the players, like Beckham, who come through the ranks are always viewed as better than those you buy. But Rooney is also regarded as that kind of player. Although he came from Everton, the fans will always look at him as one of the players who has grown up with us. He has been fantastic this season and, without doubt, his form has brought him to the high point of his career. World-class is a misused term, but with Rooney you have to say he is getting to the point where he is now one of the best players in the world.'

Champions League Round of 16 First Leg

AC Milan 2 Manchester United 3

San Siro, 16 February 2010

Wayne Rooney spectacularly validated his pre-match billing with a striking masterclass to break United's San Siro hoodoo and give the Reds a potentially decisive first-leg lead. United had to overcome a nightmare start, in which Ronaldinho put the hosts ahead and Milan passed up several other presentable chances, before a freak equalizer from Paul Scholes and Rooney's brace turned the match on its head. Clarence Seedorf kept the tie alive with a neat finish late on, but the damage had already been done.

Just over two minutes had passed when David Beckham's free-kick was only half-cleared to Ronaldinho, and the Brazilian's right-footed volley cruelly deflected off Michael Carrick and hurtled past Edwin van der Sar. The baying home support roared with delight.

Perhaps spooked by Milan's start and the deafening atmosphere, United were shell-shocked in the opening stages. Ronaldinho drew a smart stop from van der Sar with another close-range effort, and the Brazilian was perhaps a touch unfortunate to go unrewarded after being felled by Rio Ferdinand on the edge of the box.

When Jonny Evans's panicked clearance led to Klaas-Jan Huntelaar firing just past the post, United looked doomed to defeat. Out of the blue, however, came the strangest of equalizers. A superb passing move culminated in Darren Fletcher's right-wing cross, and the onrushing Scholes swung wildly with his right leg, missed the ball, and watched in amazement as it struck his left leg and spun in via the inside of Dida's post.

Quite undeservedly, United were level. The impetus then remained with the visitors throughout the second half. Although van der Sar was required to make a superb stop from Andrea Pirlo's 35-yard free-kick, Milan found chances far harder to come by as a result of the Reds' improved ball retention. Pirlo, the Rossoneri's pace-setter, had been almost entirely negated by a sterling man-marking job from Ji-sung Park.

With Milan tiring, Antonio Valencia was introduced at the expense of Nani. Within two minutes, the Ecuadorian had made his impact. Speeding past Giuseppe Favalli on the right wing, he stood up a fine cross to the back post, where Rooney rose above Daniele Bonera and sent a magnificent header back into the far top corner.

Soon after, the jubilant travelling support was cheering again. As Milan failed to cope with Rooney's influence, he nodded down for Fletcher before jogging into the penalty area. Spotting a gap between Dida and Alessandro Nesta, Rooney darted forward to nod home Fletcher's superb cross and, seemingly, bury the tie. But there was more drama to come and, once more, poor possession play would prove self-harming for United. Ronaldinho picked up a stray pass, motored into the area and crossed for substitute Seedorf to impishly back-heel past his compatriot van der Sar.

The Reds withstood a late siege from the hosts, despite losing Michael Carrick to a second yellow card, and held on for a maiden victory in the San Siro, while also setting a new Champions League record of 16 away games without defeat. Moreover, the Reds had one foot in the quarter-finals.

Team: Van der Sar; Rafael (Brown 90), Ferdinand, Evans, Evra; Nani (Valencia 64), Carrick, Park, Scholes, Fletcher; Rooney
Scorers: Scholes (36), Rooney (66, 74)
Attendance: 78,587
Referee: Olegário Benquerença

Inevitably, post-match analysis revolved around United's star striker. 'Wayne is among the best players in the world,' said Michael Carrick. 'He seems to be getting better and better, and players like him have the ability to really influence the big games. He's scoring goals and setting them up and his overall play is phenomenal. I'm sure he can get even better.'

Darren Fletcher had witnessed Rooney's evolution from rough diamond to crown jewel first-hand during their six years working together, but looking back he admits the striker's display in Milan confirmed his incredible ascension.

'I think the game in Milan was the one that made everyone think "Wow!",' admits Fletcher. 'Although he'd been scoring all season, it was his all-round performance people took note of. He was up there on his own against Alessandro Nesta and Thiago Silva – top-class defenders – and he was strong, quick, scored two fantastic headers and looked like the complete player. I think that was a turning point in Wayne's season. It was everything you could ask for from a striker.'

While Rooney took most of the plaudits, those with an eye for tactical minutiae were gushing over the contribution of Ji-sung Park, whose deployment as an advanced man-marker on Andrea Pirlo laid the foundations for United's victory.

'It was a masterstroke from the coaching staff,' says Carrick. 'He'd never really played that role for us, and Pirlo is such a big player for them. He dictates their play but I think the stats after the first game showed that he made about twenty successful passes, when he normally averages around seventy per game. It shows how well Ji did, but it wasn't just the defensive side of his game he did well; the way he broke off in attack caused plenty of problems for their defence, too. I thought it was a magnificent performance.'

For Paul Scholes, an influential member of the Reds' central pack, scoring with his standing leg and coming up against old friend David Beckham in a competitive game for the first time made for a surreal evening.

'I practise those every day, kicking the ball off one leg onto the other,' smiles Scholes. 'It's just technique! Obviously it was a lucky goal, but it was important to get in level at half time because we'd made a shocking start to the game. It got better and better for us in the second half, and it was a little bit weird playing against Becks. I've played against former team-mates before – the likes of Nicky Butt and Phil Neville – and there's not too much difference. I don't think I managed to kick Becks, though. In fact, I think he got me, which is unusual. I'll have to store that one up, I think!'

A jubilant squad jetted back to Manchester after the victory, but the Reds faced the very real possibility of being brought back down to earth with a trip to Everton to consider. Three of the champions' league defeats had come immediately after European exertions, and coming up against a resurgent Toffees side was a daunting prospect.

'It'll be a very difficult game,' admitted Sir Alex Ferguson. 'Everton's win over Chelsea shows you the potential of their team. If we could get a result I think it would be very important for us. When you get into the second half of the season and you come up against the difficult sides, you know that taking something from each match is going to be very important. That's the way I view Saturday.'

The Reds' 2007 trip to the San Siro had been scuppered by superhuman efforts at Goodison Park four days earlier. Three years on, would the roles be reversed?

Barclays Premier League

Everton 3 Manchester United 1
Goodison Park, 20 February 2010

United's title hopes were dealt a shuddering blow as a jaded performance was punished by David Moyes's fired-up Everton. Dimitar Berbatov's clinical early strike rewarded a decent start from the Reds, but a shock equalizer from Diniyar Bilyaletdinov just three minutes later stunned the visitors, who seldom looked like recovering from the setback. Late strikes from youngsters Dan Gosling and Jack Rodwell gave the Toffees only a second win over United in 30 league meetings, allowing Chelsea to open up a four-point lead with victory over Wolves later that day.

Back in the bread and butter of the Premier League, United reverted to a 4–4–2 formation, with Berbatov deployed alongside Wayne Rooney up front. The former opened the scoring after just 16 minutes in spectacular fashion, killing Antonio Valencia's drilled cross with one touch, then hammering a finish in via the crossbar with his second.

Goodison Park was stunned into near-silence, but only temporarily. Three minutes later, ex-Red Louis Saha nodded down for Bilyaletdinov, who caught everybody by surprise with an early rocket that flew inside Edwin van der Sar's left-hand post. With Wes Brown used as a shield, the Dutchman just didn't see the shot coming.

United's immediate response was defiant, as Rooney rounded Tim Howard only to be thwarted by a combination of a heavy touch and a heroic last-ditch intervention from Phil Neville. Former United players were everywhere, it seemed. Although Landon Donovan should have done better than miss the ball when it fell to him six yards out, the Reds continued to create sporadic chances in the second period, without ever fully convincing or dictating play. Darren Fletcher shot just past Howard's post and Berbatov headed off-target, but sloppy possession play still prevailed.

In a bid to inject life into his side's efforts, Sir Alex introduced Paul Scholes and Gabriel Obertan for Berbatov and Ji-sung Park, and shifted to 4–5–1. Rather than give United the edge, Everton made the more positive response and moved ahead 14 minutes from time when Gosling dragged home Steven Pienaar's cross.

The Reds almost pinched a point when Rooney's superb free-kick was deflected agonizingly past the post by Sylvain Distin's forehead, but the tiring visitors were picked off when Rodwell burst through in injury time, smashed a low finish past van der Sar and secured United's sixth league defeat of the season. Advantage Chelsea.

Team: Van der Sar; Neville, Brown, Evans, Evra; Valencia (Owen 81), Carrick, Fletcher, Park (Scholes 66); Rooney, Berbatov (Obertan 66)
Scorer: Berbatov (16)
Attendance: 39,448
Referee: Howard Webb

'We were well beaten, it's as simple as that,' admitted Sir Alex. 'Maybe we left something in Milan – there certainly looked to be a lot of tiredness in the team. But we're going for a championship and we expect Manchester United to respond to the importance of the game. The players had all been bouncing in the week, but . . . the real effect came in the second half when we were second best to everything. We started the game well enough, but you don't want to lose a goal so quickly after taking the lead, and Everton's goal galvanized them and gave them some incentive. In the second half they were the better team.'

'We are all very disappointed and upset,' added a crestfallen Patrice Evra. 'I'd like to give the excuse that we are very tired after the amazing night in the San Siro. But I won't give that excuse. We were tired – a lot of players were tired – but I think our mentality lost the game. It's not about not having spirit, it's that we didn't believe enough. We play every time for the United shirt and we want to win, we believe until the last second. But we didn't believe enough. I am very frustrated. It was not an easy day and it was a tough place to go. It was a tough time to play Everton as well. But I think it was just about having a bit more belief in getting the victory.'

Only three days would pass before the Reds would host Gianfranco Zola's struggling West Ham at Old Trafford. 'Are we are pleased we have a game so soon?' asked Evra. 'Yes and no. It's not easy. We only have three days to recover. But this is United. If we win on Tuesday we will all be pleased. But for now we need to recover and get ready for that game.'

The Reds would be boosted by the long-awaited return of Nemanja Vidić. The Serbian centre-back had not featured in 2010, but hopes that he could reprise his imposing partnership with Rio Ferdinand were dashed on the morning of West Ham's visit, when the England skipper suffered a recurrence of his back injury. Nevertheless, Vidić's return was a timely one as United looked to get back on track, post-haste.

Barclays Premier League

Manchester United 3 West Ham United 0

Old Trafford, 23 February 2010

Back to winning ways via three stylish goals, and with a clean sheet secured by a dominant defensive display, United's victory over West Ham proved the perfect tonic after the damaging defeat at Goodison Park. Two fine headers from Wayne Rooney and a late clincher from Michael Owen secured the points for the Reds, but the gloss was taken off the victory by a serious-looking injury to Anderson.

The Brazilian midfielder lasted less than ten minutes before his knee buckled on the stretch and he was quickly substituted. That unfortunate interlude interrupted a strange, if entertaining, first period in which excellent and excruciating play mingled unpredictably.

A superb James Tomkins challenge halted Rooney's marauding run and prompted a Hammers attack that ended with Valon Behrami shooting past Ben Foster's far post. Moments later, the United stopper survived a jittery moment as he fumbled Alessandro Diamanti's deflected effort, padding the ball down onto the goal-line before collecting it. Visiting goalkeeper Robert Green also had to improvise, contorting impressively to keep out Dimitar Berbatov's effort, after the Bulgarian had redirected Darron Gibson's wayward shot. The Irishman then chanced his arm three times in quick succession, once prompting a magnificent save from Green, who brushed the ball past the post.

It took a magnificent team effort to break parity shortly before half time. Substitute Ji-sung Park fed Berbatov, who chipped out wide to Antonio Valencia on the right-hand side of the penalty area. The winger opted for a first-time volleyed cross into the box, which Rooney thudded home with a diving header.

In the form of his life, Rooney almost doubled the lead two minutes later with a fabulous 25-yard volley. Seconds after the break, Park crashed a shot against the underside of the Hammers' crossbar. The Reds, not content with the narrow nature of the lead, pressed incessantly for a second goal. It soon arrived.

Berbatov's excellent pass released Valencia down the right and he delivered another perfect cross for Rooney, in space, to nod home. A hat-trick proved elusive for the striker as, despite drawing Green from his goal, Julien Faubert cleared the England striker's shot off the line. Before long, Berbatov and Rooney were replaced by Owen and Mame Biram Diouf.

It took Owen just three minutes to win possession, release it and then latch on to Paul Scholes's measured through-ball before steering home a superb finish via the inside of Green's post. Scholes missed the chance to get a deserved goal when he fired over late on, but United had already done enough to get back on track in the title race.

Team: Van der Sar; Neville, Brown, Evans, Evra; Valencia (Owen 81), Carrick, Fletcher, Park (Scholes 66); Rooney, Berbatov (Obertan 66)
Scorers: Rooney (38, 55), Owen (80)
Attendance: 73,797
Referee: Alan Wiley

'It's nice to be back,' admitted a relieved Nemanja Vidić afterwards. 'I enjoyed playing again. It's a long time since I last played, but I am happy first of all that we won the game, and also that I feel OK in terms of the injury. I feel well and that's very important for me. I didn't feel any reaction today. When I finished last season, I thought this season would be even better, but I've had the injury and this year has been very frustrating. I missed pre-season and two months recently. I hope the injury is in the past and I'm looking forward to the next games. We believe we can win the title. Confidence is a big word, but we believe we can do it. I think we will be good for the rest of the season.'

It seemed unlikely Anderson would be part of whatever befell United during the campaign's remaining ten weeks when he was sent for a scan on his knee injury. 'It's not looking great,' was Sir Alex's grim forecast. Upon learning the results of the scan, the manager confirmed the bad news. 'He has suffered a cruciate knee injury and he'll be out for the rest of the season,' confirmed the boss.

'It's unfortunate for the boy. It's a bad blow. We've assessed the situation and we know he needs an operation. That will be done in two weeks' time when the swelling has gone down. We're going to let him go to Portugal to do it. Sometimes we send them to Colorado and to Dr Richard Steadman, but on this occasion he is comfortable with the specialist he has dealt with at Porto in the past. He will deal with it. We made these decisions once we had assessed the damage. But hopefully six months should have him about right for the new season.'

Anderson joined Ryan Giggs, Rio Ferdinand, plus long-term absentees John O'Shea and Owen Hargreaves on the sidelines, while Nani was also suspended as Sir Alex planned for the Carling Cup final. In keeping with tradition, the manager had to skilfully pick a side that handed vital experience to some young, twinkling talents, while also possessing the necessary smarts to pick up silverware.

'I am thinking about the younger ones to give them that smell of success,' said Sir Alex. 'There are two or three that come into that category, like Darron Gibson, Jonny Evans and Rafael. They obviously have to be considered. But it would be nice to win the cup, having got to Wembley and got through those semi-final ties against Manchester City. You want to get to the final and do well, and it has a great attraction to it. We recognize the challenge of Villa.'

While perpetually keen to promote youth, the United manager also safeguarded the future of his oldest player, Edwin van der Sar, with a one-year contract extension ahead of the final. 'I still feel good and am enjoying my football,' said the Dutchman. 'This is a great club and I was shown a great deal of compassion and support during a difficult time in December and January, for which I am extremely grateful. I am looking forward to winning more trophies with this great team.'

With van der Sar among a host of experienced players set to miss out on starting at Wembley, Sir Alex needed carefully to consider his captain. The manager eventually plumped for Patrice Evra, who had already skippered the side against Wolfsburg, Fulham and Birmingham.

'I remember when the boss said to me, "Pat, you are my captain tomorrow",' says the Frenchman. 'He asked me what I thought and I told him I would think about it and let him know. He just laughed at me! He also said, "Pat, I believe you can be captain of that team", which was nice. It's not what I was looking for because, for me, I'm the captain in the dressing room, not just when I have the armband. It's something you need to take with responsibility and it was good to have that.'

Sir Alex had decreed who would lead United up the famous Wembley steps. Now it was over to the stand-in skipper and his colleagues to make sure they weren't the first team to climb them at full time.

Carling Cup Final

Aston Villa 1 Manchester United 2

Wembley, 28 February 2010

United retained the Carling Cup after a hard-fought victory over Aston Villa. The Reds had to come from behind after James Milner's early penalty, as Michael Owen equalized and Wayne Rooney headed a superb second-half winner. Rooney had been originally rested, but had to replace Owen after the 30-year-old suffered a hamstring injury at the end of the first half. Despite carrying a knee injury and a mild bug, Rooney entered the fray and ultimately won the cup with his seventh header in eight games.

Villa could justifiably feel hard-done-by at full time. Not for the defeat, because they had been clearly outplayed for long periods, but because of referee Phil Dowd's decision not to dismiss Nemanja Vidić in the fifth minute. The Serbian hauled down Gabriel Agbonlahor deep inside the United area, but Dowd's award of a penalty without further punishment constituted a genuine let-off for the Reds. Not that there was much relief in the ranks when Milner smashed home the resulting spot-kick.

Owen's partnership with Dimitar Berbatov was proving tricky for the Villa defence to manage, however, as they alternated dropping deep between the Midlanders' defence and midfield. The pair soon combined to level the scores, but Villa defender Richard Dunne also played a major role. The former Manchester City skipper was caught in possession by Berbatov, who carried the ball into the area. Dunne's lunging challenge temporarily averted the danger, but also fed Owen to sweep home a beautiful finish.

The Reds' No. 7 was enjoying potentially the finest game of his short United career when disaster struck just before half time. Chasing a through-ball with Dunne, Owen pulled up with hamstring trouble and was promptly replaced by Rooney.

United's control of the game continued in the second period and it took a magnificent one-handed save from the unsighted Brad Friedel to keep out Michael Carrick's low shot. Villa increasingly relied on their pace on the break, and Agbonlahor fired wide of Tomasz Kuszczak's post after one such raid.

Injury also claimed Rafael, who was replaced by Gary Neville, and the club captain was soon involved in attacks on the right flank, down which Antonio Valencia was enjoying a superb afternoon. The Ecuadorian was the architect of United's winner with 16 minutes remaining, running infield, latching on to Berbatov's flick and digging out a cross that the back-pedalling Rooney superbly directed just underneath Friedel's crossbar.

Moments later, the duo combined again. This time Rooney could only power against Friedel's post, ensuring a nervy finish in which Villa subjected United to an aerial bombardment. Valencia surged forward in injury time and fired into the side-netting with the game's final chance, but a third goal was unnecessary. United had already done enough to secure a 34th major domestic honour – an English record – and bag the first silverware of the season.

Team: Kuszczak; Rafael (Neville 66), Vidić, Evans, Evra; Valencia, Carrick, Fletcher, Park (Gibson 85); Berbatov, Owen (Rooney 42)
Scorers: Owen (12), Rooney (74)
Attendance: 88,596
Referee: Phil Dowd

'People may say it's the lesser of the cup competitions, but I think this can be a springboard for us to go on and be more successful,' said club captain Gary Neville. 'It's proved to be in previous years and hopefully it will be again this season. This competition has been really good to us in the last few years, and it's great to get a medal around your neck this early in the season.'

'It's a great feeling to lift the cup,' added Michael Carrick. 'It's a first Carling Cup win for me and it's a dream to win at Wembley. The last few matches we've played at Wembley have been quite dull affairs, but this was an open, end-to-end game and I thought we played well. We always believed we could go on to win it. We just had to be patient and trust each other. When we play our football we always believe we will get chances and it was a great finish by Michael. Thankfully Wayne came on and finished it off for us and I think we were deserved winners.'

Sir Alex Ferguson conceded there had perhaps been some good fortune in having 11 players to call upon for the entirety of the match, following Nemanja Vidić's early foul. 'I don't think there was any doubt about the penalty kick,' he said. 'As for whether Vidić should have been dismissed or not, I think we got a lucky break there. He could have been sent off.'

For Michael Owen, the game brought mixed emotions: elation at having scored, performed well and played a major role in the Reds' success, but deflation to have been forced off with a hamstring injury. Looking back, his irritation has only been concentrated by the subsequent theory that the heavy Wembley pitch played a part in his misfortune.

'I just thought I'd tweaked my hamstring and would be out for three weeks or so,' he recalls. 'My overriding emotion was one of real happiness to have scored, won my first trophy at United and feel like I'd been a part of it. I played and scored and I didn't think it would be such a bad injury. Then I went for the scan and realized it was far worse than we thought. When we realized it needed surgery it became a case of mixed emotions.

'I just feel unlucky that one injury prevented me from playing in all the exciting games at the end of the season. On top of that, there's the feeling that it could have been avoided. Everyone mentioned the pitch afterwards – there were loads of injuries sustained in that game, in the England game afterwards, then in the FA Cup semi-finals everyone was complaining, so you never know. If the pitch was a bit better, then I might have been available for a lot more games.'

At the time, it was match-winner Wayne Rooney who took the majority of the plaudits, and he was keen to continue plundering silverware over the following months. 'It's a great feeling, we're delighted,' he said. 'I think we created the better chances in the game, but full credit to Villa, they played well today. It was a good final. My goal tally isn't in my mind. If the goals come, then that's great, but I'm focused more on winning medals.'

To cap the weekend, Chelsea had earlier been dismantled by Manchester City at Stamford Bridge. The Blues' 4–2 defeat kept United just a point off top spot, while a first victory in the San Siro suggested a probable berth in the Champions League quarter-finals. Throw in the retention of the Carling Cup and the form of the Premier League's hottest striker, and the 2009–10 run-in was shaping up perfectly for United.

March

After losing Michael Owen for the remainder of the season, Sir Alex Ferguson and his coaches harboured greater-than-usual reticence as 11 senior squad members jetted off for international friendlies. Of greatest concern, given the increasingly unpredictable Wembley pitch, was the involvement of Wayne Rooney, Michael Carrick and Wes Brown in England's meeting with Egypt. Owen, the turf's latest apparent victim, garnered public sympathy from his manager, but he expressed his desire to return, fitter than ever, for the 2010–11 campaign.

'It's a bad blow for Michael,' said the boss. 'It was more serious than we thought and he'll have an operation. It's a terrible blow for the lad and disappointing for us, too. He never missed a training session all season. The heavy pitch at Wembley played some part, but it's also bad luck.'

'I've loved every minute of my first campaign with United and have already enjoyed some memorable moments,' added a philosophical Owen. 'I'm determined to come back at the start of next season in peak condition.'

Owen would have to watch from the sidelines as his team-mates fought an absorbing title race, and Sir Alex was keen to stress that Arsenal, with an evidently easier fixture list, would have some say in the outcome.

'Arsenal are bang in the frame now,' he said. 'They have the easiest programme on paper and it will be an interesting run-in. Chelsea losing to Manchester City was a good result for us, but there are a lot of hard games left. We lost to Everton, but we recovered against West Ham and we recovered again in the Carling Cup final. We have shown time and again that this football club has determination. The players don't give in and that is a good quality. You will see that in the remainder of the season.'

After a patchy first half of the campaign yielded five Premier League defeats, United's performances were benefiting from marked improvement in quality and consistency. According to assistant manager Mike Phelan, things were coming to the boil nicely.

'We're showing great signs of improvement,' he said. 'There's been a natural, gradual progression throughout the season to get us to where we are now. The players are starting to dictate matches. They're enjoying themselves, but we have to keep driving the message home that nothing's done, and we have to keep pushing them in order to get everything out of them right to the end of the season.'

With Michael Owen out for the rest of the season and Danny Welbeck on loan at Preston North End, Kiko Macheda's return to training after a series of injuries was a timely boon for a striking department featuring only two established first-teamers in Wayne Rooney and Dimitar Berbatov. But Rooney's availability for the looming trip to Wolves was hamstrung by his 86-minute outing for England against Egypt, and Sir Alex made no attempt to disguise his distaste for the situation.

'We have to assess Wayne because he played almost ninety minutes for England the other night at Wembley, which I was disappointed in,' he said. 'When you're playing on that pitch for almost an hour on Sunday [in the Carling Cup final] and then nearly a full game on Wednesday, it's far too much. He wasn't meant to be playing at all because he was feeling his knee on Sunday. I don't blame Fabio Capello – I understand he had to pick his best team – but I don't think Wayne should have played. His own enthusiasm's caused it: he can't say no.

'Wembley's a difficult pitch. Last Sunday I thought a horse show had been on it! It reminded me of a ploughed field. The Carling Cup final was a gruelling game, end to end, and that takes it out of you. I was disappointed Wayne didn't come off earlier for England and now he's doubtful for Wolves.'

Rooney's likely absence was tempered by the anticipated return of Rio Ferdinand, who was set to reprise his famed partnership with Nemanja Vidić for the first time since October. 'Having the Ferdinand–Vidić partnership is a big boost in terms of the experience and consistency they've shown over the last few years,' said the manager. 'That will be important to us in the run-in.'

The duo's first test would come with a trip to relegation-threatened Wolves, a game Sir Alex was quick to stress would not be easy. 'Wolves are fighting for their lives, so we expect a difficult match,' he said. 'But we're in a situation now where we need to win all our games. They have to gather points to stay in the league, and it's the same for all the other teams down there. It's not easy, but knowing Mick McCarthy, he's never been one to shirk a challenge. There is no doubt they will have a go at us. We'll just have to make sure we're prepared for a battle.'

Barclays Premier League

Wolverhampton Wanderers 0 Manchester United 1

Molineux, 6 March 2010

Paul Scholes picked the perfect moment to plunder his 100th Premier League goal, firing United to a vital victory at Molineux and taking the Reds to the top of the table. The veteran midfielder demonstrated his customary calm to power home a low finish in the last 20 minutes of a gritty early evening encounter.

Without the injured Wayne Rooney, United were made to work by a battling home side eager to stave off the threat of relegation. From the first whistle, Mick McCarthy's side were intent largely on stifling the champions. Anything else was a bonus for the gold-clad hordes.

Nevertheless, United still carved out half-chances. Antonio Valencia fired just past Marcus Hahnemann's near post, while the American was scrambling as Darron Gibson's half-hit shot bobbled fractionally wide. The former Wolves loanee then passed up a more presentable chance, volleying into the ground rather than straight at goal, before Michael Carrick's tame shot was comfortably fielded.

As United toiled without reward, Wolves almost took a shock lead twice before the break. Former Reds midfielder David Jones was thwarted by a superb challenge from Carrick, but the clearest chance of the half came when the unmarked Stephen Ward headed Matt Jarvis's left-wing cross straight at van der Sar from six yards.

A foot injury prompted the withdrawal of Wes Brown at half time, with Gary Neville introduced, and the Reds began the second period with intent. Alas, so too did Wolves, who redoubled their stout efforts and forfeited their own safety with a string of heroic blocks, as Dimitar Berbatov and Patrice Evra were both denied within minutes of the restart.

Seeking a breakthrough, Sir Alex introduced Mame Biram Diouf for Gibson, nudging the Senegalese striker up top, just ahead of Berbatov. With more bodies deployed in attack, United were soon ahead. Valencia found Nani inside a packed home area and the Portuguese's pull-back was only semi-cleared by Jody Craddock. Needing no second invitation, Scholes nicked possession, drove on and smashed a fine low shot past the exposed Hahnemann.

Diouf had a pair of chances to seal the three points, but he misjudged Neville's deep cross and headed well over before failing to predict that Craddock would miss Valencia's cross. The striker's heavy touch merely presented Hahnemann with the ball. The Reds were almost left to rue those spurned openings when Ronald Zubar's half-hit shot found Sam Vokes, unmarked, deep inside the United area in added time. Somehow, he fired horribly off-target and allowed the Reds to open up a two-point lead at the head of the table.

Team: Van der Sar; Brown (Neville 46), Ferdinand, Vidić, Evra; Valencia, Carrick, Gibson (Diouf 62), Scholes, Nani (Park 74); Berbatov
Scorer: Scholes (73)
Attendance: 28,883
Referee: Peter Walton

'I feared the worst,' admitted Sir Alex, of Vokes's shocking miss. 'It's one of those chances you always hope you get in a game, but thankfully he didn't take it. Molineux is a difficult place to come to; when you come up against teams at the bottom, you know they're going to fight very hard. But I think we played the better football and deserved the win. It's an important victory for us and it's good to tick another away game off the list.'

Despite securing the three points and passing a major career milestone, Paul Scholes remained self-effacing at full time. 'You need to score goals to win games and thankfully the ball fell to me and I managed to put it away.' He smiled. 'I've been on ninety-nine goals for a while, so it was nice to get my hundredth and I'm pleased with the achievement.'

Rio Ferdinand, meanwhile, was far happier to extol Scholes's enduring importance. 'He's a true professional, a great footballer and someone who has been a pleasure to play alongside,' said the defender. 'We're delighted he's got us the winner and it's great for him to have scored a hundred league goals. Scholesy's just Scholesy. He wants to be first out of the training ground when training is over to get home and be with his family, but when he's training he works very hard. He's not someone who shouts or makes a noise if he scores a goal or does something out of the ordinary that no one else can do, which he often does. That speaks volumes for the kind of professional he is.'

On a personal level, Ferdinand was simply happy to return to action after his injury nightmare. 'First and foremost it's great to be back playing,' he said. 'Me and Vida haven't played a lot of games together recently and it was nice to get a clean sheet. It wasn't just down to us, though. It was down to the whole team. I thought we worked tirelessly, stood up to the battle and answered the questions that were asked of us. That's the sign of a team who are trying to win a fourth consecutive title. The only thing I can do is take it game by game. But I've got through this match and I'm very pleased with that.'

Typically of United's season, as one defender strode from the treatment room, he would pause to hold the door for another to limp inside. Wes Brown's seemingly innocuous clash with Wolves' Matt Jarvis had transpired to be anything but.

'It was a silly injury to get and it was my own fault,' recalls the versatile defender. 'The ball came, I tried to clear it with my left foot and Jarvis just managed to nick it away and I kicked his studs. I realized that it was hurting at the time, but it pretty much went away. At half time I took my boot off and it swelled up straight away and started throbbing. The physios had a look at it and told me I'd probably broken my foot. When we went for the scan on the Monday it turned out I'd broken it in three places, so that was a blow.'

Having not even winced in sustaining the injury, Brown's brief continuation with a broken foot further fulfilled one of the terrace songs of the season, which deemed him 'hardest man in all the town'. 'I'm not going to complain with the label,' he says. 'It's funny. It's nice to be playing and have people chanting your name. For me it's more about what we do on the pitch and making sure we win, but it is a great chant to have.'

Brown's enforced absence meant either Gary Neville or Rafael would start at right-back in United's next outing, a Champions League second-round decider against AC Milan. The Brazilian had started against his compatriot, Ronaldinho, in the first leg, and relished the experience. 'It was a great privilege for me,' the teenager said. 'It made me feel that the manager really trusts me by giving me the opportunity to play in this type of match. It's a great feeling knowing the manager believes in my ability to play at this level.'

The biggest pre-match question mark hung over Wayne Rooney, having missed the win at Wolves. As the Rossoneri return edged closer, however, it seemed increasingly likely the Reds' No. 10 would be available to finish the demolition job he had started in the San Siro. 'Initially he was extremely doubtful, but he's shown a rapid improvement since Saturday morning and he's OK,' Sir Alex told his pre-match press conference.

Having built a first-leg lead, United now had the conundrum of whether to forge on and finish the job or sit back and clutch a sizeable advantage. Cautious pragmatism has rarely been Sir Alex's way. 'I don't think we should be confused by the scoreline and think we have a bye into the next round,' he said. 'I don't think we're very good at defending leads. We need to play our normal game and that includes attacking. We've got to accept it's going to be a very difficult game and one we have to win.

'It's certainly an open tie, which should make for a great game of football. We hope to kill the tie by our own attacking abilities, but obviously AC Milan have to score and that should make it a really open match.'

Champions League Round of 16 Second Leg

Manchester United 4 AC Milan 0

Old Trafford, 10 March 2010

United ousted AC Milan in a two-legged knockout for the first time, and did so at a canter as a first-leg advantage was rammed home by a Wayne Rooney brace and further strikes from Ji-sung Park and Darren Fletcher. Aside from an early flurry, Leonardo's visitors never held the belief that they could prevent United reaching the quarter-finals, and they were ultimately left shattered by a resounding home win.

The only Milan player to emerge from the match with a shred of positivity was David Beckham, who enjoyed a reception of unconfined appreciation from a home support eager to recognize his efforts prior to his 2003 departure to Real Madrid. The England international was omitted from Milan's starting line-up, though, as Leonardo set up to attack from the off. Two of his front three had decent opportunities to set home nerves jangling, but Ronaldinho headed just wide from Andrea Pirlo's free-kick, while Klaas-Jan Huntelaar's poor control allowed Thiago Silva's pinpoint pass to bounce through to Edwin van der Sar.

Given the first-leg disparity, a United goal was always going to carry greater weight. When Rooney nipped ahead of Daniele Bonera and powerfully headed home Gary Neville's superb cross, the visitors suddenly required three goals to progress. Instead, they offered nothing, thanks largely to the efforts of Ji-sung Park, again detailed to shut down Pirlo, and Neville, who denied Ronaldinho the chance to reprise his first-leg magic.

If any semblance of doubt remained that United would advance, it was obliterated within a minute of the second half. Nani advanced down the left wing and arced a beautiful outside-of-the-foot pass behind the visiting defenders for Rooney to supply an equally deft finish past Christian Abbiati. Huntelaar missed a simple headed chance soon afterwards and that error was quickly punished when Paul Scholes slipped a neat pass to Park, who grabbed a deserved goal by drilling the ball low into the far corner.

Beckham was then introduced, more for his moment in the spotlight than to inspire an unlikely five-goal spree, and the Old Trafford crowd obliged with a rousing ovation for their former idol . . . although one or two mischief-makers did spark ironic boos whenever Beckham gained possession. Even they were stunned into silence, however, when Beckham's blistering volley prompted van der Sar's first meaningful act for more than an hour. United's response to Milan's temerity was to add further gloss to the scoreline, as Fletcher stooped to head home Rafael's magnificent deep cross, two minutes before the end.

For once, nary a spectator departed early, opting instead to stick around past the final whistle and lavish applause and acclaim on both a former hero and a gang of current idols who were marching into the quarter-finals once again.

Team: Van der Sar; Neville (Rafael 67), Ferdinand, Vidić, Evra; Valencia, Fletcher, Scholes (Gibson 73), Park, Nani; Rooney (Berbatov 66)
Scorers: Rooney (13, 46), Park (59), Fletcher (87)
Attendance: 74,595
Referee: Massimo Busacca

'With the kind of team I've got, it doesn't matter who we play next,' declared Sir Alex afterwards. 'When we play with that tempo, we're difficult to play against. It was a solid Manchester United performance. We got a break with an early goal in the second half and that effectively put Milan out. After that we played very, very well. It was a marvellous second-half performance.'

Once again, Ji-sung Park had been central – quite literally – to the Reds' success and plaudits rained down on the South Korean for his limpet-like nullifying job on Andrea Pirlo. 'Park was the key to our game,' said Sir Alex. 'We can talk about Rooney – and he was great – but Park's discipline, intelligence and sacrifice won us the match tactically. Pirlo is such an important player for them.'

Park's neutralizing of the Rossoneri, married to instances of incisive attacking play, facilitated a crushing aggregate victory. Looking back, Darren Fletcher relishes making his mark in such a memorable triumph against one of European football's true giants.

'To score in the Champions League against AC Milan is something you dream about as a kid, especially to round off a four–nil

Old Trafford - 100 years in the making

Old Trafford's 100th anniversary is celebrated by a breathtaking East Stand frontage, and a three-goal win over Fulham.

Ji-sung Park wheels away to celebrate vanquishing Liverpool with a superb diving header.

A pumped-up Darren Fletcher hails Dimitar Berbatov's first of a pair in the Reds' 4-0 win at Bolton.

The cruellest twist: United's season takes a double blow as Wayne Rooney is injured seconds before Bayern Munich snatch victory at the Allianz Arena.

Minus Rooney, the Reds host Chelsea. Carlo Ancelotti's side edge a controversial game to seize the title initiative.

Nani celebrates putting United ahead on aggregate during a lightning start to the second leg against Bayern.

Following Ivica Olic's strike and Rafael's dismissal, Arjen Robben's wonder-goal puts the Germans through on away goals.

Dimitar Berbatov feels the strain as United are held to a goalless draw by Blackburn, seemingly ending the Reds' title hopes.

Paul Scholes pops up in the final minute of injury time to break City's hearts again at Eastlands as United win 1-0.

The veteran midfielder cops a smacker from Gary Neville for keeping the Reds in the title hunt.

Ryan Giggs takes the plaudits after converting two nerveless penalties against in-form Tottenham.

Welcome back! Owen Hargreaves makes a late cameo, as United win at Sunderland to take the title race to the final day of the season.

Muted celebrations greet Ryan Giggs' goal against Stoke, as Chelsea's romp against Wigan takes the crown away from Old Trafford.

Sir Alex salutes his staff and players, before telling the supporters: 'We'll come back next year. That's what United do.'

United's first signing for 2010-11 came when promising defender Chris Smalling agreed to sign from Fulham.

The Reds caught everyone out in announcing a deal for Mexico's World Cup striker Javier 'Chicharito' Hernandez.

win,' says the midfielder. 'It was an unbelievable cross from Rafa and I just had to be brave in case the goalkeeper knocked my head off. He wasn't a small guy, either! But I think Milan knew they were out of it after the first goal and it became difficult for them with our tails up and rampant at Old Trafford. We deserved it, but I think they eased off in the second half because they were already beaten.'

The following day's back pages were dominated by images of David Beckham, who draped himself in a supporter's green-and-gold scarf as he left the field. Rather than discuss that controversial act, however, the veteran waxed lyrical about his return to Old Trafford and how Milan's European dream had been dashed by the goals of Wayne Rooney.

'The reception was unbelievable. The fans were really incredible. It's nice to be back,' said Beckham. 'I'll keep saying it – everyone keeps saying it – but Wayne Rooney is such an exceptional talent. Without doubt, he's one of the best players, if not the best player, in the world. He's up there with Messi and Ronaldo. They don't come much better than that.'

Eager to keep his players' feet on the ground, however, Sir Alex soon put forward some mitigation for the manner with which an injury-hit Milan side capitulated. 'It's important we calm ourselves down a bit, especially when you look at their team,' he said. 'They lost Nesta on the morning of the game and then lost Bonera at half time and had to play Ambrosini at centre-back. That was difficult for them. It was like when we played Fulham at the end of last year with no centre-backs. It's not easy. Our performance level was good. The minute we scored the second goal it became better and, in fairness, I think that goal knocked the stuffing out of them. There wasn't really a way back after that. Of course it was a fantastic result for us, but we need to calm ourselves down a little bit.'

Remaining level-headed was particularly important in light of the Reds' next opponents: Roy Hodgson's Fulham. The Cottagers, like United, had faced Italian giants ahead of the looming Sunday kick-off at Old Trafford. Fulham succumbed to a 3–1 defeat to Juventus, but their mere presence in the Europa League underlined the sterling work undertaken by Hodgson, his staff and players.

'It's a remarkable story,' admitted Sir Alex. 'Roy has formed a team that no one likes to play against – they're well organized, they keep possession well and can pass the ball. He has brought his experience and authority to the club, and Fulham play with great discipline, which is down to the manager. He's turned the whole club around and it's not going to be easy for us.'

United's aim of retaining top spot was aided by a clean bill of health from the victory over Milan. Ryan Giggs was almost ready to play again after recovering from his broken arm, but had been pencilled in for the visit of Liverpool a week later. The only first-team squad member to have picked up an injury during the course of the week was fledgling defender Ritchie De Laet, who suffered an ankle injury in the Reserves' draw with Manchester City. Owen Hargreaves had been due to start that game at Moss Lane, but his absence from the teamsheet quickly sparked speculation that he had suffered a setback in his recovery.

'Owen went to see the specialist yesterday,' explained the boss. 'That's why he didn't play last night. There's nothing wrong: he's been training and he'll definitely play in the Reserves' next game.'

There was also good news for Nemanja Vidić and Rio Ferdinand, who had both looked solid since returning from long-term injury layoffs. Two games, against Wolves and Milan, had both yielded clean sheets, and Vidić admitted he was delighted to be back alongside his old sparring partner.

'We've both been injured for a while and I think we need a few more games before we hit top form. But nothing has changed since we've been out – we always know how to play together,' said the Serbian. 'We understand each other. He knows how I will react in certain situations and it's the same the other way around. It's frustrating when you're out and hard to watch the games because you want to be out there helping your team. But we're back now and hopefully the injuries are behind us.'

The duo would continue to rebuild their partnership against the Cottagers, in the first home game since the 100th anniversary of Old Trafford's maiden match. 'The club is immensely proud to have been at Old Trafford for a hundred years,' said outgoing club secretary Ken Ramsden. 'To celebrate the centenary with our supporters is very important.' The Reds marked the occasion in several ways, most notably with a breathtaking image of Old Trafford's evolution adorning the East Stand frontage, and in inviting relatives or descendants of every United player from the stadium's first match, plus club officials and the stadium's architect, Archibald Leitch.

While ever mindful of United's rich history, all the players could focus on was taking another step towards penning another chapter of it.

Barclays Premier League

Manchester United 3 Fulham 0

Old Trafford, 14 March 2010

Wayne Rooney strode ominously past the 30-goal mark as United retook top spot in the Premier League with a hard-earned victory over Roy Hodgson's Fulham at Old Trafford. Dimitar Berbatov capped a fine personal display with a late diving header, but United were made to work for the three points by a visiting side keen to defend in numbers. Clint Dempsey and Bobby Zamora both came close for the Cottagers during the first half, but United dominated for long periods before deservedly puncturing a defence that had conceded just once in its previous five league outings.

Had Darren Fletcher gone for goal rather than unselfishly square for Rooney, allowing Stephen Kelly to avert the danger, United may have been ahead as early as the 11th minute. Instead, it was almost the visitors who took the lead, as Dempsey fired a 30-yard snapshot just past Edwin van der Sar's top corner.

Berbatov might have done better than head over from Nani's fine left-wing cross, but it took a superb reaction stop from Mark Schwarzer to repel a stinging half-volley from Rooney. The half's final opening went to Zamora, who reached Danny Murphy's chip first, but could only loop a volley well over the bar. The interval arrived with the game intriguingly balanced.

It took just 30 seconds of the second half for that balance to be tipped irreversibly towards the Reds. Rooney played a long-distance one-two with Nani amid a packed penalty area and slotted home a cool finish in front of the Stretford End. Rio Ferdinand hooked a volley just over Schwarzer's bar as the Reds continued to push for more, but his central-defensive partner, Nemanja Vidić, had to be alert soon afterwards to atone for his own slip by racing back and robbing Zamora just as the striker looked set to level the scores.

United responded by raining down blows. Berbatov and Patrice Evra were both narrowly off-target and Schwarzer saved magnificently from Darren Fletcher, but the Australian was left powerless as Rooney finally bagged his second, sweeping home after magnificent control and approach play from Berbatov. Five minutes later, the Bulgarian grabbed a deserved goal as he dived to head home Ji-sung Park's cross, capping a fine personal display and another collective effort that suggested United had hit top gear at just the right time.

Team: Van der Sar; Neville (Fabio 87), Ferdinand, Vidić, Evra; Valencia (Park 73), Carrick, Fletcher, Nani; Rooney, Berbatov
Scorers: Rooney (46, 84), Berbatov (89)
Attendance: 75,207
Referee: Mike Jones

Sir Alex Ferguson admitted United's lightning start to the second half was the platform for victory over Roy Hodgson's wily Cottagers. 'Fulham made us work because they've got good possession of the ball. They have composure and experience and they made us chase all over the pitch, particularly in the first half.

'We had some good pieces of play in the first half and their goal-keeper made some fantastic saves, but we had to speed up the play. Murphy and Baird were completely in control in midfield and we had to hurry them up and make the game a bit quicker. The start to the second half was crucial and we got a good one to put us in a good position. Our confidence grew after that.'

While Rooney's opener was the game's most important goal, his game-clinching second was the most aesthetically pleasing for Sir Alex, largely down to the inimitable approach work of Dimitar Berbatov.

'The second was the star goal,' said the boss. 'The work by Berbatov was fantastic football and he just laid it on a plate for Wayne, who took it well. Berbatov is intelligent, he has good composure on the ball and he adds to the team all the time. The making of the second goal was absolutely superb. It was very important for him to score later because he had a few opportunities, but he took one and that's important.'

As far as the Bulgarian was concerned, however, he wasn't concerned whether he scored or provided goals, so long as United kept winning. 'It's part of my job, to assist and to score,' he said. 'I preferred the second goal I gave to Wayne today to scoring the third goal.'

So, having started the day in third position, United were back atop the Premier League. With two points separating United, Chelsea and Arsenal, and games fast disappearing, one of the tightest title races in history looked certain. Although TV coverage dictated playing times and teams took turns playing before their title rivals, Michael Carrick insisted such psychological minutiae were of little consequence.

'It's not too much of a factor,' said the midfielder. 'It's nice before the game if you see [Chelsea or Arsenal] drop points, but it really doesn't affect us once we go out on the pitch. You get into game mode and focus on winning. If you apply too much pressure too early then you start doing things that maybe you shouldn't. We just believe in ourselves. The confidence and belief's there at the moment, and we're scoring good goals and scoring plenty of them. Hopefully we can maintain that through this part of the season. It is very tight and I'm sure it's going to go down to the wire. There are eight games to go and it's about winning as many as we can.'

United's ambitions of another double success were consuming the club, with an extremely upbeat ambience around Carrington. Sharing in the cheer was Owen Hargreaves, albeit for more selfish reasons. Completing 45 minutes for the Reserves against Burnley may not have mirrored the glory of lifting the Champions League trophy in Moscow, but it marked a huge step towards the resumption of a glittering career so cruelly interrupted.

'It was lovely to be back in a team environment,' grinned the England international. 'It's been a very long time and it was great to take that first step. I don't think I could have anticipated the rehab and the whole thing taking as long as it has. It's been incredibly frustrating but you just have to deal with it, take it step by step, try to be patient and do what's best. Sometimes you can't force things. Playing again was the first step and hopefully I can kick on from here.

'The reception I've had from the fans has been fantastic. I came to United and we had a good first season, and I came back early to do some training to hopefully be fit for the start of my second season and it just didn't work; it had an adverse effect and it snowballed from there. The fans have been great. When they see me they ask when I'm going to be playing and tell me they want to see me play. I've been doing my utmost to be able to play, so I look forward to being able to run out at Old Trafford again and being able to repay the faith the fans have shown. I'm not coming back just to be back; I want to come back and have as much of an impact as I did in my first season. It means a lot to me, so those are my targets and it will happen when time's ready.'

The looming visit of Liverpool would inevitably come too soon for Hargreaves, but Sir Alex Ferguson could count on having Jonny

Evans, Rafael and Ryan Giggs available. For the latter, the return would come against doctor's orders. 'The surgeon wasn't happy,' recalls the winger. 'It wasn't a problem if I got hit on it because I had a plate in the arm. The problem was that if I landed wrong, the pressure could have cracked the bone again, so I knew I'd have to try and land on my elbow if I was falling.'

Giggs was champing at the bit to be involved against a Liverpool team who had confounded expectations throughout the season. Rather than build on running United close in 2008–09, Rafael Benítez's side were struggling to stay in the race for fourth spot, leaving them unlikely to qualify for Champions League football.

A rare highlight in the Merseysiders' season had been October's win over United at Anfield, a third successive victory over the Reds, and there was a steely determination inside the United camp that the run would be halted. 'We are looking forward to the game,' said Ji-sung Park. 'This time I hope we show our strength. The fans need to get behind us and cheer us to victory.'

'Liverpool are one of our biggest rivals and we never like losing to them,' added Rio Ferdinand. 'I'm confident we can get three points on Sunday and end this streak they have over us.'

Carrington was abuzz in the run-up to the match, with excitement at being drawn against Bayern Munich in the Champions League quarter-finals (and a subsequent semi-final tie against Lyon or Bordeaux for the winners). Mainly, though, Sir Alex's men were giddy with the promise of retribution against Rafael Benítez's side.

Barclays Premier League

Manchester United 2 Liverpool 1
Old Trafford, 21 March 2010

A welcome return to the league's summit, a timely curtailment of Liverpool's hoodoo and the significant matter of local bragging rights made for a satisfying afternoon's work at Old Trafford. The Reds recovered from an early Fernando Torres strike, as Wayne Rooney tucked away the rebound from his own saved penalty before Ji-sung Park's brave diving header secured a crucial victory for Sir Alex Ferguson's side.

A packed Old Trafford basked in glorious sunshine and resounded with racket as pre-match anticipations suggested more misery would be heaped on Rafael Benítez's visitors. Instead, the men from Merseyside stunned all bar the small band of travelling supporters by taking a fifth-minute lead. Having seized possession in midfield, Torres fed Steven Gerrard and motored into the area. As the ball was ferried to Dirk Kuyt and subsequently crossed, the Spaniard somehow slipped United's radar and rose, unmarked, to power a clinical header past Edwin van der Sar.

Vitally, United soon drew level. Antonio Valencia surged into the box and was dragged to the ground by Javier Mascherano. Referee Howard Webb deemed the offence had taken place just inside the area, a decision that sparked heated debate both on the pitch and in the dugouts, as the two managers aired their views. Having earlier displayed his class in opening the scoring, Torres resorted to scuffing the penalty spot in an attempt to hamper Rooney as the United striker waited patiently for the chance to take his kick. Pepe Reina guessed correctly and produced a superb parry, but the rebound fell perfectly for Rooney to tuck away a half-volley, haul United level and end his own five-year drought against the Anfield outfit.

Having won the penalty, Valencia was proving a fruitful outlet and he continued to torment Emiliano Insúa and pepper Liverpool's area with crosses. From one, Park headed off-target when he perhaps should have tested Reina. Nani managed that feat shortly afterwards, as the Spanish stopper tipped the winger's low shot around the post.

Park had another chance early in the second half, but could only poke a left-footer straight at Reina after a surging run. He didn't have to wait long, however, to get his goal. Gary Neville's right-wing overlap bought time for Darren Fletcher to measure a cross and Park hurled himself goalwards, heading home and taking a hefty boot to the ear in the process.

Naturally, time remained for a scare or two, although the visitors' remaining chances were both spurned by the usually remorseless Torres. He miscontrolled one effort and then skewed a second, simpler, chance to Yossi Benayoun, whose tame close-range header went straight to van der Sar. A nervy, relieved buzz gripped Old Trafford but soon evolved into a defiant roar as the Reds took three vital points and, in the process, helped themselves to a healthy dose of *schadenfreude*.

Team: Van der Sar; Neville, Ferdinand, Vidić, Evra; Valencia, Carrick, Fletcher, Park (Scholes 87), Nani (Giggs 79); Rooney
Scorers: Rooney (12), Park (60)
Attendance: 75,216
Referee: Howard Webb

For once, it was a pair of unsung heroes, rather than Wayne Rooney, who were thrust into the spotlight. The breathless industry of Ji-sung Park and Darren Fletcher – plus their immaculate combination for United's winner – had Sir Alex eulogizing at full-time.

'Ji-sung was fantastic,' said the boss. 'He's one of these players that we can give roles to play and he does it because of his control and discipline. We found another role for him, which was slightly different to the one he played against Milan, but none the less he did a really important job for us. He's such a brave little lad and that courage got him the goal.

'Darren's work-rate is fantastic, and his natural energy is important. He's got such a light frame, too, but he covers every inch of ground. It's interesting that we've lost the last three games to Liverpool and Darren has missed all of them, twice with flu and once with injury.'

'I was desperate to play against them,' admits Fletcher, looking back. 'Illness and injury always seemed to make me miss the Liverpool games, which was really disappointing. Plus we'd lost a couple of times to them and it's one of the biggest games of the season. It was nice to play a part in the winner, but the goal was impossible without Gary Neville's trademark overlap. That's partially what allowed David Beckham to get all those crosses in over the years. Gary gives you that yard to get the ball out of your feet and get the ball in, and Ji's taken a stud to the head and shed blood to dive in and score the winner. That victory meant so much to us and the fans.'

The manner with which Park celebrated his winner – repeatedly beating the United badge on his chest as he sprinted away – prompted much mirth from good friend Patrice Evra. 'He punched it so hard, it was as if he was saying, "I'm in love with Man United",' laughed the Frenchman.

'It was a great feeling,' explains the South Korean. 'Derby matches are very important games, so to score the winner in a derby is a fantastic feeling. Doing it in front of the Stretford End was unbelievable as well, because you're right next to the fans' reaction. I was very happy.'

That collective joy was extended in the day's later kick-off, as Chelsea squandered a lead to draw at Blackburn, leaving them four points behind the Reds and two behind Arsenal, with a game in hand on both.

With six days until the next outing – a tricky trip to Bolton – there was plenty of time to recover and recharge. But the rare lull between fixtures was, in some ways, untimely, as the players were eager to rattle up the victories and secure a historic fourth successive title.

'The run-in is always exciting and it's obviously better if you're one of the teams involved,' said Scholes. 'And this season we're definitely in with a shout. We always say it's important to put yourselves in a position where you're in with a chance of winning the league, even if you're not leading from the front. If you can be there or thereabouts, then that's good enough because anything can happen in the run-in. We're in that position, so now it's a case of kicking on and winning games.'

Perhaps only Wayne Rooney had a played bigger role in picking up maximum points in early 2010 than Nani, whose brimming but previously unharnessed talent had now spilled over into results. The Portuguese's reward was a new contract extension, taking his deal to at least June 2014. 'It has been like a dream come true to play for Manchester United,' said the former Sporting Lisbon prodigy. 'The coaching staff have taught me so much about the game and I'm playing alongside some of the best players in the world. I'm looking forward to winning many more trophies with this team.'

Another winger, albeit vastly more experienced, was due to make his return to the starting line-up after a month on the sidelines. A fresh, energized Ryan Giggs could provide the spark to take United to glory at home and abroad, according to Darren Fletcher.

'You only need to look at his part in the injury-time winner we got against Manchester City back in September,' explained the Scot. 'His touch and pass for Michael Owen were fantastic – he didn't panic and we got the winner. Ryan has so much experience of these types of situations. It's great to have him back. He's been revitalized. He's not the flying winger he once was; he's changed his style and adapted, but that's what great players do. He has a real eye for a killer pass and he floats into areas where he's hard to mark and he's still got that burst of pace to get away from people. He's a really intelligent footballer and a great player to play with. Having him back is very important and having another player in the squad gives the manager great options.'

Giggs was available to start at Bolton, but doubts lingered over Paul Scholes and Wayne Rooney. With the Champions League trip to Munich to factor into preparations, a rest for both was on the cards. Certainly, a taxing physical examination at the Reebok Stadium was the last thing the manager and his players wanted ahead of travelling to the Allianz Arena.

'Going to Bolton is a battle – it's always been that way,' said the boss. 'Losing points at this time of year can be damaging. I think there will be a few points dropped by the three teams between now and the end of the season – not a lot, but some. We just have to make sure we don't drop as many as Arsenal and Chelsea.'

Barclays Premier League

Bolton Wanderers 0 Manchester United 4
Reebok Stadium, 27 March 2010

No Rooney, no problem. The Reds responded to the injury-enforced absence of the team's 33-goal talisman and Chelsea's seven-goal rout of Aston Villa with a comprehensive win at the Reebok Stadium. Jlloyd Samuel's clinical own goal put United ahead at the break before Dimitar Berbatov's close-range brace ensured victory and substitute Darron Gibson crashed home a late fourth with almost his first touch. The swagger with which United picked apart the tiring hosts in the latter stages, married to the steadfast fortitude on show defensively, completed an impressive all-round performance in a traditionally tricky fixture.

Matters could have been rendered easier with an early goal, but Berbatov's thumping volley was well parried to safety by Jussi Jääskeläinen and Jonny Evans fired off-target from close range from the resultant corner. But for all United's dominance, it was Edwin van der Sar who produced the game's most outstanding saves. The first came when Johann Elmander's thumping near-post shot was beaten to safety; the second was a stunning tip-over from Fabrice Muamba's top-corner-bound effort. In between, the Reds took the lead in comical circumstances.

The on-song Giggs found space down the left flank and strode towards goal before picking out a cross for Darren Fletcher at the back post. Before the ball could reach the Scot, however, the onrushing Samuel side-footed a deadly finish inside Jääskeläinen's far post to send the travelling supporters wild.

Bolton's response was to continue to probe for openings wherever possible. Whenever it wasn't, up-and-unders were the contingency plan. However, with Nemanja Vidić in flawless, dominant form, even the aerial bombardments failed to yield a route back into the match. Instead, United made the game safe. Giggs fed Fletcher, and Jääskeläinen might have done better than parry out the Scot's left-footed effort. Instead, the ball fell perfectly for Berbatov and the Bulgarian tapped home the rebound. Nine minutes later he knocked home his second of the game, a goal that owed much to the industry of Nani, who cruelly contorted Sam Ricketts before squaring for the former Spurs striker to jab home.

United relentlessly pushed for more. Nani teased Ricketts again before sliding a cross into the centre of the box, where substitute Gibson – on the field for less than two minutes – arrived to crash in a finish via the underside of the crossbar and cap an impressive performance of silk and steel.

Team: Van der Sar; Neville, Vidić, Evans, Evra; Valencia, Fletcher (Gibson 81), Giggs (Macheda 85), Scholes (Carrick 74), Nani; Berbatov
Scorers: Samuel (38 (og)), Berbatov (69, 78), Gibson (82)
Attendance: 25,370
Referee: Martin Atkinson

The victory against Bolton looked emphatic on paper, but Sir Alex Ferguson was in no doubt about where the game had been won: in defence. 'It's a tremendous result because it's a difficult place to come,' said the boss. 'You've got to deal with the aerial balls all day and it required some fantastic defending. I don't know how many times Nemanja Vidić headed that ball clear, but it must have been in the thousands! You get a sore head just watching it.

'And Edwin made two absolutely magnificent saves, the second one in particular, from Muamba. He did well to reach that. Edwin's

211

making saves like that because he's got the concentration and composure to make sure he doesn't panic when they get opportunities like Elmander's. That's the kind of experience he brings to a situation when we have to win.'

Van der Sar was happy to share the credit not only with Vidić but United's backroom staff. Midway through his post-match interview, the Dutchman dragged fitness coach Tony Strudwick before the cameras to praise his work behind the scenes at Carrington.

'Tony and his team work hard to prepare the players in the best way possible,' said Edwin. 'A lot of the progress we are making on the pitch is down to him. With his help and the tactics of René Meulensteen, Mick Phelan and the boss, it's great to be here.

'As for today, these sorts of games are ideal for someone of Vida's quality. He won a lot of aerial battles when they were putting the high balls in. You know what you are going to get with Bolton. I've been here a few times now and it's always like this. It was great to get the first goal so we had something to hang on to. Even after the second goal we were eager to go on and score more. Chelsea have scored twelve goals in two games against Portsmouth and Villa and in the end goals can be decisive. So we knew we had to get a few.'

Two days later, the Reds travelled to Munich. The players, already in high spirits after victory at Bolton, were boosted further by the presence of Wayne Rooney and Rio Ferdinand in the 22-man party. And although Bayern had struggled to navigate the group stages and reached the last eight at Fiorentina's expense only on the away-goals rule, nobody was taking them lightly.

'We're in the quarter-finals, so they're all going to be tough games, but we're always wary of teams who have a great history in the European Cup,' said Ryan Giggs. 'Bayern have a lot of trickery in their team, with Franck Ribéry and Arjen Robben, and they have some good players and match-winners. But we fancy ourselves if we play to the best of our abilities. We've won the European Cup three times and they've won it four times. We are two teams with real pedigree, experience and great players, so hopefully it'll be a good spectacle and a great game to play in.'

For Sir Alex, the message to his players was simple: score. 'Scoring away from home gives you a big advantage,' he told reporters at his pre-match press conference. 'We must try to do that. When I came here with Aberdeen [in 1983] we drew nil–nil and everybody was delighted, apart from me. I just sensed the danger. Although we managed to go through, Bayern scored twice on our ground. So, scoring is going to be important.'

Having already set a competition record of 16 games unbeaten away from home in the Champions League, Sir Alex's side could approach the latest test with optimism. 'Our record has been fantastic,' the boss conceded. 'It's an indication of the team's maturity and their understanding of how to play in Europe. We've had some big challenges in those sixteen games. A few years ago we addressed the weaknesses in our game away from home and accepted that challenge. We're going into this game in the right form and that's important. The team's come together very well and defensively we're looking really good. That pleases me more than anything.'

How things can change.

Champions League Quarter-final First Leg

Bayern Munich 2 Manchester United 1

Allianz Arena, 30 March 2010

United's season took a devastating twist in the space of ten injury-time seconds that threatened to derail months of hard work. Seemingly destined for a 1–1 draw, despite a below-par performance, the Reds were well-placed for a berth in the Champions League semi-finals when disaster struck. Wayne Rooney suffered a serious-looking ankle injury in the final minute of added time and, as he lay beating the ground in pain, Ivica Olić pinched a dramatic late winner. The reversed reminiscence of Barcelona in 1999 was lost on few, and the last-gasp devastation was polar opposite to the euphoria with which United began the game.

Little more than a minute had passed when Nani's right-wing free-kick clipped Mark van Bommel, looped up and dropped perfectly for Rooney to steer a left-footed volley into the roof of Hans-Jörg Butt's net. Already a goal up and facing a Bayern side shorn of their star player, Arjen Robben, all looked rosy for the Reds.

Instead, having a tangible advantage to protect, subliminally put Sir Alex's men in a tactical quandary. Stick to the initial game-plan of containing and countering, or sit back and hold on to that precious lead? The uncertainty manifested itself in a ragged performance in which United's reliable passing went AWOL.

Bayern gradually recovered from the early body blow and took heart from United's ambiguity. Fortunately, Edwin van der Sar was perhaps the only visiting player anywhere near his top form. The Dutchman held efforts from Franck Ribéry and Danijel Pranjić, while Olić somehow slid wide after Hamit Altintop's shanked shot flashed across the six-yard box.

Rooney's presence had Bayern's suspect defence on edge, however, and he escaped their attentions once more to latch on to Darren Fletcher's cross, only for Butt to save well at close quarters and keep the deficit at a single goal going into the interval.

Whatever measures were taken during the break to bring focus, purpose and, most crucially, composure to United's game, they weren't heeded. Van der Sar was called upon to save from Olić (twice), Altintop and Thomas Müller (twice) before, 13 minutes from time, Bayern drew level in fortuitous circumstances. Ribéry's tame free-kick looked a routine field for United's Dutch stopper until it nicked Rooney and spun inside the post. Game on.

United briefly rallied and Nemanja Vidić thumped a Ryan Giggs corner against the crossbar. But, just as the game was meandering towards a draw, substitute Mario Gómez marauded towards the United goal. In attempting to avoid tripping the German, Rooney landed awkwardly on his ankle and dropped to the ground. Gómez's run was halted, but Patrice Evra dallied in possession and failed to spot Olić rushing towards him on the blind side. The Croatian nicked possession and slotted home a composed finish to send the Allianz Arena wild.

Bayern's victory had been largely facilitated by an off-colour display from United, one which sent the Reds' record-breaking unbeaten away record up in smoke and threatened to dash hopes of reaching a third consecutive final. But a one-goal deficit was far from insurmountable against a Bayern team with clear weaknesses. More worrying was the injury to Rooney. As he was helped from the field and down the tunnel, was he taking the season's hopes with him?

Team: Van der Sar; Neville, Ferdinand, Vidić, Evra; Nani (Valencia 70), Fletcher, Carrick (Berbatov 70), Scholes, Nani (Giggs 82); Rooney

Scorer: Rooney (2)

Attendance: 66,000

Referee: Frank De Bleeckere

'We didn't do well enough, simple as that,' added Sir Alex. 'Possession has been an important part of our game over the last few years, but we just kept giving the ball away and we caused our own defeat. It's a disappointing performance, possession-wise. Bayern were the better team. You have to give them credit because they pressed the ball well. It was a big effort by them in that respect. None the less, we should be better than that in possession of the ball. We just kept giving it away and it was our downfall.

'At Old Trafford it'll be a different game. We'll be much better, we won't be giving the ball away the way we did tonight and hopefully we'll recover. We've got an away goal, which is an advantage, but we'll go out to win the game. That's the important thing.'

But what of Rooney? As the United talisman limped away from the Allianz Arena on crutches, everybody wanted to know how long he would be sidelined for. He would almost certainly miss Chelsea's visit to Old Trafford four days later, but a definitive diagnosis would have to wait until Rooney returned to Manchester for a scan. 'Pray' urged the *Sun*'s back page, summing up most of the nation's thoughts, if only for England's looming World Cup campaign. As March drew to a close, with the Reds in charge of the title race and well-placed in Europe, despite defeat in Germany, the entire season appeared to be hanging in limbo, linked inexorably to the damage done to one man's right ankle. Sir Alex's grim assertion summed up the situation: 'We'll have to wait and see.'

10

April

Wayne Rooney was everywhere. Front pages, back pages and in super slow-motion from countless angles on every television news bulletin. All of it speculation and filler as the football world held its breath and waited for an announcement on the striker's well-being. In every image or snippet of action from the Allianz Arena, pain was etched across Rooney's face. According to him, it was a blend of agony and rage as he lay writhing on the Munich turf, aware of the short-term implications of Bayern's late winner and the wider perspective of his own season.

'I was aware they'd scored when I heard their fans. I was gutted,' says Rooney, looking back. 'To get injured and lose the game in the same few seconds was hard to take. I've never really injured my ankle that badly, but when I went over on it I felt something pop. I thought it was my ligaments but it was a blood vessel on my nerves – that's what the pain was. When I got back to England my foot was all swollen and bruised, but the scan showed it wasn't too bad. I was quite fortunate, really.'

Rooney's relief was still fresh when a United club statement announced: 'We're pleased to report Wayne has not suffered a fracture.

The scan revealed only minor ligament damage.' Sir Alex Ferguson soon added a timeframe, speculating that the striker was likely to miss 'two to three weeks' of action. That meant gargantuan clashes against Chelsea and Bayern Munich, plus an invariably sapping trip to Blackburn, would have to be tackled without the star of United's season.

Nevertheless, the boss was far from downbeat going into a potentially decisive game in his side's hunt for a history-making 19th English league title. 'Wayne is obviously a loss, but if you look at us over the season we have been missing defenders and midfielders and yet we are still a point clear at the top of the league,' he said. 'We're in the middle of the Champions League quarterfinal with an away-goal advantage and we have also won the League Cup. The players will not let Wayne's absence upset them. They know the incentive for the next two games. We've been in worse situations this season, having to win without two or three big players. And we've coped.'

'Obviously we don't want any injuries, particularly to our best players, so it is disappointing to lose Wayne,' added Gary Neville. 'But we have quality players throughout our squad and it's an opportunity for someone else to come in and show what they can do. In the past, other players have always stepped up to the plate for us and made a contribution and we have got goals throughout our team. That's something we need to show on Saturday.'

While Rooney's absence dominated the pre-match build-up, Chelsea would also be without key players Michael Essien, Ashley Cole, Ricardo Carvalho, Branislav Ivanović and José Bosingwa. 'All the teams in the run-in will point towards the fact they get injuries and suspensions,' said Neville. 'They're just things you have to cope with. It's all about who deals with them best.'

Barclays Premier League

Manchester United 1 Chelsea 2

Old Trafford, 3 April 2010

United's title aspirations were dealt an almighty blow as Chelsea exploited a sluggish first-half display to take a two-point lead in the race for the Premier League title. Visibly fresher than their hosts for having a full week to prepare for the game, the Blues forged ahead inside 20 minutes through Joe Cole's neat flick, before Didier Drogba's highly contentious late second goal settled matters. Kiko Macheda halved the arrears, but the Reds could not muster a vital equalizer.

United were left to rue a below-par start to the game in which Chelsea were sharper both with and without the ball. Dimitar Berbatov operated as a lone striker with central support from Ji-sung Park, but neither received sufficient service to trouble John Terry and Alex in the centre of the visitors' defence. The towering Brazilian flashed a header wide from Frank Lampard's corner in the fourth minute as Chelsea's intent flickered. In response, Berbatov headed comfortably over Petr Čech's bar from Antonio Valencia's cross. It was as close as United came in the first period.

Neither side could claim to be particularly productive in attack, but Chelsea took their one clear chance. Not that it was a bread-and-butter goal, by any means. Florent Malouda's darting raid between three United players allowed him to pull back from the left byline, and Cole flicked an audacious finish past a rooted Edwin van der Sar to hand Chelsea the advantage.

Then began a trend that would characterize the game: debatable refereeing decisions. Ji-sung Park was seemingly tripped by Yuri Zhirkov, while Gary Neville unceremoniously barged Nicolas Anelka to the ground. Both could easily have been penalties. Mike Dean awarded nothing. The second half began with a let-off for

United as Paulo Ferreira stormed through on goal. But the Portuguese was hindered by indecision and eventually slid a cross-shot ahead of Nicolas Anelka and past the far post.

Buoyed by that reprieve, and a clear upsurge in United's intent and tempo, the home support played its part with an uplifting soundtrack. Patrice Evra drilled wide, Ji-sung Park skewed off-target and Berbatov sent a pair of headers outside Čech's framework. Just as it seemed the Reds were building enough pressure to finally crack the visitors' defence, along came the hammer blow. Salomon Kalou slipped a pass through for Drogba, clearly a yard ahead of the United defence. Almost every pair of eyes inside Old Trafford flickered towards referee's assistant Simon Beck. No flag. The Ivorian striker, without a second thought of play being stopped, lashed a shot inside Edwin van der Sar's near post. Game over.

Or was it? Two United substitutes combined with nine minutes remaining to pull a goal back. Fine play from Nani down the left culminated in his cross being bundled home by Macheda, although Chelsea argued the Italian had been guilty of handball. Suddenly both sides had grievances to air.

With time ticking away, the Stretford End urged United forward in wave after wave of attack, probing for another route to Čech's goal. When it arrived in the final minute of normal time, Berbatov could only volley Neville's cross straight at the goalkeeper. The champions were beaten, and the challengers were suddenly in control of both sides' destiny.

Team: Van der Sar; Neville, Ferdinand, Vidić, Evra; Valencia, Fletcher
  (Gibson 86), Scholes (Macheda 72), Giggs, Park (Nani 72);
  Berbatov
Scorer: Macheda (81)
Attendance: 75,217
Referee: Mike Dean

'It's a disappointing result,' sighed Sir Alex afterwards. 'I thought we looked leggy in the first half. We took too long to get going. Chelsea were by far the better team. But in the second half we did well and we were unfortunate not to get something from the game.'

Inevitably, Didier Drogba's controversial second goal provided the biggest post-match talking point. 'What I can't understand is that the linesman was directly in line with it,' said Sir Alex. 'There's nobody in front of him and he gets it wrong. In a game of this magnitude you really need quality officials. We didn't get them today and it was a poor, poor performance. That's twice we've been undone by refereeing decisions against Chelsea; it was the same down at Stamford Bridge. So we've caught the wrong end of them this season. It's unfortunate but it happens. Sometimes you get the decisions for you, sometimes you don't.'

'It was probably a one–one game, and the fact that Drogba's off-side goal was given in such a big game just beggars belief,' reflects Gary Neville. 'That goal killed us. You look back and think those two points could have cost us the title. It doesn't bear thinking about. You could point to our individual mistakes throughout the season or say that decisions even themselves up over a campaign, but in such a big game, so close to the end of the season, against your main rivals, you'd be happy to take a point because you'd still be in control of the championship.

'It was a massive moment for us. In the second half we played well, pulled a goal back at two–nil and still had more chances after that. The big thing was them going two–nil up when we looked like we were going to score. The decision at Stamford Bridge was equally horrendous. Those decisions have given Chelsea six points and we've ended up with none, so it's a massive swing in points.'

United were no longer in pole position, and Sir Alex was quick to concede his side were at the mercy of Carlo Ancelotti's Blues for the remainder of the league season.

'Chelsea are favourites now, no question,' he said. 'There are five games left and they are two points ahead and four goals better off in goal difference. I'm certain we'll respond, but we could win our next five games and still not win the league. If Chelsea win their five, they're champions.'

With Bayern Munich due at Old Trafford four days later, there was no time to lick wounds. 'We have to raise the players,' said the boss. 'It's a European tie and an opportunity to get to the semi-finals of the Champions League with a final in Madrid beckoning. That's incentive enough.'

'We were down after the first Bayern game, but we can't allow ourselves to be down again,' added Nemanja Vidić. 'We need to face facts that we have been disappointing in the last two games, but we also need to keep our heads up and not feel sorry for ourselves.'

With each passing day, however, the likelihood of a shock boost grew. The day after Chelsea's win at Old Trafford, Wayne Rooney was undergoing strenuous recovery work at Carrington, testing his ankle to its limit in a bid to have him ready to face Bayern. As the Germans' visit neared, Rooney knew he would be available to play a part.

'I knew I'd be available three days before the game,' he says. 'I did some intense training, did another session the day after that and then the day before the game I trained with the team. The manager still had a decision to make about whether he wanted to risk me. I think there was a bit of a risk involved, but myself and the manager decided it was a risk worth taking.'

Although one or two tabloid whispers betrayed Rooney's fast-tracked recovery, Sir Alex was keen to downplay expectations, and perhaps catch Bayern off-guard. The day before the game, the striker sat out the morning training session, open for the first 15 minutes to the world's media as dictated by UEFA policy. That afternoon, however, he joined in full training. Over at Old Trafford, Sir Alex was keeping his cards close to his chest.

Asked if Rooney had a chance of involvement, Sir Alex said: 'No. We have made some good progress with the lad. The medical team have done some fantastic work, but I'm not prepared to take a risk on a player that's not a hundred per cent fit. We're looking more at the Manchester City game, or maybe Blackburn as a sub. The boy is making good progress, but it's an ankle injury. It's no different to any other ankle injury. I can't take a risk.'

As far as the public, the media and Bayern Munich were concerned, Rooney would not be playing. Regardless of his projected non-involvement, Sir Alex was keen to stress the importance of a choral onslaught from the home support in United's bid to reach the semi-finals.

'Old Trafford has got that suction towards the goal when we are in full flow and the crowd is really up for it,' said the boss. 'It's an amazing feeling. It's not always entirely because of the team, it's because of the fans too. They make it happen. Hopefully that's the case against Bayern. If we get the performance level right, then it makes a difference. It makes a difference to the supporters and to the players' belief and confidence.

'The semi-finals of the European Cup is a fantastic incentive. That would be a great achievement for the players, having been a goal down against a very good, experienced Bayern Munich team. Most people would think we have a good chance. I think we do. The tie certainly is not over, but there is work to be done.'

Sat alongside his manager, veteran winger Ryan Giggs was keen to be able to deposit another epic Old Trafford evening in his memory bank. 'We've all seen some great nights here and hopefully this can be another one,' he said. 'We are all part of that – the players, the fans, the coaches. There is no better feeling as a player than when the Old Trafford crowd is behind you on a Wednesday night. A big European game against Bayern Munich is what you become a professional footballer for; this is what you look forward to.'

Champions League Quarter-final Second Leg

Manchester United 3 Bayern Munich 2
(4–4 on aggregate, Bayern Munich win on away goals)

Old Trafford, 7 April 2010

Ten-man United exited the Champions League in heartbreaking fashion, as Bayern Munich lost an enthralling encounter at Old Trafford yet still reached the semi-finals by virtue of Arjen Robben's stunning late volley. A storming start had United two goals ahead inside seven minutes through Darron Gibson and Nani. And when Nani added his second four minutes before half time, the Reds looked certain to coast into a last-four tie with Lyon. But, little more than a minute later, a catastrophic concession to Ivica Olić changed the complexion of the tie completely.

Bayern needed only one more goal to progress and their quest was aided just after the break by the dismissal of Rafael for a second bookable offence. United spurned further chances to put the tie to bed before mounting Bayern pressure culminated in Robben's scorching volley direct from a Franck Ribéry corner. That goal capped a dramatic turnaround of fortunes on a night that had started so brightly for the Reds. Even before Gibson and Nani bagged early goals, the Old Trafford crowd had received an almighty boost when the United teamsheet revealed the shock inclusion of Wayne Rooney.

Eight days of hysterical speculation could finally die down: United's talisman was back. Bayern could also count on reinforcements, though, as Robben won his own high-profile race against time and Bastian Schweinsteiger returned from suspension. Predictably, given the late personnel boon, Old Trafford hummed with anticipation. Less than three minutes in, the Theatre of Dreams was pinching itself. Rafael rolled off the attentions of Franck Ribéry and curled a pass infield to Rooney. His instant lay-off to Gibson allowed the young midfielder to advance on goal and poke a 25-yard shot into the bottom corner.

The scenes of celebration had hardly ceased when they were intensified just four minutes later. Rooney spread a fine pass wide to Antonio Valencia and the Ecuadorian teased Bayern right-back Holger Badstuber, twice shimmying to cross before firing in a low delivery for Nani to cheekily back-heel inside the far post. United's dominance was absolute, although midway through the first period Rafael picked up a booking for an altercation with Mark van Bommel. Soon afterwards the Brazilian fired past the far post after running virtually half the field with the ball.

Bayern threatened for the first time as Olić forced a sharp save from Edwin van der Sar, but United's response was to move further ahead, as Nani fired Valencia's pull-back high into Butt's net. Just as the tie appeared dead and buried, disaster struck. United were caught short at the back, Thomas Müller headed on for Olić and the Croatian bundled past Michael Carrick before firing past van der Sar from the tightest of angles.

Within five minutes of the second half, the plot thickened as Rafael received a second caution for tugging Ribéry's shirt, although Bayern's haranguing of referee Nicola Rizzoli would later spark debate. Initially, United's response was positive, as Nani and Darren Fletcher both came close to a killer goal. Between those two chances, John O'Shea replaced Rooney, who had been visibly struggling since taking two heavy hits on his right ankle midway through the first half.

As the home side retreated, Bayern's possession carried greater menace, although without examining van der Sar. On the break, Nani forced a reflex save from Butt and Carrick fired over from the resulting corner. Then, substitute Mario Gómez glanced a header onto the top of the crossbar before Robben struck a hammer blow on 73 minutes, volleying Ribéry's corner through a crowd of players and inside the far post.

Time remained for the Reds to salvage something, but Bayern turned in a masterclass in keep-ball to prevent any further opportunities. Out of Europe and playing catch-up in the title race, eight days of misery had turned United's season upside down.

Team: Van der Sar; Rafael, Ferdinand, Vidić, Evra; Valencia, Carrick
(Berbatov 80), Fletcher, Gibson (Giggs 81), Nani; Rooney
(O'Shea 55)
Scorers: Gibson (3), Nani (7, 41)
Attendance: 74,482
Referee: Nicola Rizzoli

'I don't think the best team has won the tie,' Sir Alex Ferguson said
afterwards. 'I think we played better tonight than they did. I don't
think anything's been missing in our campaign, and I don't think
we were fatigued tonight. With them having the extra man, they
made the ball work. We defended very well and it's taken an exceptional goal to finish the tie. It was a tremendous hit by Robben. But
our performance was excellent. We were just very unlucky tonight.'

The manager was merely reiterating what he had already told
his crestfallen players. Rarely has Old Trafford's home dressing
room known such disappointment and despair, but Sir Alex was
quick to do his best to rouse the troops.

'I think the manager lifted the lads straight away by saying he
was proud of us because of our fantastic effort and work-rate, and
the performance in the first half,' reveals Darren Fletcher. 'He was
saying, "What more can I ask for?" After playing well, we were out
of Europe in the quarter-finals, and having responded from the disappointment of the first leg and then getting knocked out at home
he said he was proud of us. From there it was all about rallying the
troops because there was still a league to win.'

But after suffering such a seismic defeat in such galling circumstances, it was inevitable disappointment would linger. 'Don't
let me start about Munich,' Patrice Evra says, even now. 'That was
the twist of the season, I think. I have respect for Bayern Munich
but, for me, that game was Manchester United against Manchester
United. We killed ourselves. To be winning one–nil after seventy-
five minutes in Germany and lose two–one, then be winning here

226

three–nil and go out of the competition is such a bad memory. We did not have the right spirit in the first game. We had the right spirit in the second one but we were unlucky. Robben can try that strike again as many times as he wants and he will never score again. We threw away the chance to reach the Champions League semi-finals.'

'After the disappointment of losing to Barcelona in the Rome final, and having the experience of getting to the final in the last two seasons, we felt this year we could do the same,' adds Darren Fletcher. 'The reason the Bayern game is so disappointing is because Bayern carried the luck with them over the two games. We've got to be disappointed with the goals we conceded and the manner in which we lost the games – we gifted them goals, which you can't afford to do in Europe – but everything seemed to go their way in the tie. Having played so well in the first half at Old Trafford, we really felt we were going to go on and win comfortably. The rest is history: Olić's goal, the red card and Robben's wonder goal. There was a great opportunity there for us to get to the final. All due respect to Lyon but we'd have fancied our chances in that semi-final. The biggest thing is to learn from it. You can maybe get away with one mistake in Europe, but two or three and you're going to get it.'

Two turning points dominated post-match discussion: Olić's strike before half time and Rafael's sending-off. 'It was a foul, I thought,' recalls Michael Carrick, who was left prostrate as Bayern's Croatian striker hit the visitors' pivotal first goal. 'Olić stood on my ankle and took my boot off. I was going to let it run to Edwin and he stood on my ankle, pinned my foot down and I couldn't get out of the way of the ball. My boot came off, I couldn't really react and he's managed to squeeze it in from a tight angle. I probably should have headed it anyway, but the fact that he stood on me put me off balance. It was probably a foul but it wasn't given. Sometimes you get those, sometimes you don't. A number of things went against us that night, but what can you do?'

As the stunned players filtered into Carrington the next morning, the mood had not lightened, especially for Rafael, who, in the eyes of the media, shouldered sizeable blame for the Reds' exit. As ever, when an individual comes under fire at United, the squad quickly closed ranks.

'People are talking as if Rafael has killed someone,' said Patrice Evra. 'A player who's twenty-nine or thirty-two can make the same mistake. OK, the first yellow card for kicking van Bommel, he shouldn't have done that. But the second one, I think the German players, as well as my France team-mate Franck Ribéry, put pressure on the referee.

'You need to make mistakes to be a good player – you learn from them, you become stronger. Rafael is a good player and he will be a different-class player now he has had this experience. When I came here I was twenty-four and I had already played for France and reached the final of the Champions League with Monaco. But the first six months at Old Trafford was difficult. I didn't expect I'd receive such a big slap in the face, but I went on to show why United bought me.

'Against Bayern Munich, I think Rafael played brilliantly. The morning after the game I told him to smile, to be happy, because he has the privilege of playing for Manchester United. I know the mentality of Rafael. He has a lot of hunger and I'm sure he'll be one of the best right-backs United have ever had.'

With fresh wounds so agonizingly tender, the only way forward was to look forward. And, as if by magic, the club pulled the proverbial rabbit out of the hat to deliver some timely good news. Mexico striker Javier Hernández, better known in his homeland as 'Chicharito' or 'little pea' was to join the club subject to a work permit, making him the second prospective new signing for 2010–11 after defender Chris Smalling.

In one of the most clinically executed transfers in United's history, not a single rumour preceded the announcement. Hernández had even been a guest of the club during the Bayern Munich clash, but still nobody saw it coming . . . much to the delight of chief executive David Gill.

'We'd been tracking him for a while,' he reveals. 'He really came on the scene back in the autumn. Our chief scout, Jim Lawlor, was particularly keen on him and we sent him out there. We watched a lot of him and got as much information and detail as we could via games he played and through Mexican websites. Then we went out there and Jim met with the club. We ended up doing the deal pretty quickly. It was very unusual. To get a deal done under the radar in today's world, with the media coverage the way it is, is fantastic. We had him in a box for the Bayern game. We thought putting him in the directors' box might be a bit risky so we put him in a private box instead.'

'It's a dream and I feel so happy,' beamed the Mexican. 'I've really enjoyed my week in Manchester – the stadium, the atmosphere at the club and the history are incredible. At the game, the atmosphere was incredible with all the fans singing. It was fantastic to see and I hope I can do great things here.'

The signing of Hernández ensured United strikers present and future were side-by-side in the papers, as more speculation raged over Wayne Rooney's ankle injury. The England international was expected to be out for little more than a week, but that still ruled him out of the Reds' must-win trip to Blackburn.

'I don't think it's as serious as we said when he got the injury the first time, but I think he'll be ready for the City game,' Sir Alex told his pre-match press briefing. 'We've got more time to work on it, anyway. Other than that, everyone else is fit.

'Given the nature of the game on Wednesday and the energy spent, we have to address the situation of freshness. We've got a squad to use – we have the likes of Paul Scholes, Ryan Giggs and Gary Neville and we also have John O'Shea back now. He came on against Bayern and did thirty minutes' work – it's good to get him back because he's such a versatile player for us. Sam Allardyce's team is in fantastic form. Blackburn is always a difficult place to go and they have a good home record. Hopefully we can get the energy back in the team. If we do that we'll be all right.'

Barclays Premier League

Blackburn Rovers 0 Manchester United 0

Ewood Park, 11 April 2010

United's plight went from bad to worse as Blackburn's ploy of doggedly playing for a point frustrated the Reds for 90 agonizing minutes. Antonio Valencia and Dimitar Berbatov spurned presentable chances in either half, but Rovers and their limited ambition ultimately proved too sapping a foe for United to overcome, giving Chelsea the chance to open up a four-point lead in the title race.

As expected, Sir Alex Ferguson made several changes to the side that started against Bayern Munich four days earlier. Wayne Rooney missed out, while Darren Fletcher and Patrice Evra were rested, the latter to make way for the long-awaited return of John O'Shea. Berbatov and Federico Macheda formed a strike duo ahead of a four-man midfield of Valencia, Paul Scholes, Ryan Giggs and Nani.

The game's tone was set early as Blackburn were encamped in their own half, with two massed banks of players interested in little more than breaking up United attacks and nicking possession wherever possible. It took almost 30 minutes for the first opening, as Paul Robinson did well to keep out Valencia's low shot. Just before half time, the Rovers goalkeeper repeated the feat by saving with his legs from the Ecuadorian, who should have scored after a magnificent through-ball from Berbatov.

United's cause was hampered in the second period when Giggs sustained a slight hamstring injury, prompting the introduction of Darron Gibson. By then, Blackburn substitute David Dunn had loosened United's stranglehold on the midfield battle and it was becoming increasingly difficult to forge even half-chances.

One finally arrived in the 80th minute as Scholes's crossfield ball was headed back by Neville to Berbatov. But the Bulgarian couldn't get a clean shot on goal and managed only to stab a tame effort straight at Robinson. He managed a superior connection on his next shot, but its ambitious range and wayward direction ensured no further work for the Rovers goalkeeper. Evra replaced the injured O'Shea as United pressed but, with all Sir Alex's substitutes already made, Rio Ferdinand was forced to soldier on after suffering a groin strain and a dislocated finger.

Nevertheless, urged on by 8,000 baying away fans in the Darwen End, the Reds launched countless forays forward and resorted to several long balls. One final mêlée culminated in Neville's left-foot shot creeping just past the post before the final whistle signalled the end of the contest and, perhaps, United's rule over England.

Team: Van der Sar; Neville, Ferdinand, Vidić, O'Shea (Evra 79); Valencia, Scholes, Giggs (Gibson 58), Nani; Berbatov, Macheda (Park 66)
Scorers: n/a
Attendance: 29,912
Referee: Peter Walton

'It's going to be very, very difficult to win this league now,' a downbeat Sir Alex admitted afterwards. 'We'll have a lifeline if Chelsea blow it, but in their eyes they have an easy game against Bolton on Tuesday. They'll expect to win that and that would put them four points clear. Our play today in the last third wasn't good enough and the result isn't what we expected given the amount of possession we had. We had the chances in the game – I don't think Blackburn made any chances – but dominating possession isn't enough. We should have done better.'

After a devastating run of results, United's dressing room at Ewood Park resounded with pin-drop devastation. 'It felt like we'd lost six–nil, to be honest,' reveals John O'Shea. 'Keeping a clean sheet gave us some crumb of comfort, but not really . . . We'd needed to win. We had some decent enough chances, I suppose. Antonio's was a good chance and it was a good save from the goalkeeper, but it's just one of those games where you think an early goal would have made such a difference. Blackburn set out to draw the game and they defended doggedly. We knew we'd have to deal with that, but it felt like a defeat afterwards.'

'To be honest, we were down after going out to Bayern Munich,' admits Gary Neville. 'Drawing a game at Blackburn isn't completely out of the ordinary, but to have two-thirds of the possession, the opponents not have a shot on your goal, have all the play and not look like scoring is so unlike us. For the possession we had, we should have scored at least one in that game. We had one clear chance through Antonio and maybe a couple through Berba, and you look back at those moments and say "If only".'

United's grip on the Premier League trophy was slipping. Chelsea, as expected, overcame Bolton at Stamford Bridge, albeit by a solitary goal in an unconvincing display, and maintained their four-point lead with four games remaining.

The next stop for United was Eastlands, perhaps the last place anyone of a Red persuasion would want to be at the time, with United punch-drunk and City finally punching above their weight. Again, some speculated that the game could mark a power shift in Manchester football as the Blue faction rode into the Champions League alongside their ailing neighbours. Others suspected United could once again put City in their place and display the enduring class of champions.

There seemed little chance of the latter, though, if the football media were to be believed. 'I live locally so I'm aware of everything that's said,' says Gary Neville. 'We were almost the whipping boys, the underdogs. When you're proud to play for United and you've won so many trophies, it hurts to hear your club being talked of in that way and disrespected. It was almost as if we were a bunch of has-beens and City were the new force. All week you could sense that atmosphere.'

The ambience around Carrington remained bullish, and was further lifted when it was announced that Paul Scholes would be playing on for another year. The deal followed a hint of coercion from Sir Alex Ferguson, who had to convince his midfield maestro that one more season at the peak of the game would not be too taxing.

'I still want to be able to contribute something,' concedes Scholes. 'I don't want to be here just for the sake of it. The manager came to me before the City game and said he wanted me to stay another year and thought I could hopefully still give something next year. Of course, that's all the persuading you need. If he wants me, I'm staying.'

For Scholes, Neville and fellow veteran Ryan Giggs, few fixtures can rival clashes between United and City. For Giggs, the chance to appear in his 33rd successive Manchester derby was too tempting, and the winger was selective with the truth when evaluating his hamstring injury with the club's medical staff ahead of the game.

'I hurt my hamstring against Blackburn and I thought my season was over, to be honest,' he recalls. 'But I had treatment and it responded really well and I was desperate to play. I trained on the Friday and I could still feel my hamstring a little bit, but I was desperate to play so I just kept quiet.'

With the title seemingly out of sight, even though Chelsea would have to follow United's trip to Eastlands with a tricky away game at Champions League challengers Tottenham, the Manchester derby became a stand-alone fixture. Forget national rule: this was all about local authority.

Barclays Premier League

Manchester City 0 Manchester United 1
Eastlands, 17 April 2010

Victories are rarely sweeter. A day after extending his epic career by a further year, Paul Scholes capped another midfield masterclass with an unforgettable winner just seconds before the final whistle at Eastlands. After a tense and tight derby encounter, the 35-year-old popped up in the final minute of added time to superbly nod home Patrice Evra's cross and keep alive United's dream of a fourth straight title. Three points was no less than United deserved, and it was fitting for Scholes to procure them, having dictated the tempo of the game throughout.

Of United's three pre-match injury doubts, Wayne Rooney and Ryan Giggs both started, but Rio Ferdinand's groin injury prompted a return for Jonny Evans alongside Nemanja Vidić in the centre of defence.

With a vocal home support baying for blood, United swiftly set about silencing the masses, dominating possession and coming within inches of taking the lead through Darren Fletcher's 25-yard effort. Carlos Tévez's free-kick drew a fine full-length catch from Edwin van der Sar, but City wouldn't muster another chance all half. Instead, United spurned the two clearest openings of the first 45 minutes. Antonio Valencia held off Wayne Bridge to head to Rooney, who shimmied into space before firing uncharacteristically off-target. The Ecuadorian was soon at it again, only for Giggs to stab his low cross straight at Shay Given.

The Reds continued to boss matters after the break, but City's speed on the break yielded a close call when Craig Bellamy blazed horribly off-target when a square pass for Tévez looked a better option.

Nani replaced Darron Gibson as Sir Alex Ferguson upped the ante, only for Roberto Mancini to respond by sending on Patrick Vieira for Adam Johnson. The two substitutes were soon involved as Nani slid Giggs's cross wide under heavy pressure from Vieira. United needed to win, but City could countenance a draw and sat back, breaking sporadically. One such raid presented Gareth Barry with a glorious chance, but having worked his way into the United area, the England midfielder elected to tumble under Gary Neville's attentions rather than go for goal, and his half-hearted appeals yielded no penalty.

Giggs's lob was kept out by Given, and substitute Dimitar Berbatov – on for Rooney – headed just past the post from Nani's cross before a City set piece almost brought disaster in the final ten minutes. Nemanja Vidić produced two brilliant interceptions to thwart the hosts, first flicking a cross away from the lurking Nedum Onuoha, then toe-poking clear the danger in an almighty goalmouth scramble.

When Giggs just failed to reach Nani's cross in the final minute of normal time, it seemed Sir Alex would have to chalk this up as 'one of those days'. Instead, Evra led one final foray down the left flank, exchanged passes with substitute Gabriel Obertan and floated a superb cross into the centre of the City area. There, arriving late into the box in trademark fashion, was Scholes to execute a perfect header that nestled just inside Given's post. Cue wild scenes behind Given's goal as players and supporters blended in a cocktail of joy. It was a third injury-time winner of the season for the Reds against the Blues, and very probably the most satisfying of the lot. Cancel that shift in power.

Team: Van der Sar; Neville, Vidić, Evans, Evra; Valencia (Obertan 80), Fletcher, Gibson (Nani 59), Scholes, Giggs; Rooney (Berbatov 74)
Scorer: Scholes (90)
Attendance: 47,019
Referee: Martin Atkinson

'It's a massive game for fans of both teams and I know how much this will mean to our fans. I can assure you it means exactly the same to us,' panted a still-out-of-breath Paul Scholes at full time. 'To win in a Manchester derby is a big thing, however you do it, and that's three times this season we've managed to score in the last minute to win games. We just keep going. Some teams play for a draw but we want to win all our games and that guarantees we'll go right to the end.'

The dramatic finale made for flared tempers among the home supporters, and Darron Gibson, having been substituted, was well placed to sample the ire. 'I was going mad on the bench near the City fans,' he recalls. 'They weren't happy and there were nearly a few punches thrown in there. When we scored, a few of them leaned over to try and get to us, but there's nothing you can do about that. It's a tense atmosphere and tempers flare, but I don't mind that. To be honest, I wouldn't have minded being punched, so long as we won!'

That enduring sense of satisfaction, allied to the euphoric celebrations by all at full time, illustrates how important victory was. 'There was a lot riding on that game in the week leading up to it,' says Gary Neville.

'You could tell at the start of the game that it was carnival time for them. There was a feeling around the place that it was their day, that they were going to win, that they were going to get fourth place and we were going to end up losing the championship on the day. What they weren't reckoning on was that they were playing United, and it doesn't quite happen that way. They were up against eleven players who were determined to make sure we won the game.

'Paul Scholes was outstanding on the day and for him to pop up with the winner was unbelievable. For me, it was the outstanding moment of the season. We knew we were out of the league if we didn't win the game. We were the ones trying to win the game, whereas City were bringing defensive midfielders on for forwards. They were happy with a draw even though they were at home. Three times we've shown them that we go to the last second of every match. The mentality of the team is always to try to win every match, so late winners aren't luck. We got the break we needed with a great cross and a great header. It's the hardest way to win, of course, but the best way. If you can score in the last minute, there's no comeback – they just don't have the time.'

Neville's ever-simmering emotions boiled over at full time, as he planted a congratulatory kiss on match-winner Scholes's lips, an image captured by photographers and splashed across the following day's back pages.

'Nev did get some stick for that, but poor Scholesy couldn't do much, could he?' confirms John O'Shea. 'He was the poor victim who tried to push him off, but it was too late. That's Gaz for you. I don't think it was for his benefit, mind you. I think it was to make the City fans feel that little bit angrier!'

Looking back, Neville can see the funny side. 'A few people have given me a bit of stick, but I've spoken to a lot of my mates, who said they'd have done exactly the same if they'd been able to get to him!' he laughs. 'I was just so happy.' And what of Scholes's reaction to being pounced upon by his long-term friend and colleague? 'A kiss on the lips from Nev is worth it any time after a winner against City!' he wryly smiles.

'To be honest, it was just an incredible moment. We'd won to keep the league alive,' continues Neville. 'All week you could sense the atmosphere from their fans, and it was a sweet victory for that alone. Don't get me wrong: City will be powerful over the next few years – we've got to get our heads around that. The players they're signing, the managers they've got, the fanbase they've got . . . they will be powerful. But that was a sweet day. That's not to say we haven't suffered against them in the past or will do in the future – you have your day and you celebrate; next time it could be their day. In that case you have to go and drink for sorrow rather than drink for joy.'

With no Champions League involvement to consider and a full week before Spurs' visit to Old Trafford, United's jubilant players were allowed out to celebrate the victory. 'It's a rare occasion,' says John O'Shea. 'We did go out afterwards, a few of us. We get an extra day off here and there, but you'd gladly give it all back to be involved in the Champions League semi-final.'

There was double cause for celebration as Chelsea were

comprehensively beaten by Tottenham, while Blues skipper John Terry was sent off. Just a point off the pace with three games remaining, United were, incredibly, back in the hunt. Having also beaten Arsenal four days before overturning Chelsea, Spurs had done United a major favour. Now, however, the division's form team were set to provide stern opposition at Old Trafford.

'This is the best Tottenham team in my time at United,' Sir Alex said. 'Harry Redknapp's done a great job. Of course I was delighted with Spurs' displays against Arsenal and Chelsea. They were absolutely brilliant and could have won by more goals. That was championship form you saw from them, beating two of the best three teams in the league convincingly. We know it's a difficult game, but we need to take advantage of last weekend.'

Having been thrust back into contention, United's players were out of a rut and relishing the chance to take on Spurs. With Chelsea playing Stoke the following day, victory for the Reds at Old Trafford would temporarily take the champions two points clear.

'Last weekend was great,' said Wayne Rooney, who would miss out with a minor groin injury. 'To beat City in the last minute was fantastic, and then Tottenham went and made the day even better for us by beating Chelsea. The title race is back on and it's now between us and Chelsea. We need to win our three games and hope Chelsea slip up somewhere. But we're feeling confident. The win over City has definitely helped and I think you could tell what it meant to us by looking at the celebrations after the final whistle. We're fully focused on getting nine points from our final three games. Then, if Stoke, Liverpool or Wigan can do us a favour [by beating Chelsea] we'd be very grateful. But all we can do is win our games and hope for the best.'

Barclays Premier League

Manchester United 3 Tottenham Hotspur 1

Old Trafford, 24 April 2010

United reclaimed top spot with another impressive display of fortitude and spirit as the Reds beat on-song Spurs in dramatic fashion. Harry Redknapp's side were full of confidence after high-profile maulings of Arsenal and Chelsea, but the Londoners' cagey second-half tactics were exposed as United's greater ambition was rewarded. Ryan Giggs fired the opener from the penalty spot, only to have the scores levelled by Ledley King's header. With the match tantalizingly poised, Nani's clever chipped finish and another Giggs penalty sealed a crucial win for the Reds.

That the triumph was achieved without Wayne Rooney and Rio Ferdinand spoke volumes for United's sheer will to win, especially as Dimitar Berbatov and Antonio Valencia suffered injuries during the course of the game, while both Patrice Evra and Nani vomited on the pitch. Pre-match, the loss of Rooney and Ferdinand was slightly offset by the return to the bench of Owen Hargreaves. Having his name called out at Old Trafford for the first time since September 2008 provided a timely fillip for the home support, and he was welcomed back in rousing style.

In total contrast was the game's opening period, which contained plenty of possession and posturing but failed to yield a chance until the half-hour mark when Berbatov's goal-bound shot was superbly blocked by King. As United sought to build on that chink of light, Valencia forced a fine save from Heurelho Gomes with a fizzing low drive.

Both Evra and Berbatov volleyed off-target as United ended the half in the ascendancy, and that pattern of play continued after the break. Berbatov's header sailed agonizingly between post and the onrushing Darren Fletcher before the breakthrough arrived just before the hour. The impressive Berbatov superbly held off Benoît

Assou-Ekotto before back-heeling a pass into the path of Evra, who was unceremoniously dumped onto the turf by Assou-Ekotto. Shorn of designated penalty-taker Rooney, Giggs stepped up and confidently side-footed just inside Gomes's right-hand post.

Stung into action, Spurs' forward raids began to carry greater threat. Little more than ten minutes after falling behind, King rose highest to nod Bale's corner towards the far post, which Rafael had vacated. The Brazilian acrobatically tried to recover but was unable to prevent Spurs levelling. Kiko Macheda and Peter Crouch were introduced by their respective managers as both sides chased three priceless points, and in little more than a minute Sir Alex's change reaped dividends.

Macheda collected Darren Fletcher's infield pass, took a touch and steered a pass to Nani. The Portuguese's first touch completely negated King's presence before his second lifted a beautiful finish over the grounded Gomes and sent Old Trafford delirious. The goal merely extended the winger's fine run of form and he made another telling contribution to seal the three points. Gaining possession in the centre circle, Nani sped towards goal, tricked his way into the area and was clumsily felled by Wilson Palacios for the game's second penalty. Giggs again stepped up, opted to change sides, and drilled another devastating finish past Gomes.

Top of the league once more, albeit reliant on an unlikely favour from Stoke at Stamford Bridge, it was clear the champions would not be deposed without a fight.

Team: Van der Sar; Rafael (Macheda 80), Vidić, Evans, Evra (O'Shea 67); Valencia (Carrick 60), Fletcher, Giggs, Scholes, Nani; Berbatov
Scorers: Giggs (58 (pen), 86 (pen)), Nani (81)
Attendance: 75,268
Referee: Andre Marriner

'I must say, Nani's finish was absolutely brilliant,' said Sir Alex Ferguson at full time. 'To have the audacity to try it at that stage of the game tells you about his courage. Not many players would have tried that, particularly from such a tight angle. It was fantastic – ten out of ten for doing it.'

Courage was also betrayed in the steely nerve of Ryan Giggs, who, having never taken a penalty in open play during his epic United career, converted two in a high-pressure situation against a goalkeeper renowned for his penalty saves. 'In the back of my mind, I was thinking that he does save a lot of penalties,' reveals Giggs. 'I was more nervous for the second one because I was indecisive. The first one I knew what I was going to do. The second one, I was stood there and I still didn't know what I was going to do. I wasn't nervous for the first one because I'd been practising and I was confident I'd put it right in the corner.'

Being back atop the table was a huge boost for the United dressing room, but every squad member knew there would have to be help from others if Chelsea were to be overcome. 'Since they beat us here at Old Trafford it's been their title to lose,' said Darren Fletcher. 'We just have to keep winning and concentrate on ourselves. We've won our game and now it goes over to them. It'll be tight now for the rest of the season.'

The Reds' determination had been characterized by the mid-game exertions of Nani and Patrice Evra. Blood, sweat and tears are recognized sacrifices in football, but rarely does a player vomit and continue playing. Nani completed 90 minutes, while Evra played on long enough to win the opening penalty before succumbing to his illness.

'I didn't feel well the day before the game,' recalls the Frenchman. 'I felt something in my stomach. Then before the game I didn't have a good breakfast. I was eating and my stomach looked really full but it was almost empty. After the first half it was OK, but in the break I didn't feel well. I told the boss but tried to play on. After I vomited I felt a bit better but I put in a lot of effort and it was very warm, so I started to feel a bit dehydrated.

'When I vomited it was only water, because whenever I drank something my stomach regurgitated it straight away. It was not a beautiful experience! I remember while I was vomiting I could hear the fans shouting, 'Woah – look what he's doing!' I felt a bit embarrassed, but it was quite funny. It was funny that Nani did it as well. I was laughing when I saw him afterwards. I said, "Welcome to the club."'

Evra's queasiness had cleared, but there was nausea for all inside the United camp as Chelsea obliterated Stoke at Stamford Bridge, running out 7–0 winners. Only two potential pitfalls remained for Carlo Ancelotti's side: a trip to face Liverpool at Anfield and Wigan's last-day visit to London.

Wayne Rooney was also in the capital as Tony Pulis's side were demolished. The United striker was on hand to pick up the PFA Player of the Year award at the association's annual glitzy bash, and Rooney soon added the Football Writers' Association award to his growing collection of individual silverware.

'I've scored a lot of goals this season and I think overall my play has been good,' reflected the striker. 'It's definitely been my most prolific season in front of goal and I'm pleased with the way things have gone. Of course, as a forward player you rely on the support and service of your team-mates. A lot of what I've achieved is down to my team-mates. It's nice that people put me up there among the best players around, but I think Lionel Messi is the best in the world. The things he can do with the ball are just unbelievable and he's scoring a lot of goals as well. He's been fantastic again this year, the best player in the world.'

Rooney wasn't the only Red recognized by the PFA, as the inclusion of Patrice Evra, Darren Fletcher and Antonio Valencia in the PFA Team of the Year validated Rooney's assertion that much of his success could be attributed to his colleagues.

'It was a pleasant surprise to be included,' admits Fletcher. 'It's nice to be recognized by your fellow players; it definitely makes it that little bit more special that the team was picked by the Premier

League's players. They're the ones who play against you every week, so for them to have selected me was a real honour. Individual honours aren't as important as winning trophies with the team, but it is nice to be recognized by your fellow players.'

Amid the mutual back-slapping, Fletcher and his colleagues were pinning a season's hopes on a favour from Liverpool, perhaps the Reds' unlikeliest allies. With little to play for after a miserable season, compounded by an extra-time defeat to Atletico Madrid in the Europa League semi-finals, the omens didn't favour Liverpool or United as Chelsea prepared to go to Anfield.

'Great clubs don't throw their history and traditions away for one game,' Sir Alex told his pre-match press briefing. 'I think Liverpool will do their best on Sunday – they have to. You depend on that resilience of the British players and players playing in British football – they know they have to go out and produce Saturday and then midweek and Saturday again. They show great attitude and character all the time.'

The manager also revealed at his press conference that Gary Neville had joined Ryan Giggs and Paul Scholes in penning another year's contract extension, ending months of speculation that the veteran defender would retire at the end of the season. 'We're delighted,' said Sir Alex. 'We think he deserves it because his contribution to the club has been fantastic. As I've said time and again about certain players, they make a career out of their will and determination. Gary is one of those players.'

'Gaz definitely deserved his new deal,' says Ryan Giggs. 'He's just a great defender. Look at how he played against Franck Ribéry in Munich or against Craig Bellamy at Eastlands. He didn't give them a kick. He had an absolute blinder against City. He didn't just turn up for the game – he did his research on Bellamy's runs.

'Once he gets a run on you there's no stopping him because he's that quick and that powerful a runner. Nev was brilliant against him and coming up against one of the form players in the league and one of the quickest players in the league, he didn't give him a kick. That's testament to his professionalism and what a great defender he is. He also brings you a lot going forward as an attacking player.'

Confirmation, then, that there was still life in Neville as a top player. But whether the title race still had legs depended largely on events at Anfield as the season entered its final month.

11

May

United's title hopes may have been hinging on a favour from Liverpool, but there was still a tricky trip to Wearside to negotiate. Steve Bruce's Sunderland had suffered just two home defeats all season and Sir Alex Ferguson was well aware his side would have to fight to take three points from the Stadium of Light.

'Sunderland have hit form,' said the boss. 'My old captain has done a great job there. And it's one thing saying we hope Liverpool do us a turn, but it's Sunderland's last home game of the season. They'll do their best and we have to match that. It's not an easy game.'

Still, after the Reds' display of fortitude against Tottenham, Sir Alex had complete faith in his players to overcome the pepped-up hosts and the pre-match distractions at Anfield, where play would finish just as United's warm-up began.

'We played without nerves last week,' said the manager. 'We showed great temperament. At one–one with twenty minutes left we had to raise the bar. I thought that was the best part of our game. We showed great determination to get back in front. If you get that with three games to go, then you can be confident and trust your players for the last two matches.'

As United's players arrived at the Stadium of Light, there was time before the pre-match warm-up to take in events at Anfield. For 30 minutes, a drab, even encounter was doing enough to kindle the Reds' title hopes. Then, disaster struck as Steven Gerrard's poor back-pass allowed Didier Drogba to nip in and tap home the opener. Frank Lampard scored a second for the Blues after half time, twist-ing the dagger in United hearts.

'It was hard to go out and play well after that,' recalls Ryan Giggs. 'The manager and staff can gee you up, but it was a big blow to take. You shouldn't have to rely on other people, but we were hopeful. We've been to Anfield – I know it's a different proposition for Liverpool v United – but it's the one place you wouldn't want to go for a result. It's one of the toughest places in the world to go and get a result, so for Chelsea to do it so easily, knocked the stuffing out of us. The manager did say beforehand to just go out and express our-selves against Sunderland.'

Barclays Premier League

Sunderland 0 Manchester United 1

Stadium of Light, 2 May 2010

Earlier events at Anfield meant United would almost certainly be passing the domestic crown to Chelsea, but the Reds displayed all the hallmarks of champions with an impressive victory over in-form Sunderland. A classy display was capped by a well-worked goal from Nani and only a string of squandered opportunities spared Steve Bruce's side an embarrassing defeat in their final home game of the season.

Fresh from watching Chelsea swat aside Liverpool, United knew victory was imperative. Defeat would abruptly curtail the title race, while a draw would only string it along on mathematics. Set up to attack, with Wayne Rooney back in tandem with Dimitar Berbatov, the Reds' ambition was plain to see.

Sunderland's October draw at Old Trafford had been built on a foundation of sapping doggedness and the Wearsiders again snapped into challenges throughout. Able to mix style and substance, however, the Reds bit back with interest. Early on, Rooney out-muscled Michael Turner and latched on to Berbatov's cross, but Sunderland goalkeeper Craig Gordon reacted well to turn away the striker's stinging shot. From the rebound, Phil Bardsley – one of three ex-Reds in the home line-up – bravely deflected Ryan Giggs's follow-up for a corner.

Home skipper Lorik Cana glanced a header wide and Steed Malbranque forced Edwin van der Sar into a solid save with a rasping 25-yard effort, but those brief flurries came amid sustained United pressure. Giggs struck the outside of Gordon's top corner from just inside the area before United took the lead on 28 minutes. Neat interplay on the edge of a packed Sunderland box culminated in Rooney nodding down to Fletcher, who teed up Nani to swerve a venomous half-volley just inside Gordon's right-hand post.

Berbatov, who fed Rooney in the build-up to Nani's opener, then skewed horribly wide after another incisive United move. Frustratingly, the Bulgarian's afternoon got worse: on the stretch, he could only turn Rooney's cross over the bar from three yards out before heading over from similarly close range, albeit via a deflection off Kieran Richardson.

Michael Carrick replaced Berbatov soon after, but was left equally vexed when his low shot beat Gordon but was cleared off the line by the diligent Turner. Perhaps the biggest cheer of the afternoon from the away support was reserved for another substitute, Owen Hargreaves. The midfielder was involved for just 30 seconds and touched the ball only once, but had cleared the mental barrier of making his first senior appearance since September 2008. Despite that warming subplot and a third straight win against on-song opposition, United's penultimate outing of the season was laced with disappointment. The title race would go to the wire, but United were in the unfamiliar position of being dark horses.

Team: Van der Sar; O'Shea, Vidić, Evans, Evra; Nani (Hargreaves 89), Fletcher (Ferdinand 87), Scholes, Giggs; Rooney, Berbatov (Carrick 71)
Scorer: Nani (28)
Attendance: 47,641
Referee: Steve Bennett

'The players' attitude was terrific,' said Sir Alex afterwards. 'There was good commitment from them, they enjoyed the game and played good football. All we can do now is win next week. We want to do that in front of our fans on the last day of the season. Wigan will have a go at Chelsea and you never know in football. It's a crazy game. We are clutching at straws a little bit, but the important thing is for us to win our game and enjoy it in front of our fans. There'll be seventy-six thousand there, so we'll play the right way and play with a lot of dignity.'

As long as the Reds had a mathematical chance of retaining the title, the squad would wring every last drop of sweat from themselves, according to match-winner Nani. 'We have a chance to win the league and we will fight until the end,' said the Portuguese. 'You never know what's going to happen in football. We just have to wait and see and win our game.'

'It would be nice if we were a point ahead,' added Edwin van der Sar. 'We're not in charge and it's difficult, but we have to keep going, see what we can do this week on the training ground, see if everybody has recovered from this match and hopefully have a nice game for our supporters on Sunday. We're still hanging in there.'

The veteran Dutch goalkeeper conceded he and his colleagues had hoped for, rather than expected to receive, any favours from Liverpool against Chelsea. But he refused to apportion blame to Rafael Benítez's side. 'They've had a gruesome two weeks, played a lot of games and picked up a couple of injuries,' admitted Edwin. 'I don't think that will be the cause of us maybe not winning the league;

248

that's happened over the course of the year and some breaks we didn't get and Chelsea got, especially in the last couple of weeks.'

After returning to Manchester, a week of waiting and day-dreaming about potential scenarios whereby Wigan could reprise their shock September defeat of Chelsea at the DW Stadium was punctuated by the Reds' annual end-of-season awards bash. The entire first-team squad descended on Old Trafford for the glitzy shindig and plenty were on hand to offer pre-emptive post-mortems of the season, while still retaining an air of 'you never know'.

'It's been an exciting season,' said Rio Ferdinand. 'More of the so-called lesser teams have been taking points off the top four, while in previous seasons it's been a case of the big teams beating all the others and then dropping points against each other. It's been a weird season. Hopefully that will bode well for Chelsea's game on Sunday.'

'When you leave it in the hands of others, you've got to take the punishment for it,' added Gary Neville. 'We saw that on Sunday. We did our job, which is all we could do. Now we hope something can happen this Sunday. We'll be kicking ourselves come the end of the season if it doesn't go our way. The mistakes we have made have been unusual but I think every team can say the same. It's been a crazy season and I hope we don't come to regret it. If we do, we'll learn from that for next season.'

While the 2009–10 campaign still had one final weekend to run, 2010–11 couldn't come quick enough for Owen Hargreaves. Just a sniff of action at the Stadium of Light had him champing at the bit and eyeing a permanent return to regular senior football.

'I've missed two seasons and I'm disappointed about that. But I'm twenty-nine and hopefully I've got another six to eight years left in me,' insisted the midfielder. 'Being out for so long is obviously not something I would have envisaged myself going through. It's been a learning experience and I try and take the positives from it. It was short, coming on against Sunderland, but we've got our last game this weekend and then I'll hopefully get ready to attack next season.'

The immediate focus of the awards evening was to recognize the current campaign's telling contributors, with one man tipped to sweep the board. After Will Keane and Ritchie De Laet picked up the Jimmy Murphy Young Player of the Year and Denzil Haroun Reserve Team Player of the Year awards respectively, Wayne Rooney took centre-stage.

The gongs for supporters' Player of the Year, Players' Player of the Year and Goal of the Season all went home with the prolific striker, who singled out the recognition from the Red Army as the most meaningful.

'I'm delighted to win the fans' Player of the Year award,' he said. 'It's a special feeling and something I'm really proud of. The fans come and watch us all over the country and all over Europe and pay a lot of money to do it. The support they give us is unbelievable. If we're playing at home and the game isn't going right for us and we need to score a goal to win it, the fans push you on. You can feel that, you can sense that on the pitch. It's a magical feeling. And the fans away from home are incredible. They're the best fans in the world.'

The likelihood of United supporters celebrating a fourth successive Premier League title had diminished since a nightmare fortnight in April, but Sir Alex preferred to focus on the positives as he addressed the media for the final time, ahead of Stoke's visit.

'We've scored more goals than last season and we have the best defensive record in the league,' said the boss. 'We have good structure at the club and a good squad. I'm pleased with the way we've gone about the last couple of games. We hope we sign off in the right way but it's never easy playing against Stoke because they're a determined and powerful unit. We want to do well in our last home game.'

A packed Old Trafford steeled itself for one final afternoon of tension and drama, knowing every event unfolding in the Theatre of Dreams was secondary to those taking place at Stamford Bridge.

Barclays Premier League

Manchester United 4 Stoke City 0

Old Trafford, 9 May 2010

No more plot twists, no more romantic notions and no more title as United's comfortable win over Stoke was negated by Chelsea's destruction of ten-man Wigan. By the time Darren Fletcher turned home the Reds' opener against the Potters, Carlo Ancelotti's side were already a goal ahead. Moments after United took the lead, Latics defender Gary Caldwell was sent off at Stamford Bridge and Frank Lampard smashed in the resulting penalty. With little more than half an hour gone, Chelsea were champions-in-waiting.

There was no hint of the nine months of drama that preceded the final day, as English football's two leading lights posted a combined 12 final-day goals without reply. Emphatically, Chelsea bagged eight of them. United's professionalism ensured Stoke were never given a sniff of compounding a miserable day, and the outgoing champions were on top from the off. Dimitar Berbatov twice had efforts blocked and then headed over before another block from Robert Huth denied Patrice Evra a goal to cap his magnificent season.

The breakthrough came on 31 minutes as a Ryan Giggs corner sparked a scramble in the Potters' area, only for Fletcher to fire a finish into the roof of the net. For all Berbatov's frustration in finishing, his magnificence in providing soon set up United's second goal, with a surging run and pull-back for Ryan Giggs to steer underneath Asmir Begović.

Having had the Chelsea score confirmed at half time, it was inevitable United's second-half display would pack less punch. With every goal that flew in at Stamford Bridge, Stoke's fans would celebrate at Old Trafford and provide an irritating running commentary for those clad in Red. Slight vengeance was exacted as United added further goals, although the first came from former Reds defender

251

Danny Higginbotham, who crashed home a finish from close range after sterling approach play from Rooney.

The England striker soon departed with a recurrence of a groin injury, but his replacement, Ji-sung Park, dived to head home Giggs's corner and ensure a fourth straight victory with goal number four. Alas, there would be no fourth successive title. Chelsea's surge for the line had been too powerful and, although there had been some mitigation, United could only congratulate the new champions.

Team: Van der Sar; Neville, Ferdinand, Vidić, Evra; Nani, Fletcher, Scholes (Gibson 62), Giggs; Berbatov (Macheda 62), Rooney (Park 77)
Scorers: Fletcher (31), Giggs (38), Higginbotham (54 (og)), Park (84)
Attendance: 75,316
Referee: Mark Clattenburg

'We applaud Chelsea because we know how hard it is to win the title,' Sir Alex said. 'It's the hardest league in the world and we've won it for the last three years. I congratulate Carlo Ancelotti on a wonderful achievement. He's a good manager and a good guy. We won the last three titles. That was fantastic and the players have been great. Now we'll come back next year – that's exactly what Manchester United do. We can be proud we've challenged hard for a fourth title in a row. Next season we'll go again and bring back the title to the best place in the world.'

Disappointment and defiance mingled throughout a subdued dressing room at full time. 'We were so close,' rued Nani. 'We had a lot of chances to win the league but didn't take them. Against Chelsea at home we didn't win and that was the game where we lost the league. We still have to be confident about next season. Next year we will be fantastic because we will show we are strong and we will work hard. We did so well and it was quite equal between ourselves and Chelsea. You could say we deserved to win the title just as much.

But we have to forget about this and think about next season. United is a very strong club and we have a very strong mentality. We didn't win the league this season, but next time we will.'

The temptation to analyse where two title-tipping points could have been gained was tough to resist. Questionable officiating against Chelsea, missed opportunities at Blackburn, five points dropped against Aston Villa and a shock defeat at Burnley were all singular instances of potentially decisive slips, not to mention the small matter of decimating injuries to key players at key times. Even Sir Alex couldn't help but recall the ones that got away.

'If you think of Burnley away, we'd only just started the season and then we lost three points,' he said. 'We missed a penalty that day and if we'd scored it, we would probably have gone on to win the match or get a draw at least. That point could have made the difference. You go through the bad refereeing decision in the game at Chelsea and the one against them at Old Trafford . . . But if you look at all these twists and turns, you can torture yourself. There's no point to it. We sometimes get breaks ourselves, so you have to take the bad with the good.'

A dissatisfying denouement to the season would play on the minds of United's players, but several would have the chance to vent their frustrations at the World Cup in South Africa. Rio Ferdinand, Wayne Rooney and Michael Carrick (England), Patrice Evra (France), Nani (Portugal), Nemanja Vidić and Zoran Tošić (both Serbia) and Ji-sung Park (South Korea) were all named in national squads, as was United-bound striker Javier Hernández (Mexico), who was granted a work permit not long after the season finished. Rio Ferdinand, England's captain, however did not make it to the tournament in the end, after he picked up knee ligament damage while training in South Africa. He was immediately sent home for treatment.

One high-profile absentee from England's World Cup squad was United goalkeeper Ben Foster, who joined Birmingham City for an undisclosed fee in a bid for more regular senior action. Following the

agreed deals for Hernández and Chris Smalling, the Foster deal signalled United's first summer sale. While speculation raged as to how
dramatic a facelift the Reds would require after being deposed as
champions, chief executive David Gill gave his take on the season.

'We had a very interesting season [in 2009–10],' he says. 'Overall
we did very, very well but came up slightly short compared with the
great success of the previous three seasons. But I think we have to be
realistic. We only fell one point short in the league, did very well in
the Champions League and went out rather unluckily. We won the
Carling Cup, too. I suppose the key disappointment from a cup perspective was the FA Cup. But a lot of other teams would like to have
achieved what we achieved.

'When we go into a season, we want to be up there challenging
right to the end in all competitions. We've got the size and quality in
the squad, plus Alex with his experience and his coaches. So that's
what we aim to do: challenge. But only one team can win the
Premier League, only one can win the Champions League and so on.
We never say we must win the league or the cup – it's all about challenging because that's when the interest continues right to the end of
the season.

'That happened this season, although we didn't have much hope
on the last day. None the less, we took it to the wire. From a financial perspective we budget to come third in the league, reach the last
sixteen of the Champions League and do slightly better in the FA
Cup than we did. So we're realistic in our budgeting. If Alex wants
it, the money is there to invest from the sale of Ronaldo, plus we've
delivered on the commercial side of the club as well.'

But as the annual frenzy of transfer rumours began, Sir Alex
insisted there would be little business taking place over the summer.
'People don't recognize I've actually signed three players for twenty
million pounds,' he said. 'Chris Smalling will join us from Fulham,
Mame Diouf has done really well and, of course, young Javier
Hernández from Mexico will join us after the World Cup. Those are
three young players whose futures are guaranteed for the club. Other

young players who come into that bracket are Kiko Macheda, Gabriel Obertan and Danny Welbeck. Darron Gibson's starting to emerge very strongly and Jonny Evans has proved himself at twenty-one years of age. So we've got a good nucleus of young players.

'What I'll have to make decisions on is how we can improve the team, because when you challenge for four league titles in a row, the Champions League, the Carling Cup, the FA Cup and the Club World Cup, it can have a draining effect and you have to be aware of that. You have to spot the moment when you say, "It's time to freshen. It's time to change one or two players." It's not that I have a desire to do it, it's a need to do it, simply because the demands and the pressure on players over a longer period can be quite exacting. But we've got a good foundation to carry the club for a long time now.'

'I'm experienced enough to know you can't win them all. What you try to do is recover from every defeat and try to regain the upper hand next season. It's a challenge. A few years ago it was Arsenal, then it was Chelsea, and each time we've managed to raise the bar at our football club – and that is exactly what we are going to do next year.'

Sir Alex's players glimmer with similar intent, but recognize that there must be less reliance on the excellence of Wayne Rooney. The striker's injury in Munich badly affected the Reds' hopes of two major trophies, and Ryan Giggs admits United must be better equipped to cope without him.

'We can't rely on Wayne Rooney next season like we did this one,' says the winger. 'We need to be scoring more goals from different areas and from different players, even though as a team we scored more than we did last season. We were also better defensively this season than last, but we can't rely on Wayne as much as we have done this season in terms of goals. But whether the manager does or does-n't bring in any other strikers this summer, the other players know we need to score more. Whether that's defenders coming up for corners or midfielders chipping in, we all need to contribute a lot more.'

For a squad so accustomed to silverware and glory, beginning next term as challengers rather than champions will be an unsettling experience, but one that Michael Carrick hopes will prove a galvanizing force.

'We'll definitely be trying to win the title back,' says the midfielder. 'We've done it before and the lads here are experienced enough and hungry enough at the same time to try and bounce back. You look back and realize what an achievement it is to win the league three years in a row, but that doesn't help us now, having lost it. Our hunger will be stronger than ever next year. If something's taken away from you, then you want it back.'

The sense of bereavement has already passed, replaced by an ambition that burns brighter than ever in anticipation of the 2010–11 season. After all, it's the pain of failure, rather than the joy of success, that is the biggest motivator at Manchester United.